Glasgow's Other River:

Exploring the Kelvin

Glasgow's Other River:
Exploring the Kelvin

ALEX MATHESON

Killermont House in 1870. This fine mansion, built in 1805 on the right bank of the Kelvin, was situated two miles north of Maryhill. It has now been demolished.

FORT PUBLISHING

First published in 2000 by Fort Publishing Ltd, Old Belmont House,
12 Robsland Avenue, Ayr, KA7 2RW.

Designed by Paul McLaughlin, 48 Queen Street, Lochmaben, DG11 1PS

Maps by Justin Wilson, 01560 700208

Typeset in 10.5pt Garamond by Senga Fairgrieve, 0131 658 1763
Printed in Great Britain by Bell and Bain Ltd., Glasgow

ISBN 0-9536576-2-0

A catalogue record for this book is available from the British Library

For Lucy

Contents

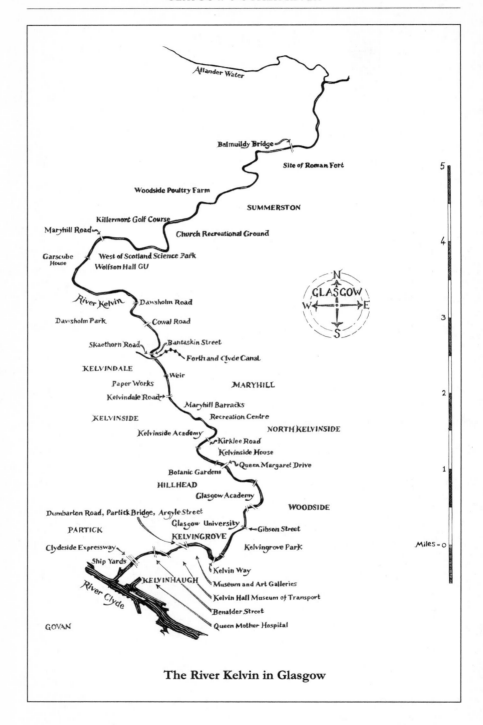

The River Kelvin in Glasgow

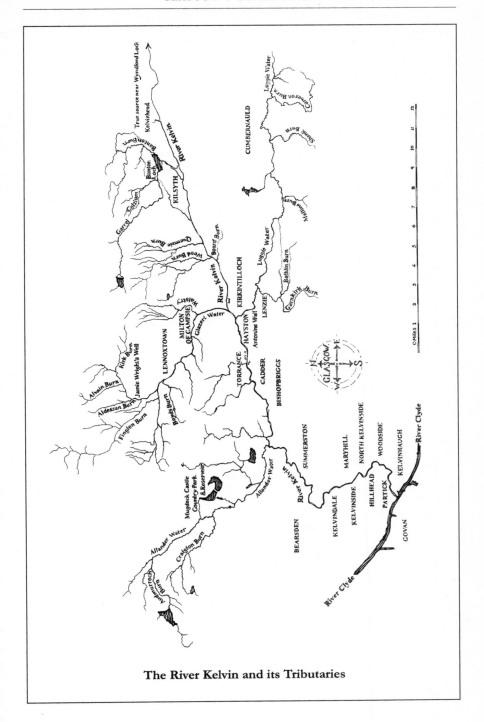

The River Kelvin and its Tributaries

List of Illustrations

Introduction

As rivers go, the Kelvin does not amount to much. It has a total length of 34 kilometres (21 miles) from its source at Wyndford east of Kilsyth to its confluence with the Clyde at Partick, but add its major tributaries, the Glazert, the Luggie and the Allander, and all the streams that feed them, and you have a river which drains a large part of three historic counties, Stirlingshire, Dunbartonshire and Lanarkshire. It is a river which offers some remarkable contrasts, between the meandering stream crossing flood plains and the more dramatic river that runs picturesquely through the wooded gorge that cuts right across one of Europe's largest and most industrialised cities. Like its eastern counterpart, the Water of Leith, the Kelvin was the indefatigable workhorse of the Industrial Revolution, an astonishing range of mills utilising the water of its lower reaches. The Kelvin has witnessed the rise and fall of many industries: flour milling, bleaching, dyeing and calico-printing, textiles, nail-making, the manufacture of paper and flint glass, chemical works and shipbuilding. For two centuries its weirs and dams impeded the natural progress of salmon, and then the effluent from riverbank industries killed every living creature. The post-industrial Kelvin is an ecological miracle. Today the river teems with all manner of fish including salmon, and birds that depend on fish, like the kingfisher and the cormorant, are now regular sights along its banks. Indeed, cormorants can now be seen at Kilsyth, which is about as far from the sea as one can get. But it is a sobering thought that, at the beginning of the twentieth century, over ninety species of birds were recorded along the Kelvin, whereas barely forty have been recorded in recent years, though admittedly the number is steadily rising.

The cormorant, first recorded on the Kelvin in 1991, has been adopted as the insignia of the Friends of the River Kelvin (FORK), a group founded in 1990, partly to encourage a greater awareness of the Kelvin and its attractions, and partly to take care that its amenities are maintained and improved. Its members cheerfully undertake the regular but thankless and never-ending task of cleaning up the river, with monthly meetings for this express purpose; they have even found a use for those supermarket wire baskets and trolleys that mysteriously end up in the river, and employ them as protection for many useful water plants which help the regeneration of the river. Moreover, *FORK News*, the quarterly newsletter, is a mine of information on current developments and nature notes as well as containing fascinating articles dealing with the more historic features of the river.

The River Kelvin Angling Association was formed on 17 March 1992 and has gone from strength to strength, now numbering over six hundred members

The Kelvin in the West End, or Kelvingrove, Park, around 1870

who regularly fish the river for salmon and trout. The Association has played an active part in river conservation as well as operating a costly fish restocking programme. Canoes are now a regular sight in the lower reaches of the Kelvin, while the riverbank footpaths have been greatly improved, and now provide an important source of recreation for walkers and cyclists. Even the police have instituted bicycle patrols, infinitely more mobile than constables on foot and more flexible than patrol cars for ensuring the safety of people enjoying the Kelvin's many attractions. In the past decade alone much has been done by the local authorities as well as conservation groups to transform the last vestiges of the industrial wasteland into a valuable amenity, and the Allander-Kelvin Link now plays a vital part in joining up the West Highland Way to the walkways along the Clyde. As a result, it is now theoretically possible to walk through 'countryside' from the Broomielaw to Fort William!

The Kelvin is a vital green corridor for the urban wildlife of Glasgow, and here I must pay tribute to the late Michael McGhee, known as the Squirrel Man. Michael was a real character, just like St. Francis of Assisi, who spoke to the squirrels and had a name for each of them. He would often stand in the Botanic Gardens or Kelvingrove Park with a squirrel on each hand and one perched on his bunnet. But he was much more than that; he was a man who cared passionately about the Kelvin and did much to record the rare plants that were managing to get a toe-hold on its banks. I have to admit that, before I read his notes, the area south of the Clydeside Expressway to the Point was just an overgrown eyesore; but now I see it through his eyes, as a veritable wonderland of plant species. And it is not just squirrels that inhabit Kelvin's urban banks these days, but otters and mink have also been sighted.

I grew up on the banks of the Kelvin and have witnessed the startling changes which have occurred in the past thirty or forty years, largely as a decline in the manufacturing industries of Glasgow. When I came back to the City ten years ago after a long absence I began walking along the Kelvin, at first renewing my acquaintance with the haunts of my youth and then exploring farther and farther afield, until I determined to walk both banks, so far as was practical, all the way from its mouth to its source. Inevitably this drew me to explore its tributaries. The Allander I knew quite well from boyhood, but the Glazert and the Luggie were new to me, and soon I came to know the very different terrain that surrounds these rivers and the burns that feed them.

This book is essentially about a complex system of rivers and streams, but it is, I hope, much more than that, for I have tried to describe the towns, villages and urban districts that are touched by the Kelvin, to point out the places of interest along the way and mention the events and personalities associated with them. Inevitably this cuts across much that has been written about Glasgow and its environs in the past, and I have drawn my facts from many books. A detailed list of authors and titles will be found at the end of this volume. Some of these sources are fascinating works by local historians and amateur antiquaries, long out of print little gems of arcane information. I am primarily indebted to the staffs of the Mitchell Library (especially the Glasgow Room), the Glasgow University Library and the Libraries and Museums Department of what was until quite recently Strathkelvin District Council (particularly the Kirkintilloch Museum which has published an invaluable series of leaflets covering every aspect of that town and district). It would be invidious to single out any one book when every title listed in this book has been so helpful, but I must pay special tribute to the Glasgow volume by Elizabeth Williamson, Anne Riches and Malcolm Higgs in the Penguin series *The Buildings of Scotland*. This tightly packed 700-page tome has been my constant companion stravaiging the City's streets these past ten years, and its detailed descriptions of buildings, often accompanied by acerbically witty comments, have opened my eyes and, I hope, given me a much keener appreciation of Glasgow's architectural delights. To these three authors I am deeply indebted for dates of design and construction, and the names of architects and contractors.

A number of individuals have also helped with this project in various ways: first and foremost Mark Eden-Bushell of FORK whose enthusiasm for the Kelvin is infectious, Professor Emeritus Gary Roach of Fintry for details of the burns that feed the Glazert, Bruce Allan for additional information on Kirkintilloch and Bishopbriggs, James Crawford for material concerning the golf courses of the Kelvin Valley, Charles Reid for details regarding Torrance and Baldernock, James C. Macleod for information regarding Mugdock, Roderick

Macpherson on the Scottish Historical Exhibition of 1911, Colin Hunter-McQueen on Kelvingrove and the Museum of Transport, Dr David Boyce for invaluable data on the bridges over the Kelvin, and Bill Spaulding for out-of-the-way material regarding Partick.

This is by no means the last word on the subject of the Kelvin. Even as I write, there are exciting developments in train, plans to revitalise the Kelvingrove Bandstand and rebuild the Halfpenny Bridge at the Botanic Gardens, as well as the canalisation currently under way at Kilsyth. Nor is there any room for complacency regarding the preservation of the river and its amenities. While good progress is being made along the Urban Kelvin, there is a need for vigilance along the Rural Kelvin and its tributaries, especially to monitor the activities of farmers in allowing the tipping of rubble and industrial waste on the river banks. I hope that this book will play a part in the continuing revitalisation of this beautiful river and make people more aware of its attractions.

Alex Matheson
Glasgow 2000

CHAPTER ONE

From the Source of the Kelvin to Kilsyth

Guidebooks and gazetteers are divided as to the source of the Kelvin and even the meaning of the name. It has been variously described as rising in the Campsies or the Kilsyth Hills; both are true, in the sense that streams that feed the Kelvin have their origins in the ranges of hills that lie to the north of Glasgow. A more accurate description places the source of the Kelvin about three miles east of Kilsyth, without being more specific. Finally, an examination of large-scale Ordnance Survey maps traces the river unequivocally to a thin blue line running alongside the Forth and Clyde Canal, so close to it in fact that one might be forgiven, at first glance, for thinking that they are one and the same. Clarity is not helped by the fact that the Kelvin at this point forms a political boundary; once the dividing line between Stirlingshire and the detached part of Dunbartonshire, then, for a quarter of a century, the boundary between Strathkelvin District and Cumbernauld and Kilsyth District. Today Strathkelvin has become East Dunbartonshire, while Kilsyth is now in North Lanarkshire, but the Kelvin is still the frontier. At this juncture the thin blue line disappears underneath the line of black dashes, obscuring the very point at which the Kelvin springs into being. Indeed, one gets the impression that the Kelvin is of much greater length, for there is a thin blue line running farther east.

The mystery is solved by checking it out on the ground. Drive along the A803 from Kilsyth, heading towards Banknock, and at the approach to that village turn right. About 200 metres down this side road you come to a bridge over a stream and, just beyond, the steep embankment which leads up to the Forth and Clyde Canal. The first thing you note from the bridge is that the river is running in the wrong direction. Stand on the bridge and look eastward and you can see this stream quite clearly. Cross the road and look over the other side of the bridge and you will see a small stream disappearing into a forest of sedges and rushes. This is the Bonny Water, fed by the outfall from Banton Loch and streams running down from the hills past Banton.

A few metres to the south, at the base of the canal embankment, there is a small drainage ditch. The water oozing out of the bed of the canal into the ditch does not appear to be going anywhere. It is stagnant, brackish and foul-smelling, and its course, running straight as a die through a marsh, is obviously man-made. Why it has not been joined to the Bonny Water nearby seems a mystery, but as you trudge westward you realise that there is an almost imperceptible tilt of the land. That bridge over the Bonny actually marks the watershed even though it is only 47 metres (152 ft) above sea level. The Bonny runs due east to join up eventually with the Carron which in turn debouches into the Forth, while the Kelvin runs due west and eventually enters the Clyde at Partick in Glasgow. A small farm near this spot is called The Sheddings and alludes to this geographical curiosity. It must have mystified the Dutch cartographer Johannis Blaeu for his map of 1654 shows the Kelvin and the Bonny joined at the hip, like Siamese twins, coming down from a common stream before going their separate ways.

The actual source of the Kelvin is in this marsh at Wyndford, near Banknock

Digressing slightly, it should be noted that the Carron and the Kelvin are the only rivers in Scotland to lend their names to inanimate objects (if we accept that tweed cloth has no connection with the Tweed, but is derived from tweel, the Scots word for twill). The Carron bestowed its name on the ironworks (apostrophised in an epigram of Robert Burns) whence came the world-famous carronade, the Royal Navy's not-so-secret weapon in the war against Napoleon. Kelvinator, on the other hand, was a brand of refrigerator which enjoyed such a measure of popularity that, for a time, kelvinator became synonymous with fridge, just as hoover, both noun and verb, meant a vacuum cleaner. The brand and its generic usage have, sadly, long since vanished into oblivion.

At the top of the embankment you are standing on the highest point of the canal, at Wyndford Lock, twentieth of the thirty-nine locks on the entire canal system. A brass plaque set into a boulder on the canal bank is a sort of mile-post, indicating Kilsyth, 8 2/3 km in one direction, and Falkirk, 11 1/4 km in the other. Using vulgar fractions instead of decimals in the metric measurement seems to be contradictory; but in round terms Kilsyth, the first town on the Kelvin, is five miles away. An excellent towpath on the north bank of the canal doubles as the footpath for the Kelvin and you can follow the course of both waterways for four kilometres. At the mid-point there is a footpath at right angles which runs due north to the cluster of houses at Kelvinhead, on the A803 which runs parallel to the river and canal, about 400 metres distant. This path runs south along a prominent, narrow ridge, a man-made feature for it is the vestige of the embankment that once carried a narrow-gauge mineral railway from the collieries at Banton. Hutches (small wagons) were hauled by horses down to the canal where the coal was loaded on to barges for the voyage to Edinburgh or Glasgow. Where the ridge peters out on the canal bank there are the remains of a wharf, still marked on some maps as Kelvinhead Jetty, and the ruins of a stone building where the wharf-keeper once resided.

Halfway up the ridge path there is a break where a bridge once spanned a cattle track. An examination of the masonry at the sides of this gap reveals that the mineral line was of considerable antiquity, probably dating from the early nineteenth century. The line marks the eastern boundary of Kilsyth parish, the Kelvin itself forming the southern limit of the parish. Looking at this sluggish stream, so narrow that a small child could easily leap across it, it is hard to imagine that before the Ice Age this was a mighty watercourse, the bed of which now lies more than a hundred metres below ground level and stretches as far as Grangemouth. It was apparently the original course of what is now the Clyde, turned aside most mightily by that process of glaciation which carved out Loch Lomond and the Gareloch. Over many thousands of years a glacier more than 500 metres thick slowly gouged and ground and filled the valley, then wind and weather did the rest.

To the west of the ridge track there is a small stream coming down from the hills above Banton, so small and insignificant that it does not even figure on the large-scale Ordnance Survey maps. It passes under the main road at the western edge of Kelvinhead and runs into a deep gully on the south side. From the name of the hamlet it is obvious that this lively, babbling brook is also regarded (by local people at any rate) as the true origin of the river, and certainly it puts life into what is a very torpid stream up to that point.

The Kelvin begins to look more like a stream by the time you come to the first of the many bridges that span it. This is on the back road from Kilsyth to Dullatur and thence to Cumbernauld, both developed considerably in relatively recent times. At this point there are good footpaths on both banks of the canal, but the Kelvin itself meanders off in a northwesterly direction, with a fantastic loop which almost describes a full circle near Cadger's Sheuch. The river crawls through very flat land, prone to flooding after heavy rain. By the time it reaches the southern outskirts of Kilsyth the river is beginning to lose its rather artificial, ditch-like appearance, although man has a final assault on the Kelvin by directing its waters through an enormous concrete culvert. When these words were written (early in 2000) both the Kelvin and the canal, at this point, were undergoing the brutal attentions of giant mechanical diggers and other infernal machines which, by the end of that year, would transform them both. The nearby stretch of the canal, in fact, had been blocked off and drained, affording a rare glimpse of this waterway without water. This mammoth operation forms a small part of the Millennium Link, an ambitious project costing many millions, designed to restore the canal to full working order, not for the carriage of freight as in days of yore but as a valuable leisure and recreational facility. Other times, other customs indeed.

Round the corner from Kelvin Gardens, just north of the bridge which carries the B802 over the river, there is an attractive picnic area on the east side, located in a disused quarry which has now been beautifully landscaped around a stretch of water. 'No swimming' notices warn of the deep waters in this quarry pool which is best left to the mallard and other waterfowl. You will even see cormorants on this pool; these seabirds have now colonised the Kelvin and are a not infrequent sight in and around the river as it runs through the city of Glasgow. The sheer cliffs of the old quarry below Manse Road are a popular training area for rock climbers.

This is a convenient point at which to cross to the south side of the canal and retrace your steps past Auchinstarry and pay a visit to the Roman fort at Croy and inspect the remains of the Antonine Wall. A few kilometres to the east, just beyond Dullatur, there is another Roman fort, and westward these relics of the mighty Roman Empire are spaced at roughly two-mile intervals all the way to Bearsden and beyond. To be sure, the area is also rich in Pictish remains. There were, at one time, two Pictish forts in the vicinity of Kilsyth, at Coneypark and Balcastle. The first was obscured by nineteenth-century development but the latter is still very much in evidence and, of course, gave its name to Balcastle (from Gaelic *baile chaisteal*, 'castle town'). Balcastle, in fact, lies due north of the Roman fort of Bar Hill, while Coneypark is due north of Croy and one can just imagine the opposing forces keeping a vigilant eye on each other across the Kelvin.

Standing on the escarpment known as Croy Hill, you can get a good view of the vestiges of the wall which was erected in AD 143 to mark the outer limit of the empire and keep the savage Caledonians at bay. Where you are now standing, Roman legionaries, many of them recruited in Dacia on the shores of the Black Sea, would have stood guard. As we move towards a United Europe, it is strange to think that the Kelvin was just beyond the pale of Roman civilisation and did not quite enjoy the benefits of that *Pax Romana* that extended all the way to the mouth of the Danube, for a few centuries at least before it all went sour and the barbarians took over.

Standing on the bridge at Auchinstarry and looking westward, you can see the Kelvin still running straight but now looking more like a river. Despite its somewhat artificial character up to this point its antiquity as a landmark is borne out by its name which is pure Celtic. In modern Gaelic it is *Caol abhuinn* ('narrow river'), which is a very good description. Nevertheless, this did not deter some eighteenth-century antiquarians from trying to make out a good case for some mythical Celtic hermit called Ban or Bean whose cell was nearby. Thus *Cill Bhean* (the cell of Bean) seemed to suggest a very ancient ecclesiastical connection. It was a man of the cloth, however, the Revd J.B. Johnston of Falkirk, who shrewdly pointed out that as the name was accented on the first syllable that part must be an adjective, hence *caol*, and he drew attention to the contraction of *abhuinn* in other place names, such as Irvine, Methven and Ruthven.

Of course the ecclesiastical party would have none of it, and even if they had to admit defeat on that score, they remained adamant in the case of Kilsyth. In this name the accent was placed on the second syllable, so they suggested that the name was derived from *Cill sithe* (cell of tranquillity) or perhaps from some otherwise unknown Celtic saint called Syth. This ignored the fact that the original name of the parish was Kelvesyth, an early form of Kelvinside which appears in documents and inscriptions in the fifteenth and early sixteenth centuries. By 1550, however, the name had changed utterly to Monyabrach or Monaebruch (from Gaelic *Monaidh abrach*, 'hilly place of streams') and, indeed, the Ebroch is one of the streams feeding into the Kelvin. The present form Kilsyth was adopted in the eighteenth century, although Killsyth Castle appears on Blaeu's map of 1654.

Doubtless there was always a stream meandering across the marshlands on the western side of the watershed towards Auchinstarry, but it was given both definite form and purpose by Sir Archibald Edmonstone of Duntreath who purchased the Kilsyth estate in 1782 for £41,000. One of the great improving landowners of the period, he dug out the channel at his own expense in order to drain the Dullatur Bog. This experiment was so successful that other proprietors of land in the vicinity then joined with him to complete the project. Robert Whitworth, one of the foremost civil engineers of the time, was commissioned to carry out the work. The channel was deepened and widened at the beginning of the nineteenth century.

Looking at this 'canal' today as it runs straight as a die through the flat plain, it is hard to imagine what a difficult task faced Whitworth and his successors. The problem was that the Kelvin had no gradient; even today there is hardly any drop in the level of the river between its source and Auchinstarry, so there is really no incentive for this lazy little stream to get moving along. When you consider that the river drops only 47 metres in a total length of 34 km (and most of that drop occurs in the final stretch) it is hardly surprising that it often seems to wander so aimlessly, as if seeking the slightest assistance from the laws of gravity. This would not matter too much in normal weather, but after winter snows and heavy rainfall in early spring the streams like the Woodburn and the Queenzieburn that plunge headlong from the Kilsyth Hills swell into raging torrents and at one time transformed the placid Kelvin into a broad lake, inundating the fields at the south side of the parish. A local poet, William Muir, published a nineteenth century ode evocatively entitled 'Kelvin, Keep Low'. This problem was alleviated by further dredging of the channel and the installation of field drainage, but even nowadays this part of the Kelvin Valley is prone to flooding.

If the Antonine Wall was designed to prevent communication between the Roman world and the barbarians beyond the pale, Kilsyth epitomises two forms of communication which developed dramatically in the eighteenth century, both running parallel to the Kelvin. The first is the A803 which traverses the parish and was proudly described by the Revd Robert Rennie in his description of the parish for the *Old Statistical Account* (1796) as 'the great highway leading from Edinburgh to Glasgow'. In turn it would be superseded by the A80 and later the M8 motorway, but in its heyday the stagecoaches rattled and the freight-wagons rumbled along its dusty unmetalled surface.

Then there was the Forth and Clyde Canal. For many years shipowners and merchants had wished for some short waterway linking the estuaries of the Forth and Clyde and thus cutting out the hazardous route round the north of Scotland. As a result, several surveys were carried out between 1726 and 1762. In 1764 Robert Smeaton, best remembered as the architect of the second Eddystone Lighthouse, came up with a plan to construct a canal 43 km (27 miles) long for the sum of £79,000. The project was bedevilled by bickering and politicking by rival interests and almost three decades elapsed before it was completed. Work began at the eastern end in 1768, giving rise to the prosperity of Grangemouth, and proceeded at a leisurely pace. The canal reached Wyndford at the end of 1771, skirted the south side of Kilsyth the following year and extended as far as Kirkintilloch by August 1773. Two years later it had progressed as far as Stockingfield when the promoters ran out of cash. The project was bailed out by a consortium of Glasgow merchants, but as they paid the piper they called the tune and the course of the canal was now diverted due south and terminated in the basin at Hamiltonhill by November 1777.

Almost seven years elapsed before work on the canal was resumed. As it progressed westward along the original course it diverged from the Kelvin, but in the end their paths crossed, quite literally, when the canal was carried on a massive aqueduct that traversed the river valley. Smeaton was succeeded as chief engineer by Robert Whitworth in June 1785 and thus it fell to him to construct what was widely regarded at the time as one of the engineering wonders of the world. After that, it was plain sailing and by 1790 the canal had reached its destination at Bowling on the Clyde. Simultaneously, the southern spur was taken forward from Hamiltonhill and terminated at Port Dundas in the very heart of Glasgow. By the time it was completed, the costs of building the canal had risen fourfold, although it was now much longer (62 km, 39 miles) than originally envisaged and at least a metre deeper, thereby enabling vessels of a much heavier draught to navigate it. By 1773 the eastern section of the canal was open to traffic and this undoubtedly stimulated the growth of industry in and around Kilsyth, followed shortly by Kirkintilloch. From 1790 to 1840 there was a half-century of phenomenal growth as all manner of industrial enterprises, from textile mills to coalmines and iron foundries, profited from the improved coast-to-coast communications, and by 1816 shareholders were receiving a generous dividend of 25 per cent.

That was literally the high water mark. The depression in the aftermath of the Napoleonic Wars was followed by the development of better and faster communications. By 1831 Scotland's first locomotives were running on the Glasgow-Garnkirk Railway which ran parallel to the canal and the Wall but to the south of them. In vain, the canal proprietors tried to operate barges tugged by steam locomotives, but they could not possibly compete with the railway and from 1840 onwards the canal went into decline as a commercial waterway, although it remained a major tourist attraction for many years thereafter. Even as late as the 1930s pleasure craft could often be seen on the canal, but it was closed for good at the end of 1962. Since then, however, stretches of the canal have been dredged and locks put back into working order. Once more it is possible to take an excursion on a canal boat, the *Caledonian*, which operates dining cruises from its base at Glasgow Bridge on the Cadder-Kirkintilloch road, and when the Millennium Link is completed the canal will become a major tourist attraction.

The Glasgow-Garnkirk Railway, and later the Edinburgh and Glasgow Railway, lay well to the south of the town, and it was not until the closing years of the nineteenth century that Kilsyth got direct rail communications. The Kelvin Valley Railway opened in 1885 and connected Kilsyth to Glasgow, via Lenzie and Maryhill. Three years later the Kilsyth and Bonnybridge Railway was established, with a station in the Duntreath Arms Inn on the western side of the town. The Caledonian Railway obtained running powers over this line from Kilsyth to Larbert. This rail link survived the rationalisation and regrouping of the railway companies after the First World War, but fell victim to the Beeching Axe in the 1950s, at the time the mining industry was coming to an end. Today, you can walk along parts of the disused railway line, westward from Dumbreck and south of Queenzieburn or eastward along the south side of Banton Loch. Sadly, in a few short years, this monument to late-Victorian transport has become as much an ancient ruin as the Antonine Wall.

For centuries the lands of Kilsyth were in the hands of the Livingston family, with their seat at Kilsyth Castle, and it was from the parish that Lord Kilsyth took his title. Of the castle, on the banks of the Garrel below Allanfauld, there is now very little to be seen. It was destroyed by Oliver Cromwell in 1650, in retaliation for Sir James Livingston, Lord Kilsyth, having supported the Marquess of Montrose. Sir James had a more modern mansion in the town (where the garden of the parish church is now located), but this was briefly garrisoned by a party of Highlanders who razed it to the ground before they departed, to prevent it falling into Cromwell's hands.

Later generations of the Livingstons preferred to reside at Colzium House, whose extensive grounds lie on the north side of the main road at the east end of the town. It was the home of the third Viscount Kilsyth, an ardent supporter of James VII and II, who was imprisoned in Edinburgh Castle in the aftermath of the battle of Killiekrankie in 1689. That had been a great victory for the Highlanders, even though their commander, James Graham of Claverhouse, Viscount Dundee, had been mortally wounded. Shortly after the battle, but before his capture, Lord Kilsyth met Dundee's beautiful young widow and fell madly in love with her. Due to his confinement, their courtship had to be conducted by correspondence but soon after his release in 1694 they married. They went into exile in the Netherlands and lived for some time in extremely straitened circumstances at Utrecht. The house where they lived had a mound of peat stacked on the roof and one night in October 1695 the roof caved in under the weight, burying the inmates. Lord Kilsyth and a guest were pulled from the debris but Lady Kilsyth, their baby son and his nurse were killed. The grieving husband and father had the corpses of his loved ones embalmed and eventually he was allowed to return to Scotland to have them interred in the family vault in Kilsyth kirkyard where a plaque recounts the tragic story. Ironically, Lady Jean Cochrane, the wife of two such ardent Jacobites, was the granddaughter of the first Earl of Dundonald and a member of one of the most staunchly Covenanting families in Scotland who regarded Claverhouse as the devil incarnate.

It was to Colzium that the newly widowed Viscountess Dundee came just after her first husband had been killed, and it was on long walks around the beautiful walled garden that she and Lord Kilsyth fell in love. It was in these gardens that the lovers exchanged gold rings as a token of their betrothal. The following day, Lady Dundee, while walking alone, lost her ring. The superstitious lady regarded this as a terrible omen and offered a large reward for its recovery, but to no avail. Then, to make matters worse, Lord Kilsyth lost his ring as well. Almost a century later, when the gardens were being altered to suit Sir Archibald Edmonstone, first Lady Dundee's ring was found by a gardener, and then Lord Kilsyth's ring turned up a few days later.

Today, the walled garden at Colzium is a riot of colour even in wintertime.

The estate passed from the Edmonstones to the Lennox family by whom Colzium House was rebuilt in 1861. Nearby was a building erected in 1815 and for many years used as a laundry. Its chief feature was a tower accommodating a clock by Wood of Glasgow, erected in 1863 and recently restored by students of Barmulloch College. For many years, however, this outbuilding fell into disuse and was derelict by 1974 when it was restored as the Clock Theatre. In the 1930s W. Mackay Lennox of Craigengoyne gifted Colzium and its extensive policies to the people of Kilsyth as a permanent memorial to his mother, Margaret Lennox. For a few years the house was used as a youth hostel but it is now a community centre and museum, maintained by North Lanarkshire Council.

Colzium Burn, near Kilsyth

On the eastern side of the grounds is the spectacular glen of the Colzium Burn, another Kelvin tributary which rises on Garrel Hill and follows a more or less parallel, though more easterly, course past the disused quarries and then enters the estate near Riskend. After tumbling through cascades and boulder-strewn linns, it mellows in its lower reaches. In springtime the eastern slopes of this burn are a dazzling carpet of daffodils, forming the Marie Curie Garden of Hope. Farther up the burnside is a picturesque little cemetery for cats and dogs and other household pets.

The ruins of a medieval motte can be seen at the southwestern end of Banton Loch, sometimes referred to as Townhead Reservoir as it was created artificially to drain the streams from the hills above Banton and act as a top-up for the canal, by way of a channel from the loch to Craigmarloch. At its western end, however, there is an outfall which joins the Colzium Burn and thence, by the Garrel, feeds into the Kelvin. Three and a half centuries ago, however, this was relatively dry land, a large plain with a slight depression in the centre, and an ideal place for two armies to confront each other. On this very spot was fought the battle of Kilsyth on 15 August 1645 between the Royalists and the Covenanters. Montrose's Highlanders were drawn up on the rise to the north of the modern reservoir, while Baillie's Covenanters were ranged on the high ground to the south, grimly determined to stop the wild men of the north from advancing on Glasgow or Edinburgh. For several hours the opposing forces glowered at each other. It was an oppressively hot day in high summer.

The story goes that Montrose removed his kilt and commanded his men to do likewise - perhaps it was this bizarre order that gave Mel Gibson the idea for one of the more dramatic scenes in *Braveheart!* At any rate the Highlanders, clad only in their shirts, taunted their adversaries with their bare behinds, but this was more than the dour Covenanters could tolerate. Some hotheads immediately broke rank and charged in their fury, and their comrades joined in. As they reached the dip in the middle of the plain, however, the Highlanders counter-attacked, screaming wild Gaelic slogans as they charged down, claymores flashing. This was the Highlanders' one and only battle tactic but it was usually extremely effective, and on this fateful day it ended in the complete rout of the enemy.

In the greater scheme of things this was merely a side show in the course of the Civil War but General Baillie was no match for the great Montrose, and before the day was done more than six thousand Covenanters lay dead or dying on the battlefield, a third of all the casualties sustained in the entire half-century known as the Wars of the Covenant. Slaughter Howe at the eastern end of the loch alludes to the massacre. Weapons, armour and grisly mementoes of that carnage can be seen today in Colzium House while a low circular monument in its grounds poignantly recalls the tragic event. It was Montrose's greatest triumph, the culmination of a bloody campaign in which the men of the Lowland counties felt the severity and barbarity of the Highlanders. Kilsyth was seemingly a decisive victory for Montrose, and Glasgow, which surrendered to him soon afterwards, was to have been the venue of a Royalist parliament which he summoned for the following October, in defiance of the legitimate authorities in Edinburgh.

But nemesis was at hand. The Royalist cause might momentarily be in the ascendant in Scotland but after Cromwell's crushing victory at Naseby in June, it was shattered in England. Early in September David Leslie crossed the Tweed with a huge well-trained and battle-hardened army. The Highlanders, sated with booty, drifted back to their glens and straths and Montrose, desperate to win new recruits, had unwisely advanced far to the southeast of his power base. At Philiphaugh on 12 September Leslie caught up with him. Although Montrose managed to escape, his followers were shown no mercy and even their female camp-followers were ruthlessly butchered as revenge for the wholesale slaughter at Kilsyth a month earlier. Montrose was hunted down and when he continued to evade his pursuers the government exacted a brutal revenge on those of his lieutenants who had been present at Kilsyth. Montrose himself was not captured till 27 April 1650, and was hanged, drawn and quartered in Edinburgh a few days later.

The Livingstons suffered for their allegiance to the Crown during the interminable civil wars of the seventeenth century but were eventually rewarded with a viscountcy. Their connection with the parish ended in 1716 when William, third Viscount, was attainted for backing the wrong side in the first Jacobite Rebellion. The Livingston lands were forfeited and eventually sold to Sir Archibald Edmonstone who made extensive additions to Colzium House as well as funding many projects in and around the town. After 1716 the Livingstons made their mark elsewhere. From a cadet branch came the Revd Alexander Livingston, the first minister of the parish after the Reformation in 1560, and his direct descendant was Robert Livingston, a signatory of the American Declaration of Independence in 1776 (see separate box).

The Kelvin skirts the parish and at one point runs close to the town, but it has never been in any real sense an artery for the town. That status belongs to the Garrel Burn which rises in the Kilsyth Hills to the north of the town. Whereas the Kelvin has the least auspicious start of any river I know, the Garrel springs spectacularly out of the Birkenburn Reservoir (or Johnny's Dam, to give it its local nickname), just above the Birken Muir. As the Birken Burn it flows due east, skirting the northern slopes of the Laird's Hill or Craigamphel, and only becomes the Garrel when it tumbles over the escarpment known to this day as the Laird's Loup. A hoary old legend (of which there are many variations) maintains that this landmark derived its name from a Highland laird who was being pursued by his enemies. He and his tired steed managed to struggle as far as the crags but when he spurred it on in his desperation the poor beast stumbled and both horse and rider plunged over the rocks to their deaths.

The picturesquely boulder-strewn stream hurtles between the Laird's Hill and Garrel Hill, and descends rapidly through rugged defiles and spectacular cliffs by a series of cascades and cataracts, gradually becoming more tranquil as it reaches more level ground in Garrel Glen, a favourite haunt of Kilsythians since time immemorial. The various linns, pools and waterfalls were distinguished by such picturesque names as Upper Craidlens, King's Linn, Witches Linn, Long Tom, Thunder, Strawberry and Treacle. There were numerous springs which provided an abundant supply of pure water for picnickers' kettles and these were known by such names as George's Well, St Mirren's Well, Katy's Well, Christie's Well and Ross's Well. This idyllic scene was not immune to Victorian progress. Limestone quarries were opened in the mid-nineteenth century, and a narrow gauge railway laid to transport the stone to the canal. The Revd Peter Anton, who published a history of the parish in 1893, wrote nostalgically about the Glen:

> The emigrant recalls it in tears, and the old folks at home, whose feet, when they were young, used to wade around its crags, and spring so nimbly from stone to stone, regret their inability to renew the joy. The Glen is not now what it was before the Neilston railway spoilt it, when its western side, above the Mill dam sluice, over to the Allanfauld road, was covered with birches, blaeberry bushes, and wild roses. Quarryman's wedge and crowbar have in places farther up sadly

hurt the rocks. This vandalism, however, has stopped, and Nature in its hate of ugliness is fast healing the Glen's wounds, with fresh verdure of ferns and wild flowers; is hiding the disfigurement with new rowan trees, hazels and sloes, and is every winter sending spates down the burn to clear out the channel. When there is no one left to recall the old times, the Garrel Glen will be as full of beauty and romance as ever.

And, just as the minister prophesied, so it has come to pass. Although Kilsyth has grown enormously in the past century and the Revd Anton might be startled to see the Kelvinway housing scheme sprawling up the lower slopes on Garrel Hill, the Glen itself, extending northwards from Allanfauld, is today beautifully restored to its pristine glory and is well worth a visit. If you drive eastwards through the town, turn left at the quaintly named Tak-ma-Doon Road, then left again to the car-park near the golf course. From there a public footpath runs northwards up the right bank of the Garrel Burn. From the top of the ridge you can walk eastwards to the summit of Tomtain (453m). Though not as lofty as Garrel Hill it affords the most spectacular views. According to Chambers' *Gazetteer* (1885), 'parts of fourteen shires can be seen from Tamtane (*sic*) with a good telescope in a clear day'. If you are lucky, you will see Ben Lomond and Berwick Law and all points in between. A curious landmark on this path is a stone removed from a mansion long since demolished, informing the passer-by that it was 'built in 1856 by A. Dennistoun'. This was the Alexander Dennistoun who feued land in the southwest of Glasgow and laid out the suburb named in his honour. Just above Allanfauld, the Garrel joins the Ebroch and together they run right through the centre of the town, passing under the main road and emerging at Bogside, then running in a southwesterly direction to join the Kelvin beyond Wellshot and forming the western boundary of the burgh.

On the opposite side of the main road, at its junction with Tak-ma-Doon Road, there is the beginning of the McCann Walkway, named in honour of one of the town's most popular provosts, Patrick McCann, MBE. The well-paved footpath, intermingling with several pedestrianised streets, runs along the Garrel. At the mid-point, beside East and West Burnside Streets, the walkway widens into a tiny piazza at the centre of which stands the Miners' Monument. On top of a pedestal stands a block of black stone with vertical polished faxes on both sides, headed simply 'The Miners'. On one side can be seen the figure of a miner at work; on the other three scenes of collieries and pithead winding gear. Along the base on both sides is the stark motto NO DAWN, ONLY BLACKNESS. This simple but very moving little monument was designed and constructed by pupils of Kilsyth and St Maurice's Academies. It was unveiled on 25 March 1996 by Councillor John Cullen and Patrick Kennedy, a retired coalminer. A plaque commemorating Provost McCann is affixed to the railings alongside. Nearby is Burngreen Peace Park, inaugurated on 13 September 1986 by Provost Pollock

The Garrel at Burnside Gardens, Kilsyth

and Marie-Therese Pirolli, the mayor of Kilsyth's French twin, Meulan. A few steps away is the Rotary Time Capsule, containing coins and documents interred in August 1990 and not scheduled to be disinterred till the year 2040.

Although Kilsyth in former times lay at the centre of an area of immense mineral wealth, stone quarrying and coalmining were carried on in the periphery of the parish, especially around the neighbouring village of Banton. Mining for coal and ironstone was pioneered by the Carron Company in 1760 and lasted almost two centuries; but the closure of the last pits in 1959 threw more than four thousand miners out of work, a very heavy blow for the district. The ornate ironwork on the numerous bridges spanning the Colzium and Garrel burns in and around Kilsyth came from this foundry. The largest employer of labour in Kilsyth itself was Murdoch and Company who specialised in the production of coffins, but could not compete with larger and more modern factories in Birmingham, so this industry has likewise vanished. Where Murdoch's imposing premises once stood there is now a new housing scheme. The family which once provided so much of the town's prosperity is now remembered solely by the memorial to its munificence which stands in Burngreen Park.

Kilsyth is the birthplace of the revolving blackboard, its father being William B. Garden (of Wilson and Garden Limited), who also invented a machine for counting coins as well as the racecourse totalisator. When he was not busy inventing useful gadgets he was fashioning walking-sticks, and fine examples with Garden's distinctive fiddle handles are much prized to this day. Robert Graham of Tamrawer, factor of the Kilsyth estates, is credited with introducing the potato to Scotland. It seems incredible that this useful tuber, which had been brought from America by Sir Walter Raleigh in Elizabethan times, was confined at first to Ireland, and only invaded England in the early eighteenth century. It was thought that the Scottish climate was too rigorous for the plants to survive, but Graham obtained a tuber which he planted in his own kitchen garden. When this proved successful he embarked on a full-scale experiment. On 21 April 1762 he planted a field at Neilston, east of Old Garrel Mill, and for every peck planted he got 269 pecks when the crop was harvested on 26 October that year. A shrewd businessman, Graham leased farms all across the central belt of Scotland from Angus to Ayrshire, from the Tay to the Clyde, and within five years the cultivation of potatoes had spread to every part of the country, making Graham a fortune in the process.

The American Connection

When the English politician, essayist and wit, Horace Walpole commented on the secession of the American colonies that 'Cousin America has run off with the Presbyterian parson' he was nearer the truth than he realised. From the Revd Alexander Livingston, the first minister of Kilsyth following the Reformation in 1560, was descended a family which played a prominent part in the founding of the United States. Robert Livingston (1654-1725) settled in the colony of New York after it was ceded by the Dutch and played an important part in the development of the British administration. His son Philip (1686-1749) likewise rose to prominence in the colony, while Philip's son William (1723-90), appropriately born on St. Andrew's Day, took a leading role in the foundation in 1756 of the New York St Andrew's Society, now one of the world's oldest and most prestigious Scottish societies. He graduated from Yale, practised law and served in the colonial legislature and exerted an extraordinary political influence through newspapers and magazines which he edited. He took the leading role in the long-running campaign to prevent King's College (now Columbia University) from falling under the control of the Church of England, and used the New York Mercury to advance the Presbyterian viewpoint. In 1772 he moved to New Jersey, which he represented in the first and second Continental Congresses, but abstained from voting on the Declaration of Independence which he considered an unwise move. Later he became Governor of New Jersey.

His cousin Robert R. Livingston (1718-75) was a justice of the New York Supreme Court from 1763 till his death. He was the father of two of the outstanding political figures of the American Revolution. Robert R. Livingston Junior (1746-1813) graduated from King's College and was called to the bar in 1773. He was a member of the New York provincial congresses (1775-7) and delegate to the Continental Congresses (1775-80). He was one of the small committee appointed to draft the Declaration of Independence, taking as its model the Declaration of Arbroath (1320). Ironically, he never signed the Declaration, as he was absent from Philadelphia on that historic day, being detained by more pressing political business in New York. In 1777 he was appointed Chancellor of New York State, an office he held until 1801, and it was in this capacity that it fell to him to administer the oath of office to George Washington when he was sworn in as first President of the United States on 30 April 1789. In 1801, he was appointed US ambassador to France and two years later, with fellow American Scot, James Monroe, he negotiated the purchase of Louisiana from France for $15million. When it is considered that 'Louisiana' signified not just the present state of that name but most of the central belt of states, including Arkansas, Colorado, the Dakotas, Iowa, Kansas, Missouri, Montana, Nebraska, Oklahoma and Wyoming, it will be realised what incredible value for money that was. Effectively, it was Livingston and Monroe who paved the way for the USA to extend right across North America.

In 1804 he retired from politics but became President of the New York St Andrew's Society and busied himself with agricultural improvements, such as fertilisers and scientific sheep-breeding. This period is best remembered for his partnership with Robert Fulton (another Scottish-American who had worked on steam propulsion with William Symington on the Forth and Clyde Canal), with whom he launched the first steamboat on the Seine in 1802 and the world's first commercial steamboat on the Hudson in 1807, named *Clermont* after his family home. He died at Clermont, New York in February 1813.

His brother Edward (1764-1836) became one of America's leading jurists and the architect of the country's criminal code. He was a Republican member of Congress for many years, later a senator and then Secretary of State under Andrew Jackson (1831-3) before becoming US ambassador to France.

CHAPTER TWO

Kirkintilloch and the Luggie

From Kilsyth there is a footpath along the north bank of the Kelvin for about a mile, but as it approaches the road branching off the B8023 to Queenzieburn, it crosses the river by a small bridge and joins up with the towpath along the canal at Twechar. As you stroll along this footpath you get a fine view of the Roman fort at Bar Hill, especially the forty-foot ditch which the Romans dug out in front of the wall for added protection. For the most part, this ditch has long since been filled in, but sufficient remains at Bar Hill to form an impression of what it must have looked like more than eighteen hundred years ago. The Roman well has survived intact, although the wrought-iron grating is of much more recent vintage, inserted to prevent small boys from falling in. Part of the bath-house, a prerequisite of all Roman establishments, has also been preserved.

The village of Twechar is mainly a creation of the mid-nineteenth century when the rich seams of coal in the vicinity were opened up by William Baird and Comines. It was also the location of a workshop which supplied plant, machinery and services to many of the collieries in the surrounding district and even farther afield. The mines have long since vanished and today the village is mainly occupied by people commuting to Kirkintilloch or Bishopbriggs, although a valiant attempt to attract light industry to the village has been created in the Twechar Enterprise Park including such exotica as Charcuterie Continental. Anglers have a high regard for the coarse fishing hereabouts, but only in the canal; the Kelvin itself does not gain piscatorial interest till much farther downstream.

From the bridge on the Twechar-Queenzieburn road you get excellent views up and down the Kelvin. This is arguably the least interesting stretch of the river as it flows sluggishly through a flat and featureless flood-plain. When the Kelvin leaves Kilsyth it is at an altitude of 40 metres (130 ft) above sea level; by the time it reaches the outskirts of Kirkintilloch it has dropped by only 2 metres (6.5 ft) in a distance of 5 kilometres (3.125 miles). The only features of interest on this stretch are the Wood Burn, the tributary which marks the western extremity of Kilsyth parish, and the long-disused railway line which runs from Kilsyth in a southwesterly direction towards Torrance. As an alternative to following the banks of the river, one can walk along the line from Dumbreck, past Netherinch and Auchinreoch to Burnfoot, then follow the A803 southwards to Kirkintilloch where it crosses the Kelvin. About a mile east of the town, on the B8023 road, however, the Kelvin runs quite close to that road again and at this point there are traces of the Antonine Wall between the river and the road, with the remains of a Roman fort on the south side of the road and extending towards the canal.

Just as the Kelvin skirts Kilsyth on the south but does not touch it, so the Kelvin forms the northern boundary of Kirkintilloch without impinging on the town in any real sense. Kirkintilloch has changed mightily in the half-century since I first knew it, but it is still a very attractive town, perched on a cluster of rolling hills that mark the southern edge of the Kelvin Valley, with commanding views across the plain to the Campsie Hills. You get different perspectives of the town from the Campsies and the banks of the Kelvin: from the latter there are panoramic vistas of the town with the spires and towers of its more venerable buildings sharply silhouetted.

There are four bridges across the river on the north side of Kirkintilloch. From east to west, there is Inchbelly Bridge carrying the A803 towards Kilsyth. Then there is a smaller bridge about a mile to the west, carrying the unmarked road from the A803 past the hospital to Inchbelle Farm and eventually rejoining the main road. Goyle Bridge is on the B757 running due north from Kirkintilloch to Milton of Campsie, while the fourth is the Campsie Road Bridge on the minor road to Springfield that eventually connects with the B822 between Torrance and Lennoxtown. The lastnamed is a fairly recent addition of steel construction, standing alongside a much older stone bridge, now defunct but still standing. Running through the fields of Inchbelle Farm is a stream which connects the Kelvin to Antermony Loch, east of Milton of Campsie. Just beyond the confluence of this burn and the river there is a curious tract of water. It comes from nowhere and goes nowhere, but is merely the vestige of the original meandering course of the Kelvin, cut off when the river was canalised. There are several other 'oxbows' or disconnected loops to the west of Kirkintilloch, testifying to the river's original meandering character before it was disciplined by dredging and channelling.

In truth, the Kelvin, as it bypasses Kirkintilloch, is something of a fraud. It is an insignificant stream when it reaches the town, but by the time it leaves it has become quite recognisable as a river. This transformation is wrought by its amalgamation with the Luggie and the Glazert, both of which really deserve the appellation of 'river' but which have always had to be content with the lesser title of 'water'. The Luggie is about 18 km (over 11 miles) in length, rising on Herd's Hill in north Lanarkshire and flowing in a westerly direction, skirting the southern side of Cumbernauld and giving its name to the suburb of Luggiebank. Gathering strength as it goes, notably from the Shank Burn, the Mollins Burn, the Gain Burn and the Cameron Burn on the south and the oddly named Shannon on the north. The Shannon, which bears absolutely no resemblance to its famous Irish namesake, rises in the hills south of Croy, within metres of another stream which, on the north side of the watershed, runs east to Drumglass, then due west through Twechar, under the canal and the B8023 to empty into the Kelvin near Shirva Farm.

On the Luggie, near Luggiebank

Herd's Hill is, in fact, a watershed, as the River Avon has its source nearby before running in an easterly direction to join the Forth near Bo'ness. The Luggie and its tributaries drain a wide area west of Palacerigg and Greengairs. At Luggiebank, two kilometres south of Cumbernauld, the Stirling Road (B8054) heading south towards Airdrie crosses the Luggie on a high road bridge, but nearby is the original bridge, still standing though closed to motor vehicles. At this point the Luggie flows through a gorge, with wooded cliffs on the south bank but a narrow strip of level ground on the north bank. From here, footpaths run westward to Condorrat and eastward to Palacerigg Country Park. The footpaths, designated the Cumbernauld Greenspaces, are maintained by the Scottish Wildlife Trust as a Millennium initiative. The paths tend to be very muddy in places, especially where they are crossed by the small streams draining off the high ground, so wellies are essential footwear except in high summer.

The Luggie and its own tributaries pass through a number of villages that are fast losing their rural character, due to the spread of housing. Moodiesburn, which takes its name from one of these streams, arose in the eighteenth century as a hamlet alongside the Glasgow-Stirling turnpike road, but it was considerably expanded in the nineteenth century as a result of coalmining in the district. Many of the present houses were erected only in the 1960s, following the transfer of miners and their families from Bridgend. As a result of the Auchengeich colliery disaster, Bridgend was closed down and its miners' rows demolished. There is a monument listing the names of those who perished in the tragedy, a constant reminder of the hazardous conditions in which men laboured to hew coal out of the ground. The Garnkirk Burn rises on the northern outskirts of Millerston and bypasses Stepps to run in a northeasterly direction, through Glen plantation and Crow Wood golf course. It begins to turn back on itself north of Chryston then heads northeast again to join the Bothlin Burn. Back in the late eighteenth century there was a plan to divert the course of the Luggie, via this burn, to Hogganfield Loch which would then serve as a reservoir for Glasgow, but this interesting project was never implemented.

Like Moodiesburn, Chryston was originally a cluster of cottages that congregated about the medieval packhorse track that ran eastwards from Glasgow, but in the eighteenth century the village was bypassed when the turnpike road was built some way to the south, thereby calling Muirhead into existence. Unlike Moodiesburn, however, the development of Chryston and Muirhead in the late nineteenth century was mostly residential.

The Luggie is also served by a drainage ditch, known as the Canal Feeder, which runs due east and west, mostly west where it eventually joins up with the stream from Moodiesburn to form the Bothlyn (Bothlin) which empties into the Luggie at Oxgang on the south side of Kirkintilloch. Long before that point, the Luggie has become a sizeable river in its own right, giving its designation if not its name to the suburb of Waterside where the banks are attractively landscaped. On the banks of the Luggie at this spot there was a watermill expressly dedicated to the tiresome business of flax-dressing, whereby lint was separated from the pithy stalks of flax-plants. This lint-mill was the direct outcome of an eighteenth-century project to encourage the cultivation of flax in Scotland for the indigenous linen industry, and lessen its dependence on the products of northern Ireland. Not only was flax grown in the surrounding countryside, but the lint was spun locally and supplied to weavers who worked at handlooms in their cottages. By the late eighteenth century, however, mechanisation was overtaking the textile industry and the spinning of cotton thread in factories, such as James Stirling's mill on the Luggie, brought the cottage industry of damask linen to an end.

The handloom weavers were at the peak of their prosperity over the ensuing four decades and as late as 1839 there were more than two thousand looms in and around Kirkintilloch, making it third, after Glasgow and Paisley, as a leading textile centre. Interestingly, handloom weaving survived longer in Kirkintilloch than it did elsewhere in southwest Scotland, the weavers concentrating on lappets, fine decorative muslins with raised floral patterns which continued in demand till well past the middle of the century. Remarkably, there were still a few handloom weavers in Kirkintilloch at the end of the nineteenth century, and the last to ply his craft was William 'Paw' Handley of Hillhead. His wife prepared the shuttles while one daughter assisted as a weaver and another daughter peddled bolts of cloth around the neighbourhood. The Handleys gave up their business in the early 1920s.

The weavers were the aristocrats of labour; not only were they earning relatively high wages but the solitary nature of their work inclined them to contemplative study. They were above average intelligence, read widely and thought for themselves, so it is not surprising that the weavers generally held radical views in politics and religion. Kirkintilloch has some Covenanting connections (the Martyr's Stone commemorates John Wharry and James Smith, executed on 13 June 1683 for their part in the ambush of soldiers transporting the Covenanter, Alexander Smith, to Edinburgh). Later, the town was a stronghold of the Auld Lichts and Seceders, long before the rise of the Free Church in the 1840s.

The weavers were always in the forefront of radical politics, from the Friends of the People in the 1790s to the Chartists of the 1840s, although it should be noted that one of the most prominent figures in the radical agitation of the 1790s was a lawyer and member of the landed gentry. The remarkable story of Thomas Muir of Huntershill is recounted in Chapter 4.

During redevelopment in Waterside, a political banner dated 1832 was discovered in the former cottage of a weaver. Although it had the Union Jack in one quadrant, the field of the flag was occupied by a device showing the scales of justice suspended from the cap of liberty, with crossed weaver's shuttles behind. The banner bore three slogans: NOTHING SHALL EXTINGUISH LIBERTY, REFORM, REDRESS, RELIEF and THE VOICE OF THE PEOPLE IS THE SUPREME... (a fragment is missing from the lower right-hand side of the banner). The date, of course, places this banner firmly in the period of the demonstrations in support of the Reform Bill, whose passage democratised parliament.

The condition of the weavers suffered drastically as their industry was increasingly mechanised. Whereas formerly the middlemen had handled piece-work from hundreds of handloom weavers, they now found it much more economical to employ millhands (mostly girls) in factories. The handloom weavers could not compete, and were either forced into the new factories at a fraction of the money they had previously earned, or to emigrate or starve. Tragically, many of them could not afford to emigrate, and subsisted on handouts and the soup-kitchen which was conducted in the town throughout the Hungry Forties by the more affluent or charitably inclined citizens. These hard times must have come as a terrible blow to men of a proud and independent turn of mind. Out of this searing experience came many of the pioneers of socialism. One of these was Tom Johnston, the weaver's son who became a Labour cabinet minister.

His writing desk, and a collection of his writings, are on display in the reference section of the William Patrick Memorial Library. Tom Johnston House is the headquarters of local government for the district.

Kirkintilloch lagged well behind other textile towns in embracing the new technology and it was not until 1859 that Brodie's steam-powered mill was opened in Southbank Road. It had no sooner commenced operations than it was hard hit by the outbreak of the American Civil War which cut off vital supplies of raw cotton. After the mill burned down, most of the millhands moved to factories in Glasgow, though they returned home at the weekends. James Slimon was much more successful, opening a mill at Kelvinside in 1867. At the turn of the century Slimon's mill had about three hundred looms, employing over two hundred girls in the production of cotton cloth for shirts, skirts and suits. More than 90 per cent of output was destined for the American market, although during the First World War the factory switched to the production of khaki for army uniforms. The factory closed down in the 1920s. Slimon built Camphill House which was sold in 1929 and eventually became the town's public library. It closed in 1994 when the present library at the top of the Cowgate was opened and, at the time of writing, is boarded up to prevent vandalism.

Although Kirkintilloch has grown and changed out of all recognition in the past century, the banks of the Luggie have retained something of their rural character. Near the bridge leading to the town centre stands an obelisk, erected in 1876 to the memory of a seventeen-year-old Glasgow youth named Hazelton Robert Robson who lost his own life on 5 September that year while attempting to save a child from drowning when the Luggie was in spate. Robson himself was interred in the Glasgow Necropolis where his grave is completely obscured by larger and more opulent tombstones; but here in Kirkintilloch his obelisk of red granite, standing in the centre of a small garden, is still one of the town's principal landmarks. Across the street is a sandstone building which still bears the name LIBERAL CLUB in raised lettering above the doorway; but the doorway and adjoining windows have long since been walled up and a new sign proclaims it to be the Turret Theatre.

A hundred years and more ago, the Luggie perennially inundated the low-lying lands on the east side of the town, but then a project was put in hand to deepen the channel and tame the Luggie by retaining walls of masonry, much of which survives intact to this day. Some of the lower courses of stonework in the bridge at Eastside, in fact, date back to the Middle Ages and reflect the importance of this river-crossing on the packhorse route. There is a milestone at one corner of the bridge, indicating the importance of this route in bygone times. Alongside stands one of the oldest buildings in the town, an eighteenth-century house which was at one time the residence of Sir John Stirling, the pioneer of cotton in Kirkintilloch.

Robert Burns wished to extol the merits of his Ayrshire rivers in poetry but conceded that sometimes their names were 'horribly prosaic'. David Gray, the bard of Kirkintilloch (1838-61), showed considerable promise in the posthumous volume entitled *The Luggie and Other Poems*:

Beneath an ash in beauty tender leaved,
And through whose boughs the glimmering sunshine flow'd,
In rare ethereal jasper, making cool
A chequered shadow in the dark green grass,
I lay enchanted.
Before me streams most dear unto my heart -
Sweet Luggie and sylvan Bothlin — fairer twain
Than ever sang themselves into the sea -
Were rolled together in an emerald vale.

Significantly young David never apostrophised the Kelvin in similar vein. He spent his all too short life at Duntiblae on the southeast side of Kirkintilloch and his favourite walks were along the banks of the Luggie and the Bothlin. The weaver's cottage where he was born has long since vanished and his only memorial is a modest monument over his grave in the Old Aisle Cemetery. But he gave literary form to these two streams and his memory lives on through his verse which has enjoyed renewed interest since A.V. Stuart's biography (including the collected works) was published in 1961 to mark the centenary of Gray's death. The son of a weaver, young David showed extraordinary merit as a boy and his parents scrimped and saved in order to send him to Glasgow University in the hope that he would enter the ministry, but even as a teenager David excelled as a versifier and when scarcely out of his teens he went to London to further his poetic career. He had little money and slept rough in Hyde Park where he caught a chill. Malnourished and worn out, his body raddled by tuberculosis, he returned to Kirkintilloch to die. In the last weeks of his life he feverishly put his poems in order and arranged for their publication. He had just finished reading the proofs when he died, so he had the satisfaction of seeing his verses in 'guid black prent'.

Beyond Eastside is Hillhead Road which runs in a southeasterly direction up a slope to the canal, steep enough but not as steep as Hopkins Brae which it replaced in the 1930s. At the top of the slope was one of Kirkintilloch's best-known landmarks, the narrow bascule bridge over the canal. This wooden bridge which rose and was lowered in much the same manner as Tower Bridge in London, was perfectly adequate in the days of horsedrawn traffic, but the advent of motor cars and buses in the 1920s placed an intolerable strain on it, so it was replaced by an all-metal swing bridge in 1938. Immediately beyond the bridge, the canal widens to form the Hillhead Basin, terminus of the canal in the 1770s when it first opened to waterborne traffic from Grangemouth.

For a quarter of a century Kirkintilloch was the capital of Strathkelvin, one of the nineteen districts of Strathclyde Region, formed from the parishes of Kirkintilloch, Cadder, Campsie and Baldernock and extending from the Campsies to Bishopbriggs, Stepps and Gartcosh on the outskirts of Glasgow. Strathkelvin, the valley of the Kelvin, was an excellent name and it seems a pity that, in the latest round of local government restructuring, it has given way to East Dunbartonshire. The district is roughly rhomboid and its river system quarters it like a Saltire cross, the Glazert and Luggie running from northwest to southeast, and the Kelvin from northeast to southwest, intersecting at Kirkintilloch itself.

The name of this bustling town is misleading for, although it boasts many churches, it does not derive its name from any of them. The original name was Caerpentaloch, which is pure Welsh (or rather Strathclyde British) for 'the fort at the head of the ridge'. The line formed by the Kelvin and the Glazert seems to have formed the frontier between the kingdoms of the Picts and the Britons of Strathclyde. The latter spoke a variant of Brythonic or P-Celtic, so called because of the p sound in words such as *pen* (head) or *map* (son) whereas Goidelic or Q-Celtic, from which Gaelic is descended, used a hard q sound as in *ceann* (head) or *mac* (son). As the Gaelic of the Picts and Scots supplanted the Welsh of the Strathclyde Britons, so there was a subtle change in the sound of the name and a substitution of the second k for p. The people of Kirkintilloch, however, have shortened the name variously to Kirky, Carney or Caurnie, all forms which occur in local literature and lore as well as in brand names (such as the Caurnie Soaperie, famed these days for its wonderful selection of aromatic glycerine soaps).

The *caer* of the ancient Britons was, in fact, adapted from one of the Roman forts on the Antonine Wall which, at this juncture, lay very close to the lofty south bank of the Kelvin. Stone from the wall provided a very convenient source of masonry for the peel or castle erected by the Comyns, the remains of which, on a commanding site high above the river, are now in the care of the Secretary of State for Scotland and maintained by the Ministry of Public Buildings and Works. Turn left at the junction of the Cowgate and the West High Street and go up the steep brae, through the beautiful war memorial wrought-iron gates and into Peel Park and you are standing on the very oldest part of the town. The Antonine Wall traverses the park, close to whose western boundary are the remains of the stone foundations of the wall. On the eastern side of the park is the distinct mound which is all that survives of the Comyn stronghold.

At the west end of the town, just beyond the confluence of the Luggie and the Kelvin, stands the remains of a second Roman fort, while a Roman fortlet is located about a kilometre farther to the southwest, on the north bank of the canal. Not surprisingly, the town is rich in classical and medieval antiquities, many of which are preserved in the Hunterian Museum of Glasgow University, although there is a good selection to be seen in Kirkintilloch's Auld Kirk Museum, a 1960s conversion of the original parish church of St Mary's at the north end of the Cowgate but recently considerably refurbished and upgraded. Kirkintilloch was a royal burgh by the middle of the twelfth century and a stronghold of the Comyn family who supported John Baliol in his bid for the kingship. The name Oxgang by which a central part of the town is known alludes to the piece of land, amounting to an oxgate, which was conferred by William Comyn, Lord of Kirkintilloch, about 1170 upon the monks of Cambuskenneth. Some thirty years previously Kirkintilloch's first church, dedicated to St. Ninian, was erected by Thorold, High Sheriff of Stirlingshire and lord of the barony of Kirkintilloch and Cumbernauld. Of the original twelfth-century foundation, at the west end of the town on a height overlooking the Kelvin, nothing now remains. Even the Auld Aisle is all that now remains of St. Mary's Church, erected in 1644 from stones of the original church.

Nearby stands the Barony Chambers, formerly the town hall and now also converted into a museum. This imposing building was erected in 1814-15 on the site of the old Tolbooth. The ground floor was occupied by the courtroom and the town jail, while the middle floor held the council chamber. The top floor contained a schoolroom, known locally as the Steeple School. This closed in 1875, the pupils being moved to Lairdsland School, and for many years thereafter the room was the venue of the local Masonic lodge. The building was surmounted by a steeple containing a bell and a clock, erected about 1823. The original bell cracked and had to be recast in 1829 and 1849. It was removed from the steeple in 1977 and is now housed in the Auld Kirk Museum. On weekdays it was tolled at six in the morning and ten at night, and on Sundays it called the faithful to divine worship, being rung four times, 'at rising time, family worship time, dressing time for kirk, and again at kirk time'. The clock was replaced by an electric timepiece at the end of 1950. The civic use of the building ceased between 1906 and 1920 when a new town hall was erected, and subsequently it was employed as a lawyer's chambers until 1979 when it was taken over by the district council and refurbished as a museum of local life, opened in 1982.

Sir John Comyn, also known as the Red Comyn, supporter of King John Baliol and later a staunch upholder of English rule in Scotland, kept an appointment in the Church of the Greyfriars, Dumfries one fateful day in 1306 with Robert Bruce, the young Earl of Carrick, who hoped to win over the Comyn faction in his own bid for the throne. The two men quarrelled, blades were drawn, and in the white heat of anger Bruce thrust his dagger into his adversary. Reeling in shock at what he had done, Bruce staggered from the church and cried to his supporters, 'I doubt I have slain the Comyn'. His henchman Roger de Kirkpatrick riposted, 'You doubt! Then I'll mak siccar (sure).' With that he ran into the church and finished the job. Turning this act of folly and grave sacrilege to advantage, however, Bruce and his friends rushed off to Castledykes south of the town, took the stronghold by surprise, and raised the standard of revolt, a renewal of the struggle for national survival that led eventually to Bannockburn (1314) and the Declaration of Arbroath (1320). In the early years of the struggle Bruce had to face not only the English but also hostile Scottish factions. Among the latter, the Comyns continued to take a prominent role, determined to avenge the murder of their kinsman. The Comyn castle, reinforced by an English garrison, held out against Bruce, but it was eventually reduced by the King's ally Robert Wishart, Bishop of Glasgow, a muscular Christian who once defiantly informed the Pope, no less, that it was better to fight for Bruce in Scotland than crusade against the Saracens in the Holy Land. Timber from the islands of Loch Lomond was used to construct catapults and other siege engines, with which Wishart besieged the castle.

Inevitably, with the triumph of Bruce, the power of the Comyns was destroyed. Their lands were seized by the King and transferred to the Flemings as a reward for their loyalty. They preferred to rule the district from their castle at Cumbernauld, so the Comyn peel tower fell into disuse. Long defunct, this picturesque ruin was plundered for building materials in the eighteenth century, and little remains today of a once impressive landmark, although the local authorities have made the most of it, with a nicely landscaped pathway running round its base. The site was gifted to the burgh in 1898 and was then laid out as a public park belatedly celebrating the Diamond Jubilee of Queen Victoria. Seven years later the Perry Bandstand and Hudson Fountain, both cast at the Lion Foundry, were inaugurated. Peel Park is an ideal vantage point from which to get a good view of the Kelvin in the valley below. It seems strange that all the development in the town has been towards the south, so that it and neighbouring Lenzie are now indistinguishable, but until now there has been no development beyond the Kelvin, due to the susceptibility of this plain to flood.

After the Wars of Independence, Kirkintilloch seems to have largely escaped from later tumults. Doubtless the armies of Montrose and Cromwell came and went, but they left no mark on the town. In 1746, however, the Highland army of Prince Charles Edward passed through the town on its retreat northwards. A Kirky lad rashly discharged his fowling piece at a Highlander in the rearguard. Although the shot missed, the incident was swiftly reported to the prince who was so incensed at this outrage that he determined to turn around and sack the town as a reprisal. Fortunately the bailies of Kirkintilloch rode out of the town and pleaded for mercy, so Prince Charles settled for a stiff fine instead before heading for Falkirk. Three quarters of a century earlier the Highland Host had been turned loose to terrorise the Lowlands and though there is no record of specific incidents in connection with this royal act of terrorism, there is no doubt that a staunchly Covenanting town like Kirkintilloch would have suffered the rapaciousness of the kilted savages who were forcibly billeted there. Ironically, much of the construction of the canal, a generation after the Jacobite Rebellion, was carried out by Highland navvies, many of whom courted local girls, married and settled in the town. Incidentally, the costs of building the canal were largely met from money raised by the government from the sale of the estates of Jacobite lairds.

Although the Kelvin does not flow through Kirkintilloch it has made its poetic mark. D. Weir, who published *Kirkintilloch as it Existed Fifty Years Ago* (1887) quotes an anonymous poet at great length (probably himself), of which this is but a stanza:

Kelvin! Thy banks are classic ground,
Where minstrel's foot is often found.
On thy green sward young lovers rove,
And breathe eternal vows of love.
Thy turbid streams rolling down,
And leaves of autumn's tinted brown
Are hurrying on to meet their doom
In the far sea's eternal tomb.

Otherwise the Kelvin has made remarkably little impact on the town. In the plethora of illustrated books about the town, published in recent years, it scarcely rates a mention. Kirkintilloch, like many other towns, now boasts a crop of booklets reproducing old postcards that pander to the nostalgia boom but there is not a single picture of the river to be seen, and the much more photogenic Luggie steals the limelight every time. The name of the river has inevitably left its mark, most notably in Kelvin Court, a new development of flats on the ridge overlooking the Kelvin at the west end of the town.

Another place to get a good view of the river valley and the sweep of the Campsies beyond is the car park at the rear of Kirkintilloch's splendid new public library. Although the present building dates only from 1994 it retains the name of the William Patrick Memorial Library which was borne by its predecessor. It pays tribute to the memory of the Revd Dr William Patrick (1852-1911), a native of Glasgow, who was minister of St David's Free Church from 1878 to 1892, when he was translated to Dundee. The fourteen years of his ministry in Kirkintilloch were often stormy as the energetic and innovative Patrick constantly locked horns with the stuffier members of his flock. A powerful orator and charismatic preacher, however, he soon had his church overflowing with new adherents. Not content with the pulpit, he bestrode a wider stage, becoming involved in many aspects of local affairs but thereby falling foul of some of the more fundamentalist congregants who believed that such activities were unseemly for a man of the cloth. In 1892 he became the first minister to serve on a burgh school board and later he was appointed Chairman of the Kirkintilloch Educational Trust.

Reverend William Patrick

Apart from the library, which was endowed by his brother David, William Patrick is remembered chiefly for the prominent part he took in the Kirkintilloch temperance movement from 1880 onwards. His efforts to stamp out drunkenness were so successful and long-lasting that, ten years after his death, Kirkintilloch voted for Prohibition. It would be misleading to give him all the credit for this, for Kirkintilloch had a long history of campaigns against the demon drink. It is recorded that there were forty ale-houses in Kirkintilloch in 1828 to slake the thirst of the weavers and flax-dressers after a hard day's darg. These places of liquid refreshment were even open on Sundays and one of the duties of the kirk elders was to tour the pubs and drive the drinkers off to the Sabbath services. As long ago as 1830 a society was formed, its members pledging themselves to abstain from drinking spirits (whisky, gin, brandy and rum), but there was no ban on 'fermented liquors' (ales and beers). Five years later, however, the Kirkintilloch Total Abstinence Society was formed, its members promising to abjure alcohol in any form. Later on, such movements as the Rechabites (1841) and the Good Templars (1870) established branches in the district. Up to that time the movement against alcohol had been passive, but thereafter a more aggressive position was taken. In 1871 the Star of Lenzie Lodge and the Roman Fort Lodge were founded, both aiming at a reduction in the number of licensed premises in the area. In 1872 they amalgamated with the Lifeboat Lodge of Good Templars, acquired a permanent meeting place in Alexandra Street and went from strength to strength from then onward. The Revd Patrick became involved in 1880 and gave the temperance movement a new sense of purpose and direction, even communion wine in the churches being replaced by non-alcoholic wine. Under the Temperance Act of 1913 a No-Licensing Committee was established and led eventually to the referendum on 2

November 1920. The prohibitionists ran a zealous campaign under the slogan 'Beer or Boots' (indicating that money spent on drink could be far better spent on footwear). The Publican Party countered with a poster campaign. On the day of the poll, the pubs were closed as required by statute. Their windows were plastered with posters: 'Closed today by law. Vote No Change or we shall be closed for ever by the fanatical prohibitionists. Electors stick up for your rights.' This was one of the earliest occasions on which women exercised their new-won right to vote, and they did so in large numbers, overwhelmingly in favour of Prohibition. The results, announced at 10.25 p.m. that night, were conclusive. No new licences would be issued, while the licences of ten public houses and one grocer expired the following May. Kirkintilloch was 'dry' until the ban on alcohol within the burgh limits was revoked in 1968. For forty-seven years Kirky topers had to go to Milton of Campsie, whose solitary tavern did a roaring trade as a consequence.

After his stint in Dundee, William Patrick answered a call to Canada and crowned his brilliant career as Principal of the Presbyterian College in Winnipeg. On retirement he returned to Kirkintilloch where he died at the relatively early age of fifty-nine. He never married, and eventually shared his manse with his bachelor younger brother David who moved from Glasgow to Kirkintilloch to practise law. He became Town Clerk in 1887, and between them the Patrick brothers held temporal and secular sway over the town. David Patrick was one of Kirkintilloch's best-loved figures and noted for his many benefactions to the town. Apart from providing public parks he bought Camphill House from the textile manufacture James Slimon and in 1929 gifted it to the burgh for use as a public library in memory of his brother.

Kirkintilloch was fortunate in having prominent citizens who felt that they had a duty to give back to the town some of the wealth which they had generated there. This particular Victorian ethic inspired Miss Beatrice Clugston to endow the Broomhill Home for Incurables, recalled in an impressive memorial erected in 1891.

Of infinitely greater importance to Kirkintilloch than the Kelvin, the Luggie and the Glazert is the Forth and Clyde Canal which extended as far as the town by 1773. The following year the Kirkintilloch Aqueduct was constructed to carry the canal over the Luggie and (later on) the railway. Although the railway line is long defunct, and the canal is in a state of suspended animation, the aqueduct survives.

With the advent of the canal, what had hitherto been a rather sleepy little village was transformed virtually overnight, as canal barges took the coal, ironstone and limestone from its mines and quarries eastwards to the Forth and Edinburgh. Kirkintilloch is justifiably proud of its pre-eminence in the history of Scottish transport. Not only could it boast that it was the country's first inland port, but it was also very quick to take advantage of the railway system. The Monkland and Kirkintilloch Railway, opened in October 1826, ranks second only to the Irvine-Troon line, developed in 1809 but confined to horse-drawn wagons. The Monkland railway used malleable iron rails from its inception, capable of carrying steam locomotives, although during its first five years in operation its freight-wagons were likewise hauled by horses.

In June 1831 the Garnkirk and Glasgow Railway was opened, using steam locomotives from the outset. Its line ran westward to Townhead in Glasgow from Gartsherrie which was on the Monkland Railway, but the latter company refused to grant the use of locomotives on its track and so passengers had to transfer to horse-drawn coaches for their onward journey to Kirkintilloch or Airdrie. From then onwards, these railway companies were at each other's throats, waging an often vicious campaign to prevent the opposition gaining any advantage.

The Monkland and Kirkintilloch Railway was compelled by the competition to introduce steam locomotives, so the general travelling public at least benefited from the deadly rivalry. This railway had its terminus in Southbank Road, near the Hillhead canal basin and thus provided a means of conveying freight, by rail and canal, from one side of Scotland to the other. The railway was promoted by a consortium of colliery owners and ironmasters who wished to circumvent the high freight charges of the Monkland Canal Company whose waterway (completed in 1793) linked Glasgow to the coalfields and ironworks of the Monklands district (Airdrie and Coatbridge). By building a railway from Palace Craigs near Airdrie to Kirkintilloch, a distance of ten miles, the syndicate hoped that the extra journey by the Forth and Clyde Canal to Port Dundas would be offset by the advantage of being able to ship minerals eastwards to Edinburgh. The line continued in operation till 1966 but was then closed and dismantled, although parts of the track are still in evidence between Whitegates and Garngaber.

The main rail route between Edinburgh (Haymarket) and Glasgow (Queen Street) was opened in 1842 and a station, named Kirkintilloch, was erected at Garngaber. In 1848 a spur from the main line ran to Lennoxtown and in this connection the original station at Garngaber was abandoned in favour of a new one farther west and now named Kirkintilloch Junction. Two years later this station was renamed Campsie Junction, but when the line was extended in 1867 through Campsie to Killearn, the name was changed yet again. This time it was called Lenzie Junction, reviving an ancient name by which the entire district had been known in medieval times. Alongside the railway station, one of the company's directors built himself a fine house on a hilltop. Pleased with the prospects, he acquired parcels of land in the neighbourhood and then formed a partnership with a speculative builder who laid out plots and built a number of villas. Selling those houses, however, proved to be quite difficult, despite the convenience of a station that gave ready access to Edinburgh and Glasgow; but in the end the railway superintendent hit upon a great idea. He persuaded his fellow directors to make a startling offer. Anybody buying or building a house within a mile of the station costing at least £500 would be granted free travel on the railway for five years from the date of purchase, and for every £100 over that sum a year would be added to the privilege. This ruse was highly successful and soon the local builders and masons had more work on their hands than they could cope with. In this highly original manner the largely residential town of Lenzie came into existence

The branch line had a station at Eastside, known as Kirkintilloch (Town) and later a halt at Back o' Loch was opened in 1925 for the convenience of the farming community but increasingly used by day trippers from Glasgow as well as serving the new housing development at Woodilea. The Southbank Road station on the Monkland and Kirkintilloch Railway was only briefly open to passenger traffic, being for most of its career a goods depot only. The Eastside station and Back o' Loch halt closed to passenger traffic in 1964 and two years later both lines were axed. Lenzie, of course, is still an important station, now mostly used by people from the district commuting to Edinburgh or Glasgow. The Edinburgh and Glasgow Railway was taken over by the North British Railway in 1865 and this, in turn, became part of the London and North Eastern Railway in 1923, being nationalised in 1948.

The canal closed to waterborne freight in 1962, but in its heyday it was also an important medium for public transport as well. Narrow horse-drawn scows were used to convey passenger traffic on the canal between Falkirk and Port Dundas from 1809 onwards, but this business was threatened by the advent of the railways. To combat this, Thomas Grahame devised the Swifts, streamlined iron vessels capable of carrying up to a hundred passengers, and towed by a pair of horses. Attaining a maximum speed of 10 m.p.h., these vessels covered the distance between Falkirk and Port Dundas in three hours. Inevitably the expansion of the rail network put paid to this rather leisurely mode of travel; but James Aitken, proprietor of a store in Kirkintilloch, revived passenger traffic on the canal in June 1893 when he inaugurated sailings by the *Fairy Queen*, the first of three vessels to bear that name. Later came two others, the *May Queen* and the *Gipsy Queen*. These were excursion steamers which plied between Glasgow and Kirkintilloch in the summer months and were normally berthed at Port Dundas. Normally these pleasure boats sailed only as far as Kirkintilloch but occasionally went as far as Craigmarloch near Kilsyth. Aitken kept the service running throughout the First World War, but in September 1939 the canal was closed to all but military traffic and shortly afterwards the third and last of the *Fairy Queens* was ignominiously towed by horses down to the breaker's yard at Paisley. In recent years, however, the stretch of the canal between Kirkintilloch and Bishopbriggs has been dredged and repaired and it is hoped, in the foreseeable future, to restore the entire length of the canal to proper working order. Already, from the Stables by the Glasgow Bridge west of Kirkintilloch one can now dine afloat on the MV *Caledonian*, a reincarnation of the old Queens, as it sails west towards the Sports Centre at Bishopbriggs.

Remarkably, Kirkintilloch was also a thriving shipbuilding centre for many years. Although it is about as far as one can get from the sea, this is where many of the puffers, backbone of the Firth of Clyde and West Highland coastal trade, were constructed and launched. In order to relieve unemployment caused by the mechanisation of the textile industries, a Workingmen's Association was formed with a view to building barges and scows for the canal. This gave rise to a co-operative enterprise pioneered in 1866 by Samuel Crawford who built only one ship, the *Rainbow*, before selling his shipyard near Townhead Bridge to James and John Hay. The site is marked today by a large pneumatic hammer, removed from the former South Bank Ironworks. The hammer was erected on this site in 1981 as a monument to the town's industrial past. Hays specialised in puffers, the sturdy little cargo vessels immortalised in Neil Munro's *Para Handy* stories. The average puffer had a gross tonnage of 80 to 100 but was capable of carrying over 100 tons of cargo. Broad in the beam, with a relatively shallow draught, these little ships were ideally suited to the temperamental waters of the West of Scotland. With a maximum length of 66 feet (22 m) and a breadth of 18 feet (5.5 m), they could navigate the Crinan Canal and thus avoid the dangerous voyage round the Mull of Kintyre, and they could sit high and dry at low tide beside many a Hebridean island and discharge coal and miscellaneous stores on to the sand where they were loaded on to carts. These vessels were also used as cargo-boats on the Forth and Clyde Canal itself and were known as 'inside' puffers, distinguished by their flush decks, tiller steering and lack of bulwarks, whereas the 'outside' boats, capable of riding out the worst Hebridean storms, had continuous bulwarks, wheel steering and derricks for loading and offloading cargo.

Puffers were launched at Hays Yard broadside on rather than stern first, owing to the narrowness of the canal. A rival firm, Peter McGregor and Sons, had a yard in Southbank Road alongside the canal basin and produced a diverse range of small vessels: tugs, launches, pinnaces patrol-boats and assorted ferry-boats as well as puffers. From McGregors Yard came some of the famous Queens that plied on the canal itself, but many of this firm's contracts were for steamships and motor vessels destined for the far corners of the globe. Although it, too, launched boats on the canal, some of the larger vessels had to be partially dismantled and transported by road or rail to a seaport for re-assembly before sailing off to their destination. McGregors Yard closed down in the 1920s but Hays were still producing puffers as late as 1945, the last to be launched being the *Chindit* in September that year. The yard continued to operate for boat repairs until 1961.

From Southbank Road, turn left and cross the bridge into the Cowgate. Until 1933 this was another wooden bascule bridge but it was then replaced by the present structure. Note the carved granite finials which bear motifs symbolic of the town's former industries. The Cowgate is much the same as any other town centre these days, with a fine array of shops and a good shopping mall on the left. Across the street, however, is the Watson Fountain surmounted by an arch bearing the motto 'Ca' canny, but ca' awa''. It was presented to the town in 1893 by Sir John Watson of Earnock, who made his fortune and reputation from coal. The local boy who made good, he rose from very humble beginnings to become one of the foremost coalmasters of the late Victorian period.

Traditionally, Kirkintilloch's fortunes were bound up in its mineral resources, especially coal, ironstone and limestone which were extensively worked from the middle of the eighteenth century onwards and gave rise to a number of support industries as well as four iron-foundries. The Luggiebank Ironworks was erected by Archibald Gilchrist in 1832 alongside the Luggie, a fortuitous choice of location, for it proved to be very convenient when the Campsie branch line of the Edinburgh and Glasgow Railway was opened a few years later. For a time it flourished, specialising in sleeper chairs and other ironwork for the railways, as well as pots and stills for the chemicals and gas industries. It fell into disuse in the 1890s, though the buildings lingered on a further century before they were demolished.

Workers in the Pipe Bay at the Star Foundry, Kirkintilloch, founded in 1861 and closed in 1981

The Star Foundry was established in Shamrock Street in 1861 by Alexander Smith and specialised in water-pipes and heating appliances. A century later it was taken over by an English company, Glynwed, but a massive programme of upgrading plant and machinery failed to stave off closure when the building trade switched to plastics for water pipes, and the foundry closed down in 1981.

The Basin or Etna Foundry derived its more familiar name from its location alongside the canal basin. It was established in 1872 by John Napier on a site which had previously been used for a sawmill and later an engineering workshop. Napier, later joined by David Dow of Falkirk, concentrated on small precision castings for the manufacture of sewing machines, but later diversified into kitchen ranges and stoves. The rise of gas and electric cookers in the 1930s led to a decline in its fortunes, although it continued to produce and repair boilers until closure in 1951. The best-known was the Lion Foundry which commenced operations in 1880 and rapidly built up a wide reputation, mainly for ornamental ironwork, such as public fountains and street furniture. While the great Carron ironworks added to its Napoleonic fame by casting many of the nation's pillar boxes, the Lion Foundry got a slice of the postal contract in the 1930s when it was given the task of manufacturing the K6, and later K8, models of telephone kiosks. When British Telecom decided in 1984 to replace the familiar and much-loved red phone-boxes with a more modern, all-glass form of open booth, it was the end of the road for Lion, and the foundry closed at the end of that year. A handsome fountain, topped by a female figure, was presented by Robert Hudson, one of the founding partners, to the burgh to celebrate the firm's silver jubilee in 1905 and this stands in Peel Park to this day, a poignant reminder of a Kirky company which once occupied a very lucrative niche in the development of telecommunications.

The red phone-box, once as familiar a sight as the red pillar-box, has now vanished from the urban scene in Britain, although many of them are still doing yeoman service in rural districts. They were exported to many other parts of the Commonwealth and, painted in many colours other than red, they are still to be seen from Hong Kong to the West Indies. The Kelvin provides a curious link between the humble phone-box and one of the region's most prominent land-marks, the majestic neo-Gothic pile atop Gilmorehill which is the University of Glasgow on the banks of the Kelvin. Whereas the University was the crowning glory for the Victorian architect Sir George Gilbert Scott (1811-78) it was his grandson, Sir Giles Gilbert Scott, who designed the phone-box. Giles, like his celebrated grandfather, was essentially an ecclesiastical architect and was knight-ed in 1924 shortly after the consecration of Liverpool Cathedral. In the same year he was invited to take part in a competition organised by the British Institute of Industrial Art for the design of the telephone box and beat off stiff compe-tition from Sir Robert Lorimer and Sir John Burnet. Although his design was approved in 1925 three years elapsed before the first kiosks went into production, and the Lion Foundry was the main manufacturer from 1931 till 1984.

Coal was being mined from outcrops in the Campsies in late-medieval times and a number of small pits were in operation by the early seventeenth century, often associated with the working of ironstone and limestone deposits, which were extensive. The mining industry developed rapidly in the late eighteenth century as the demand for lime for fertiliser and coal to power the Industrial Revolution escalated. The collieries at Bar Hill, Shirva and Strone developed in the late 1830s and provided much-needed employment for many handloom weavers who had been thrown out of work by the advent of mechanisation. The mining enterprises of Kirkintilloch reached their zenith at the turn of the century, when St Flannan's at Twechar boasted the deepest vertical shaft in Scotland. By the early 1900s there were numerous pits in the district, but they were hard hit by the national miners' strike of 1912 and the General Strike of 1926. Meiklehill, one of the district's largest collieries, closed down in the latter year. Woodilee Colliery lingered on a further five years.

The story of the rise and fall of the industries of the Kelvin Valley makes sombre reading; textiles, engineering, shipbuilding, ironfounding and mining have all come and gone. After a long period of post-industrial decline and decay, however, Kirkintilloch has picked itself up. The heart of the burgh was modernised and suburbs of new houses, both council and privately owned, sprang up on former 'brown' sites. The rejuvenation of Kirkintilloch was so remarkable that the burgh was awarded the very first of the Saltire Prizes as the 'most alive community in Scotland' to develop between the end of the war and 1960. Although the town has grown enormously in more recent years, it still retains a sense of community, epitomised in the large number of civic amenities and activities. Indeed, the Kirkintilloch Male Voice Choir has attained international renown.

The Japanese Connection

Shortly after the First World War a young Japanese named Masataka Taketsura came to Scotland and enrolled at Glasgow University where he studied distillation processes. Later he worked at the White Horse Distillery gaining practical experience and it was during this period that he lodged for a time with the Cowan family in Kirkintilloch. He fell in love with the elder daughter, Rita, and they were married in 1921. With his young bride, he returned to Japan and joined the firm which eventually developed into the Suntory Corporation, for whom he erected their first distillery at Yamagaki in 1925. Later he left and established his own distillery, the Nikka Yoichi Company at Hokkaido in the north of Japan where he felt that the climate was more similar to that found in Scotland. This distillery commenced operations in 1934, concentrating initially on the production of fruit juice which did not require a lengthy period to mature. The following year he initiated the long and time-consuming process of distilling brandy and whisky although the first spirits in commercial quantities were not ready to go on sale until October 1940. The outbreak of the Pacific War in December 1941 and the subsequent disastrous course of the conflict were major setbacks, but Taketsura persevered and eventually built up a Japanese whisky empire, second to none. Rita Taketsura did her best to assimilate, but during the war she was often spat on in the streets and was constantly shadowed by Kempai Tai, the dreaded secret police, but with Scottish doggedness she survived and lived to enjoy the fruits of her husband's phenomenal success. Rita, who left Kirkintilloch in the very year that the burgh went 'dry', died in 1961. Her husband, who outlived her by twenty years, erected a very touching memorial to her in her adopted land. The remarkable story of Rita Taketsura (1896-1961) will be found in Olive Checkland's riveting account *Japanese Whisky, Scotch Blood* (1998).

CHAPTER THREE

The Campsies and the Glazert

If the Luggie may be said to have a fairly humdrum existence, flowing placidly throughout the year except in brief periods of heavy rainfall, the Glazert provides a violent contrast. Both tributaries of the Kelvin are picturesque, especially in those parts of their course where they flow through woodland, and certainly in its lower reaches the Glazert presents an image of a wide, shallow river, heading with quiet resignation to its marriage with the tiny partner who robs it of its name. But in its upper reaches the Glazert is a wild beast, sharing the characteristics of the Garrel. Its sources are many and extremely varied. At the farthest point west are the Pow Burn and several other streams which unite east of Strathblane and Muirhouse and run due east along the north side of Bank Wood to Lennoxtown, south of the A891 and a long-disused railway line. Along the way, this stream receives accretions from the tumbling brooks running off the Campsie Fells, but just as the water enters the grounds of Lennox Castle, it is joined by the Finglen Burn which, with its tributaries the Almeet, Alfagie and Horse Burns, drains the western and southern flanks of Hog Hill. A walk up Fin Glen is a test of endurance as you scramble over rocks and gang warily through peat hags and marsh, but the effort is worthwhile for the atmosphere alone. Even if you get no farther than the top of the woods at Knocknair this is a very pleasant walk, passing the cairn believed to commemorate the Revd James Crichton, minister of Campsie parish in the troubled reign of Charles I.

Shortly after the confluence of the Finglen Burn with the main stream, the Aldessan Burn enters Campsie Glen and joins the Glazert just west of Lennoxtown village. Farther east is the Campsie Burn which rises at the very top of Campsie Glen, at an altitude of 333 m (1083 ft). This is another watershed, for only a few metres to the north is the source of the River Carron. This stream has many tributaries and also changes its name. At its source it is the oddly named Nineteentimes Burn, watered by the Newhouse and Priest Burns on its western flanks. Just above Alnwick Bridge on the Crow Road from Fintry, the Alnwick Burn, fed by Katrine's Burn and Shearer's Burn, joins the stream which now becomes the Kirkton or Kirk Burn. Its main tributary on the final stretch is the Alvain Burn draining Inner Black Hill. It runs past the old kirk at Clachan of Campsie and then under the Strathblane Road to follow Glen Road, and joins the Glazert near the eastern entrance to Lennox Castle.

Before the upheavals in local government in the 1970s, the Glazert was a river which ran through Stirlingshire and Dunbartonshire. The boundaries of the new regions and districts were then redrawn, placing the Glazert firmly within Strathkelvin District in Strathclyde Region, but the headwaters of the Finglen Burn obstinately remained outside this demarcation, several hundred metres of the stream running through Stirling District of Central Region, even though the headwaters of this burn, by and large, served as the regional boundary. The frontier then ran eastward along the summits of the Campsies, Hart Hill and Holehead, before following the course of the embryonic Carron. Looking across this magnificently bleak and rugged expanse, it is hard to imagine that one of the ancient tracks along which drovers brought cattle down from the Highlands crossed the hills at this point.

Jamie Wright's Well, Crow Road, Campsie Hills

Driving southwards on the Crow Road (B822) from Fintry to Lennoxtown, with the Kirk Burn on your right, you pass its junction with the Alvain Burn. A few metres farther down the road on the left is Jamie Wright's Well, named in memory of the man who is said to have 'tapped the rock' about the middle of the nineteenth century to provide the thirsty wayfarer with cool, refreshing spring-water. By profession, Jamie was a colour-mixer in the calico printworks at Lennoxtown but his consuming passion was coarse fishing on the Endrick, across the fells near Fintry, and he regularly tramped along this hill road with his boon companion Sandy McKay. They must often have paused at this spring to slake their drouth on a hot summer's day, and thus Jamie formed the idea of converting the spring into a crude stone basin. What Jamie Wright had begun in a primitive manner, others, later on, improved. In the 1870s Robert Gilchrist, with the help of some local workmen, installed a tank and fitted a ladle for the convenience of passers-by. Subsequently James Slimmon, a Kirkintilloch poet, wrote 'The Packman's Salutation to the Mountain Well' which spread the fame of Jamie Wright far and wide. Shortly after Slimmon's death in 1898 there was a move to do something to perpetuate his memory, and this took the eminently practical form of improvements to the well that figured in his best-known poem. A fund was set going and permission was sought from the owner of the land, Peareth Lennox of Lennox Castle, to create the granite well. The work was entrusted to John Baxter, a stonemason of Kirkintilloch who constructed the memorial of grey stone obtained from nearby Queenziemill, tastefully carved across the top with scrolled finials and the inscription JAMIE WRIGHT'S WELL in raised lettering. Below the lintel, a slab of polished red Peterhead granite was inserted. On this were inscribed two stanzas from the poem:

Hail to your dimplin', wimplin' drop,
  Clear, caller, caul',
That bids the drouthy traveller stop
  And tak' his fill!
Hail to your heart-reviving tipple
Enticing slee wi' twinklin' ripple
Thou crystal milk frae Nature's nipple,
  Wee Mountain Well.

  * * *

You joukit frae the furious blast
And seepin' doon the mountain past,
Till here my craig you weet at last,
  Sine ower the stour.

Below Slimmon's name was added ERECTED BY FRIENDS OF THE POET and the date 1900 was inscribed at the base of the well. A basin of Peterhead granite was inserted and fitted with a drinking ladle. The memorial was inaugurated on 23 June 1900 but within weeks it had been vandalised, part of the raised lettering having been chipped off and various sets of initials and names scratched into the stonework. Probably as a result, the Jamie Wright's Well Club was formed in 1903, life membership being fixed at the modest sum of a shilling (5p), although its main purpose appears to have been to promote interest in Slimmon and his poetry. When the well was again vandalised in August 1904 the *Kirkintilloch Herald* went so far as to publish the names and initials freshly incised by vandals. Despite this and later mindless acts, including the theft of the drinking cup from time to time, Jamie Wright's Well is still there. There is a car park about a hundred metres farther down the road, affording splendid views south and west.

Like the Garrel, the tributaries of the Glazert provide abundant examples of narrow gullies and ravines, linns and waterfalls, gloomy chasms and sudden suntraps which make ideal picnic spots on long summer days. Apart from the beetling crags above the Finglen Burn, the steep valleys of the hillside burns may be hard going but they are not impossible, and at the summit the hill walker is well repaid for the effort by the panoramic views of Glasgow as well as the mountain scenery farther north and west. At its southern end Campsie Glen opens out to accommodate the still picturesque village known as Clachan of Campsie, although the erection of yuppie villas in recent years for sharp-suited Glasgow commuters has made *clachan* (Gaelic for hamlet) a misnomer.

Well worth a visit is the ruin of the ancient church of St Machan at the top of the village, named in memory of a sixth-century Celtic saint. Machan was a Scot of Dalriada, a disciple of Columba who studied in Ireland and made a pilgrimage to Rome before settling in Campsie Glen. After a life spent in ministering to the people of the Campsies he died and was buried here. Doubtless his monastic cell was the nucleus for a later church, although the earliest of which there is any record was erected about 1175. In late-medieval times it ranked as a parsonage and among its incumbents were William Lamberton, the influential prelate who backed Robert Bruce, and David Beaton who rose to the eminence of a cardinal in the time of Mary Queen of Scots. To look at this tranquil spot today you would scarcely imagine that it was once a place where people not only took their religion very seriously but also, one might say, in deadly earnest. Loretta Mulholland, author of the *Campsie Glen Picture Album* (1988), notes that of the thirteen ministers of the parish between 1560 and 1780, five were deposed and one was murdered. Between the Reformation in 1560 and the Revolution in 1688 was a period of violent upheavals throughout Scotland in general, but Campsie Glen appears to have been a microcosm of the fanaticism and sectarianism of the times.

The Revd John Collins was killed by a local laird who had fallen in love with the minister's wife and subsequently married the widow. Ironically, Collins had appeared to be a confirmed bachelor, wedded only to his vocation, but not long after he came to the parish he fell in love with a young lady, widely regarded as the fairest and most eligible of the local girls. She had had many would-be suitors, including the Laird of Balglass, but had rejected them all. Now she reciprocated the ardour of the handsome young minister and soon they were married, amid general rejoicing, for both bride and groom were very popular in the district. The Laird of Balglass was outraged and swore to be revenged, but he bided his time and even went out of his way to befriend the minister. He was a frequent visitor at the manse, but as time passed he realised that he could never worm his way back into the lady's affections so long as her husband was around. Eventually he hatched a plot to get rid of his rival. One day in November 1648, Collins had gone to Glasgow to attend a presbytery meeting, but on his journey home he was waylaid by a masked man on horseback who dragged him to the ground and slew him. Balglass then stripped the corpse of watch and valuables to give the impression that he had been the victim of a highwayman.

When the minister's garron turned up at the manse riderless, Mrs Collins was immediately alarmed for her husband's safety and roused her neighbours to go and search the road. Balglass joined the search party and even helped to carry the corpse back to the manse, breaking the tragic news to the widow who collapsed in his arms. In the weeks that followed he was tenderness and solicitude personified, attentive at all times and particularly helpful when the time came for the grieving widow to vacate the manse for her husband's successor. Choosing the right moment he proposed marriage to her, arguing that he could provide a roof for her. Mrs Collins at first rejected the notion, but finally in desperation she gave way and married the laird.

For a time all seemed well. The mystery was unsolved and the murderer was not apprehended. But the laird's conscience was mightily troubled and he became prone to fits of rage and depression. Alarmed at the change in his condition, his anxious wife sought an explanation, but that only made him worse. Eventually she began to pry into his business papers, wondering whether some clue to his troubled state might be revealed. One day, when he was absent from home, she found the key to a mysterious box which he had hidden away and on opening it she discovered her late husband's watch. At this juncture she was caught in the act by Balglass; his guilty expression confirmed her worst suspicions. The lady, who seems to have been prone to fainting at such sudden shocks, passed out and when she came round Balglass had fled. In these troubled times, when law and order had all but broken down, a man could easily lose himself. Perhaps Balglass enlisted in one or other of the armies that roamed Scotland as the struggle between Royalists and Parliament came to an end, or he may have fled to the Continent where Scots mercenaries were very much in demand. Who knows? The story would be completely forgotten were it not for the tombstone of the unfortunate minister which is to be seen to this day in the old kirkyard.

The last two ministers at St Machan's were both notable, although for quite different reasons. Loretta Mulholland describes the Revd James Lapslie (1783-1824) as 'forever outspoken and controversial', which is, if anything, an understatement. Apart from his innate tactlessness which offended many of his parishioners and led to their secession to form a relief church, he was an inveterate creep, continually sucking up to the Tory gentry. Ten years into his ministry, he earned undying notoriety for his ignominious part in the arrest and prosecution of Thomas Muir of Huntershill whose story is recounted in Chapter 4. What makes Lapslie's behaviour all the more reprehensible was that he had been for several years an intimate of the Muir family, but after Muir was indicted for sedition Lapslie went out of his way to betray his friend. At Muir's trial Lapslie was one of the chief witnesses for the prosecution, not only perjuring himself in a brazen manner but being no better than a paid informer; his reward from the Crown took the unusual form of £50 a year for life, in return for which he was required to preach an annual sermon in Stirling. Muir, an accomplished and experienced advocate, conducted his own defence and easily exposed Lapslie for the Judas he was, but to no avail. The jury brought in a guilty verdict and Lord Braxfield sentenced Muir to fourteen years' transportation to Botany Bay. This harsh sentence raised a nationwide protest, but in Campsie parish feelings ran high and Lapslie was forced to lie low for a time; but backed by the threat of military intervention his sullen parishioners were compelled to leave him alone. He continued as minister a further thirty years, until his death in 1824.

In 1825 the Revd Norman MacLeod received a call to the parish, and he ministered there until 1835 when he was translated to St Columba's in Glasgow. Later he became Moderator of the General Assembly and a Dean of the Chapel Royal. Though born in Morven in 1783, where his father, also Norman MacLeod, was minister, the happiest years of his long and fruitful life were spent in Campsie parish and it was here that he was laid to rest in 1862. A charismatic figure, he was all that Lapslie was not, and within a very short time he had healed the differences and re-united the congregation. With the influx of factory workers and millhands to the district, however, the old church was no longer large enough, but under MacLeod's direction a much larger church was erected in 1828 in nearby Newtown of Campsie (now Lennoxtown).

St Machan's fell into disuse, its masonry was dismantled for house building and its fixtures and fittings sold off, much to the annoyance and disgust of the more conservative parishioners. Its bell-tower survived a further quarter of a century, and the bell tolled for funerals at the kirkyard and to summon worshippers to the Sunday evening prayer meetings held in the nearby schoolhouse; but in the 1850s the bell was transferred to the Oswald School in Lennoxtown and then relocated in the church opened at Milton of Campsie in 1888. Today St Machan's is a picturesque ruin, little now remaining apart from one end wall. In 1993 the little square below the ruined kirk was restored, the single-storey buildings are now craft shops and the old church bell has been installed on a low pedestal. It bears an inscription indicating that it was cast in 1729.

The kirkyard is worth close inspection. Apart from the Collins headstone you will find the graves of William Muir of Birdston, author of the 'Ode to the Kelvin' previously mentioned, as well as the last resting place of the much-travelled John Bell of Antermony (1691-1780) whose wanderlust took him to Russia as personal physician to Peter the Great on whose behalf he later headed various diplomatic missions to Persia, Turkey and far Cathay. He returned to Scotland in 1746, married and settled down to write an enthralling book about his career in the service of the Tsar. His descendant, the eminent geographer James Bell, who died in 1833, is also buried here. Antermony Loch, east of Milton of Campsie, is drained by a stream which enters the Kelvin near Inchbelle Farm.

Antermony House itself no longer exists, having been demolished in 1926. Apart from the Bells it has connections with Charles Macintosh (1766-1834) who leased it from the Lennox family as his country seat. A pioneer of many chemical processes, he is best remembered for inventing a method of waterproofing cloth by a mixture of indiarubber and naphtha, hence 'mackintosh' as a form of rainwear. Charles Macintosh King (1836-1920), son of one of Macintosh's partners, likewise leased Antermony after his marriage in 1867.

Doubtless he had grown to love the place as a result of visits to his godfather. He took a leading part in the affairs of the district and rose to the rank of colonel in the Volunteers. After his death, his family gave up their lease in 1923, and as no other tenant could be obtained, the house was allowed to deteriorate and later the site was occupied by a poultry farm.

As well as a martyr's stone, remembering the execution of William Boick at Glasgow on 14 June 1683 for his adherence to the Covenant, the old Clachan kirkyard also contains many tombstones pertaining to the Stirlings of Craigbarnet and Glorat, as well as the impressive mausoleum of the Lennox family. Most family vaults erected by the landed gentry are single-storey structures but this is a building on two floors surmounted by a dome and an elaborate finial. It was constructed in 1715 but repaired and enlarged in 1819 at the behest of Margaret Lennox, the heiress of the Lennox estates. According to local lore, Miss Lennox used the upper chamber as a restroom between Sabbath services, and following her death in 1832 she was interred there. It was last used as a family vault following the funeral of Mrs Kincaid Lennox (nee Frances Maxwell Cunninghame) in 1876 and closed eight years later. Ironically it was sealed with some ancient tombstones of the Kincaids who feuded with the Lennoxes for centuries.

This family were lairds of Kincaid as far back as 1280, their lands extending all along the west bank of the Glazert and bounded on the south by the Kelvin. Despite (or perhaps because of) their extensive landholdings, the Kincaids are conspicuously absent from the roll-call of the great and the good in Scottish history although it has been suggested that successive generations may have held office as constable of Edinburgh Castle in the sixteenth century. They seem to have preferred to keep to their home territory where they were often feuding and fighting with their Lennox neighbours. In his book *Milton of Campsie: People & Places* (1992), James Lindsay cites a number of documents describing instances of lawlessness involving the Kincaids, including the kidnapping of John Lennox (September 1571) and the murder of another John Lennox as he came out of church after Sunday morning service (March 1613). Interestingly, Sir John Kincaid was eventually brought to book for the latter outrage, although profaning the Sabbath seems to have been regarded as a far more heinous crime than murder. At any rate, Kincaid was only required to appear on the stool of repentance every Sunday from August till mid-October 1614.

The long-running feud was eventually resolved by the marriage of John Kincaid to Cecilia Lennox. Their son, John Lennox Kincaid, succeeded his father in 1832 and a year later he fell heir to the Lennox estates on the death of his unmarried Aunt Margaret. To signal this event he changed his name to John Lennox Kincaid Lennox and petitioned the House of Lords to revive the ancient earldom of Lennox. Anticipating a successful outcome to his petition, he decided

The junction of the Finglen Burn and Glazert Water near Lennox Castle

to give up his existing mansions of Woodhead (Lennox) and Kincaid House and move to a purpose-built structure which rejoiced in the name of Lennox Castle. Interestingly, this name has vanished from the metric version of the Ordnance Survey maps which merely designates this landmark as a hospital. There may well have been a castle here in bygone centuries, and as it is, remarkably, one of the very few complete structures dignified by that name to be found on the banks of the Kelvin or its tributaries, it deserves special mention. The pseudo-Gothic pile which lies at the heart of the hospital complex and which gave it its name was erected as recently as 1837 to a design by the celebrated architect David Hamilton. Kincaid Lennox was unsuccessful in reviving the title of nobility. In previous centuries the Duke of Lennox was the Scottish title borne by the Duke of Richmond. One of the Lennox beauties was a mistress of Charles II and is remembered nowadays as the model who posed for the figure of Britannia on the copper coinage (and ultimately the 50p coins of the present day). Lennox Castle, with its fake crenellated towers and battlements, was not untypical of the great baronial mansions of Victorian times, but taxes and death duties as well as the practical problems of maintenance led to its transformation in the 1920s from rich man's retreat to an insane asylum for females.

Changing attitudes to the treatment of mental disorders led to the expansion of the original fortress, overflowing into a motley collection of single-storey buildings and even huts occupying much of the grounds. The mental hospital is still in existence, but the castle itself has now been abandoned as unsuitable.

Currently it is boarded up, a mute reminder of the careless affluence of yesterday's leisured classes rather than a grim monument to the thoughtless barbarity of the Scottish penal system; for most of its original inmates, before the Second World War, were not mentally disturbed, far less mad, but feckless lassies who were deemed to be incorrigibly promiscuous because they had got pregnant, or the unfortunate victims of sexual abuse who had run away from home to escape the unwelcome attention of fathers, uncles and older brothers. As an occasional treat, they were allowed to go down to the village, under strict supervision of course, to spend what little pocket money they had, on toiletries and embroidery material. Older residents of Lennoxtown recall the girls from the Castle, dressed in regulation hats and trenchcoats, proceeding along the street two by two, like the crocodile from some well-bred young ladies' seminary, under the watchful eye of a couple of burly female wardresses.

All three towns or villages in the valley of the Glazert have or had the word Campsie in their name. The oldest is Campsie, otherwise Clachan of Campsie, although its post office is called Campsie Glen, while the local people generally refer to it simply as the Clachan. According to the archaeologists it has been a human settlement since prehistoric times although few of the buildings now extant can be traced back before the middle of the eighteenth century. It was a place of some importance in the Georgian period, because it was the site of the parish church, around which the present village developed. At its zenith, the Clachan boasted a weavers' workshop with fifty looms, a smithy, a bleachworks and a corn-mill with kiln. The lastnamed were operated by John Lapslie, father of the infamous minister, who sold the mill to John Lennox of Woodhead in 1800. The last blacksmith was John Cassells, waylaid and murdered on the Crow Road in the early nineteenth century; a cairn near Jamie Wright's Well marks the spot.

The bleachworks developed out of an eighteenth-century printfield (a calico printworks), and under the direction of William Cunninghame was giving employment to over fifty hands by the middle of the nineteenth century. Subsequently this flourishing concern was taken over by a company that believed in down-sizing. The loss of jobs as a result signalled the end of the Clachan as an industrial village. Many people moved to nearby Lennoxtown. At the 1841 census there had been twenty-eight houses in the village, but by 1881 this number had fallen to nine. The bleachworks closed in 1874 and by the end of the century only one house stood on the site. The manse, originally built in the 1620s, was replaced by later buildings in 1661 and 1727. Parts of the latter are still extant, although it was severely damaged by fire in 1798 when enemies of the notorious Lapslie torched it in revenge for his treatment of Thomas Muir. A new manse was erected in the nineteenth century and continued as the residence of the parish minister until 1956.

Nearby stood Ballencleroch House which has had an extremely chequered career. The lands of Ballencleroch were granted to John Brisbane in 1423. His descendant, of the same name, sold the estate to Patrick McFarlan of Keithton in 1642 and he built a new mansion on the site in 1665. It was extensively refurbished and enlarged in 1852-3. The laird of Ballencleroch in the late eighteenth century was John McFarlan (1767-1846), known as the Liberal Laird for his political views as well as his generosity in opening his estates to the public in 1785. He was a true friend of Thomas Muir and made no secret of his detestation of the parish minister. The estate was sold to the Lennox family in 1921 but forty years later was converted into the Campsie Glen Hotel, a retreat of the rich and famous (including Bob Hope and the Beatles). In 1982, however, the hotel was burned down, a desperate act of the proprietor in a bid to gain a million pounds from insurance but which netted him a four-year prison sentence for arson instead. In more recent times it has arisen phoenix-like from the ashes to become Ballencleroch again, a retreat run by the Schoenstatt Sisters of Mary, a Catholic order.

Following the shining example of John McFarlan, Margaret Lennox opened up the east side of the glen to the public in 1830. Local volunteers then created the footpath extending northwards along the rugged banks of the Kirk Burn. This entailed some minor feats of engineering, notably the bridge over the ravine and the vertiginous ascent known appropriately as Jacob's Ladder. This was a favourite haunt of the more adventurous courting couples: needless to say, the girl ascended first, with the man below to break her fall, although some might think uncharitably that the men held back to catch a glimpse of 'a gently turned foot or ankle' as one nineteenth-century observer discreetly put it.

Newtown of Campsie was established in the late eighteenth century to accommodate the millhands at the calico factory but it was soon renamed Lennoxtown in tribute to the Lennox family. Some of the millworkers' cottages, dating from about 1795, are still in existence, although they have been extensively modernised and refurbished in more recent times. As the Clachan declined, so Lennoxtown went from strength to strength, especially after it was connected with the railway branch line from Kirkintilloch. In addition to calico printing and bleachworks Lennoxtown boasted a chemical works and a factory making nails, but nowadays the village is a dormitory town for Glasgow

The Glazert, having accumulated the waters of its many tributaries, is tamed by a weir just beyond the hospital. The water has a pronounced reddish hue, as a result of the oxidation of the ironstone through which it runs. Standing on the bridge just south of the village in springtime you can see a reddish tidemark on the surrounding banks and even quite far up the trunks of trees, indicating the height of the Glazert in spate. From here onwards, however, it runs in a well-trained channel along the southern side of Lennoxtown towards Milton of Campsie. There is now little evidence of the mills which gave this village its name, although, like other towns on the Glazert and the Kelvin itself, mills of many different kinds sprang up in the eighteenth and nineteenth centuries to take advantage of the abundance of water-power which they provided. To be sure, there is still a place called Newmill which alludes to the district's industrial past, but little of interest now remains to excite the industrial archaeologist.

Credit for initiating the industrial development of Milton must go to the Stirlings of Glorat who established a bleachfield on their estate in 1749. This was taken over in 1768 and expanded by John and David Muir from Glasgow who were pioneers in advertising and building up a network of sales agents all over central Scotland. The bleachfield was sold in 1772 to John Hunter but a short time later he disposed of his interests to Messrs Bogle and Campbell of Glasgow who converted it into a calico printworks. Thereafter, however, it appears to have functioned sporadically, with intermittent periods of enforced idleness. In *The Parish of Campsie* (1892) John Cameron implies that the business had closed down before the end of the eighteenth century.

The Kincaid family (whose mansion is now a hotel) seem to have had more success in this field. In February 1786 John Kincaid contracted with two Glasgow merchants, James Henderson and John Semple, who leased lands on the banks of the Glazert north of Birdston for a calico works, known as the Kincaid Printfield but soon shortened to Kincaidfield. A very full account of this works and its various processes will be found in James Lindsay's *Milton of Campsie: People & Places* (1992). The business underwent various changes of management before closing down in 1901. The premises were briefly occupied by Shand Brothers when they transferred their chemical works from Cumbernauld but this operation closed down following a serious accident in 1920 when two workmen were killed. The Kincaid works formed part of the Lennox estate when it was auctioned off in February 1927, but no use could be found for the buildings which thereafter fell into disrepair, a sad memorial to a once great industry.

A rival calico works was established in 1794 by William and Alexander Bankier at Lillyburn, on land leased from the Stirling family of Glorat. If anything, Lillyburn had an even more chequered career than Kincaidfield. It failed to pay its way and was then converted into a dyeworks and when that failed it became a whisky distillery. In turn, this came to an inglorious end as a result of wholesale pilferage of the amber fluid by the workmen and their families who spirited off (no pun intended) thousands of gallons in pails and water-cans. Under a change of ownership the distillery fared no better, and in 1831 it was closed down and its stills and other equipment sold off. George McFarlane took over and re-activated the printworks, specialising in handkerchiefs and shawls, but, like other calico businesses, Lillyburn was embroiled in the wave of strikes that rocked the industry in the 1830s.

The year 1834 was particularly marred by strikes at both printworks which resulted in a number of workmen being charged with affray. For a time an uneasy peace was maintained only by the presence of the constabulary backed by military detachments. The McFarlane family lost a lot of money from this luckless venture and were forced to sell everything by public roup in 1843. Later the Macnab family from Kirkintilloch took it on and for a time ran the business profitably, but it fell victim to the Depression and closed down in 1929. This brought the history of calico printing in the Campsie area to an end. The site lay vacant for six years before it was acquired by John Porteous for a pulp packaging plant. Under the name of Universal Pulp Packaging Limited it continues to this day. At the entrance of the works stands an enormous piece of pumping machinery with an impressive array of pipes and connections. Painted red, it has been transformed from a functional article into a quasi-sculptural monument to bygone engineering.

North of the Glazert at Newmill there is a series of ponds and dams, a legacy of the period when the Stirlings of Glorat operated their bleachfield at Alloch. These dams collected water from the streams running south from Courtma Law, and their construction brought Sir James Stirling, third Baronet, into conflict with his litigious neighbour John Kincaid of Kincaid. The dispute eventually reached the Court of Session, Kincaid alleging that Stirling had dammed and diverted the stream which had previously passed through his land to join the Glazert. It turned out that Stirling had originally diverted the stream to provide power for his own corn-mill. Consequently no satisfactory decision could be made, although this case illustrates the great importance attached to water as a source of power as well as for use in the bleaching, dyeing and textile printing processes.

The Stirling family have been associated with Glorat since the early sixteenth century when they were granted the estate by the Earl of Lennox. Despite a feud between the Stirlings of Craigbernard and the Edmonstones of Duntreath the two families eventually became reconciled in the time-honoured manner by a marriage between John Stirling and Annabella Edmonstone whose family, it will be recalled, played a notable part in the development of Kilsyth and the Kelvin itself. For their support of the monarchy King Charles II conferred a baronetcy in 1666. Sadly, both sons of Sir George Stirling, ninth Baronet, predeceased him, so the title became dormant in 1949 as a result of his death at the age of ninety-nine. The mansion was largely rebuilt by his father in 1869, and the tower added a decade later.

About a kilometre due north there are two archaeological sites of a very different character. One rejoices under the refined name of Maiden Castle, but a short distance to the northwest, nestling under the escarpment of the Campsies, is a second structure known by the much more pithy and expressive name of the Muckle Reive. The first is a medieval fortification consisting of a motte and bailey, while the latter is of much greater antiquity, invariably described as an ancient British hill-fort, if not pre-Roman then at least coeval with the construction of the Antonine Wall in the middle of the second century.

The north bank of the Glazert immediately east of Lennoxtown deserves a mention for its involvement in an early episode in the annals of British aviation, for it was in a field at Easter Muckcroft farm on the banks of the Glazert between Milton and Lennoxtown, that Vincenzo Lunardi, the Neapolitan diplomat and pioneer balloonist, made his descent on 5 December 1785. A crowd estimated at over a hundred thousand had gathered round St Andrew's kirkyard in Glasgow to watch the intrepid aviator make his ascent. The stately progress of his balloon was closely monitored by Glaswegians on horseback or gig and quite a crowd converged on Milton and Lennoxtown as the strange contraption rapidly lost height. A vivid account of the event was submitted to the Glasgow newspapers by the Revd James Lapslie, concluding that the concourse of spectators who gathered near his kirkyard to watch the descent was 'numerous and genteel'. In a letter to a friend, however, Lapslie gave a much more vivid account of local people's reaction to the weird sight. He eavesdropped on a weaver 'expressing the most vehement desire to see this great sight and crying to his wife to take care of the bairns'. His wife wanted to see the balloon for herself and repeated the same order to her servant who responded tartly that 'she wondered what people imagined servants were made of... Let those who got bairns take care of them for by her faith, she would both see and touch Lunardi with the best of them' and threw the child from her.

Lapslie apparently organised the local people into helping the intrepid aviator to dismantle, deflate and pack away his balloon so that it could be transported back to Glasgow by road. Lapslie invited Lunardi to accompany him back to the manse for a suitable repast, but at that moment Sir Alexander Stirling came on the scene and insisted that Lunardi go back with him to Glorat House. The minister was momentarily put out, but mollified when Sir Alexander expansively included him in the invitation. They set off for the mansion, led by a small boy brandishing the flag which had bedecked the balloon. On the way they paused to admire the view, when an old man addressed them:

> Sir, I am an auld man, I am aulder than the Union, I have seen many things, but the like of this I never saw. I have seen Mar's year, and the Highlandmen's Raid and about twelve years since, I gaed o'er by yonder (pointing to the canal) to see ships sailing thro' dry land, but the like of this I never saw. Dinna ye think the world will soon be at an end.

After a hearty meal at Glorat, Sir Alexander summoned his carriage in which

Lapslie convoyed Lunardi back to Glasgow. Although Lunardi made the first flight in England, from the Royal Artillery Grounds at Woolwich, on 13 September 1784, he was beaten to the honour of being the first in the British Isles by James Tytler who made a brief ascent by hot air balloon over Edinburgh on 27 August and later made a longer flight from Edinburgh across the Firth of Forth to Ceres in Fife. Tytler, the first editor of the *Encyclopaedia Britannica*, was ever afterwards known as 'Balloon' Tytler, but has otherwise been forgotten. The colourful Italian, using hydrogen balloons, gave numerous demonstrations all over England as well as six ascents in Scotland. An infinitely better showman and self-publicist than poor Tytler, he even lent his name to the balloon bonnets which were the height of fashion that year, and rate a mention in Burns's famous 'Ode to a Louse'.

Beyond Milton of Campsie the Glazert turns south. The footpath that faithfully shadows the river from Lennox Castle passes through landscaped riverbanks and parklands and then runs all the way to Kirkintilloch along the west bank. Near the hamlet of Birdston it passes under a bridge, sole relic of the Kelvin Valley Railway that once ran to Kilsyth. In a cottage at Birdston in 1766 was born William Muir, the Campsie poet whose 'Ode to the Kelvin' has already been mentioned. The footpath terminates at the B757 on the outskirts of Kirkintilloch, where the Glazert suffers reverse takeover by the comparatively diminutive Kelvin, opposite the hospital. Just beyond the bridge over the B757 the Luggie joins the Kelvin and thereafter the river is worthy of that appellation.

CHAPTER FOUR

Hayston to Summerston

As far as Kirkintilloch the Kelvin and the canal advance side by side, but now they part company. Out along the A803 at the west end of the town is the suburb of Hayston. A footpath runs north from the main road, opposite the site of the Roman camp, and passes through open fields to the Kelvin, whence a footbridge gives access to Hayston Golf Course on the north bank. An ancient cobblestone track runs north from the bridge to connect with a public footpath to Milton of Campsie, but there is also a path running due west along the riverbank. After about a mile this path comes to an unmarked track which runs due north, passing over the disused railway line, and heading towards Carlston on the B822 road between Torrance and Lennoxtown. Ignore the track and keep going along the footpath and after a further mile or so you arrive at the outskirts of Torrance. Before the upheavals in local administration a quarter of a century ago, this stretch of the Kelvin formed the boundary between Stirlingshire to the north and Lanarkshire to the south.

This walk, from Hayston to Torrance, is straightforward. The only landmark of note is on the south bank of the river and consists of a large sewage works beyond which is the fast receding A803, the canal and the site of another Roman fortlet. The Kelvin Valley sewage works is currently undergoing extensive upgrading at a cost of £6,120,000. There is a huge rectangular culvert leading from the sewage works into the river, although I am assured that any liquid discharged into the Kelvin is now crystal clear and as pure as the driven snow. On the north bank of the river the footpath skirts the golf course and passes a number of those curious loops and whorls of disconnected water indicating the original course of the river. Between Hayston and Torrance there is hardly any drop in the river level at all and in bygone times the plain was prone to heavy flooding, with considerable loss of crops and destruction of livestock; but from about 1770 onwards the farmers and proprietors of the lands adjoining the river began the creation of enormous embankments on both sides, rather like the levees along the Mississippi. If not on the same massive scale, the Kelvin embankments are quite impressive, rising about 7 metres (21 ft) above the mean river level in some places. From the top of one of these banks you get good views back up the valley, with the towers and steeples of Kirkintilloch silhouetted on the horizon. If you feel like making a slight detour, you can walk up the track to Carlston on the B822; otherwise continue along the riverside footpath towards Torrance. Near the village the path forks, the right fork heading in a northwesterly direction to join the old railway line, and the left fork curving southwards to follow the river.

On the face of it, Torrance is a sleepy little village whose houses, pubs and shops along the main street do not appear to have changed much in the past century, but appearances can be deceptive. Discreetly tucked away behind the main street, which is actually the southwestern end of the B822, there are numerous detached houses which reveal the true nature of Torrance as a dormitory town for Glasgow. New housing of this kind now extends along the A807 to Balmore and has probably doubled the size of the town in the past two decades alone. The old London and North Eastern Railway formerly ran through Torrance but the line has been defunct for the past three decades. In the village itself parts of it have been landscaped as public parks. The town's commuters make their daily journey to Glasgow by road. At the southern end of the village is a traffic roundabout where the B822 meets the A807 from Milngavie, and about a mile to the southeast this road joins the A803 at another roundabout before it heads in a southwesterly direction to Bishopbriggs and the city centre. Torrance is barely a mile from the outer limits of the greater Glasgow conurbation, and yet it lies in open country and has somehow managed to preserve its rural atmosphere. Just south of the junction of the A807 and B822 is a fine modern road bridge spanning the river, the first to be distinguished by the name of Kelvinbridge by which the roundabout is also known.

Torrance, with Balmore, had a population of just over eleven hundred at the 1931 census; today it has grown fourfold, but without any corresponding increase in the number and size of shops and other facilities, all of which are so readily accessible in Bishopbriggs or Kirkintilloch.

There is no footpath on either side of the Kelvin past the Kelvinbridge roundabout, and it is very heavy going along the top of the embankments; but at Balmore there is a crescent on the left as you head westward and at the midpoint there is a garden centre. A rather ominous sign warns that cars parked there without proper cause are liable to be towed away. Of course, if you are patronising the garden centre, it is perfectly permissible to park there. Otherwise, you would be well advised to leave your vehicle in a rather more hospitable place. From the garden centre, there is a rough track that runs in a perfectly straight line in a southeasterly direction for about a kilometre or so through vast, flat fields. The track peters out, but continues as a footpath leading to the Kelvin. A slight turn to the left and then right brings you to a footbridge over the river, which leads on to the Keir golf course at Cadder.

There is a public right of way along the path on the Cadder side, which leads eventually to the village of that name. Along the way, we encounter our old friend the Antonine Wall again, and thanks to the immaculate manicuring of the greens on the golf course, the vestiges of the wall can clearly be discerned, with another fort (the sixth, counting from the western end of the wall) visible on the south side of the canal. The wall, in fact, serves as the boundary between two golf courses, the Keir and the Cawder (retaining the archaic spelling of the parish name). As late as 1790 one of the watch-towers was still extant, but some time afterwards it was dismantled for house-building materials. No attempt was made systematically to excavate this site until 1929-31, when archaeologists discovered that it had been occupied on three separate occasions. The first was early in the first century, by a legion under Agricola who used it as a marching camp; the second was in the period around 143 when the wall was being constructed; and the third was between 170 and 190 when it was apparently destroyed by fire. What stirring tales these mute stones conceal.

Where there is now a metal footbridge over the river, at the confluence with the Cadder Burn, there was at one time a set of stepping stones, remarkable enough to appear on countless Edwardian picture postcards. The Cadder Woods which cover the south bank of the Kelvin are particularly beautiful in spring, when the trees are clothed in fresh verdure and the bluebells provide a dazzling carpet underfoot. Just after you cross the footbridge in the direction of Cadder there is a track on the right leading up to the clubhouse, formerly a country mansion. Beyond the clubhouse is a good track along the riverbank. Along this track, look out for what at first glance looks like a medieval air-raid shelter, a small stone structure built into a tiny hillock, but in fact this was an ice-house, a relic of the bad old days before the invention of the kelvinator (sorry, the refrigerator). Blocks of ice were packed into this stone chamber in wintertime and, with luck, would still be providing ice for drinks and ice-cream right through the summer months. Farther along the path there is a very beautiful ornamental lake, providing a hazard for golfers. It has no obvious outlet to the river and is, in fact, yet another of those mysterious oxbows. On this stretch it is advisable to stick to the track for the riverbank extending about ten metres to the right is very soft and treacherous. Although the top appears to be well knit together with lush vegetation it is a very soft clay, liable to crumble away and tumble the unwary into the river. You can observe the action of the current on the opposite bank, worn smooth and now of a sinister slickness. Fall in there, and you would never be able to scramble out again.

Cadder Church and its adjoining kirkyard are the focal point of the hamlet. Doubtless there has been a church on this spot for centuries, although the present building dates only from 1830. A plaque on the wall, erected in 1909 following extensive renovation, recounts its long history. According to this plaque, there has been a church on this spot since 1150 if not earlier. The parish at one time belonged to the bishops of Glasgow; and the memory of this connection is perpetuated in such placenames as Bishop's Bridge (now Bishopbriggs), Bishop's Loch and the Bishop's Moss. Following the Reformation in 1560

Cadder, along with all the other temporal estates of the sub-deanery of Glasgow, passed into the hands of the Hamilton family which sold the land to the University of Glasgow about 1656. None too happy with this arrangement, the people of Cadder took advantage of an Act of 1690 and raised the 600 merks in hard cash necessary to pay off the University authorities. By this means they acquired the rights of patronage, entitling the parishioners to appoint their own minister without outside interference. This was no mean undertaking, for the parish of Cadder was very extensive and encompassed over 14,000 acres which contained the villages of Bishopbriggs, Moodiesburn, Garnkirk, Auchencairn, Auchenloch, Chryston, Muirhead, Mollinsburn and the western side of Lenzie. The parish is drained by the Bothlin Burn which joins the Luggie at Kirkintilloch. In bygone times this fast-flowing stream provided the power for numerous mills, from Bedlay (site of the medieval bishop's corn-mill) and Croftfoot to Drumcavil and Auchengeich.

Cadder Parish Church

Cadder kirkyard is worth a closer look. Apart from some tombstones of the Stirlings of Keir dating back to the early eighteenth century, there is a cast-iron coffin known as a mortsafe and a stone hut where corpses were kept under guard on the eve of burial, a legacy of the days of the body snatchers. These elaborate precautions became necessary when it was discovered that body snatchers were removing the lately deceased and loading them on to scows for a fast getaway along the canal to Glasgow and a ready sale to the infamous Dr Knox and other anatomists at the University. A marker board on the canal towpath highlights this lurid aspect of the kirkyard's past. Under the Millennium Link project, this part of the canal has now been restored, complete with a new bridge and approach roads.

While the hamlet of Cadder, clustered around the old church, has managed to retain something of its rural character, it now represents the very tip of an iceberg; across the canal, in reality, is the northeastern edge of Glasgow, even if the City boundary lies some distance to the south. The day cannot be far off when the housing at Westerhill on the eastern side of Bishopbriggs joins up with the development sprawling outwards from Boghead on the western side of Lenzie, although a deterrent to the complete infilling of this area is the ominous presence of Low Moss Prison, east of Cadder and south of the Antonine Wall. Low Moss cemetery is no different from any other, except in one respect and that is the granite statue of a Clydesdale horse on top of one of the tombs. It was erected by James Young Alexander who had made his money in the haulage business, in memory of his son William who died in July 1936 at the early age of thirty-seven. The managers of the cemetery strenuously opposed this erection but the family of the dear departed fought back, tooth and nail, and eventually won. As the statue is quite close to the road from Cadder village it could hardly have been placed in a more prominent position. The parents of the young man died within days of each other early in 1939 and were duly interred in the same grave. From haulage and freight this family diversified into passenger transport and built up a fleet of buses distinguished by their bluebird insignia and blue and white livery. Nearby is the Strathkelvin Business Park and a drive-in fast-food joint. Cadder thus unites the relics of Roman civilisation with the symbols of American civilisation.

Bishopbriggs ranks after Kirkintilloch as the second town of Strathkelvin. As its name suggests, it had ancient ecclesiastical connections with the bishopric of Glasgow, and derived its name from the Bishop's Bridge that spanned the Cala or Callie Burn. Around the medieval church beside the bridge developed a kirkton, but the present town sprang up farther south as a result of the opening of the Edinburgh and Glasgow Railway in 1842, with a station which served a cluster of colliery villages in the surrounding district. Bishopbriggs benefited enormously from its excellent communications, astride the medieval packhorse route, then the Forth and Clyde Canal and latterly the criss-cross network of railways. In the past half-century, however, it has grown considerably as a result of speculative building. The population quadrupled between 1951 and 1971 alone, from 5,272 to 21,684 in two decades.

Geographically part of Strathkelvin, this burgeoning town suffered from its historical affiliation to Lanarkshire; being situated at the northwestern tip of that

The car terminus in Kirkintilloch Road, Bishopbriggs in the early part of the twentieth century

county it was all too often a case of 'out of sight, out of mind'. In January 1960, at a meeting of the local ratepayers' association, it was decided to petition for burgh status. This was eventually achieved in 1964, and the new burgh proudly matriculated its arms showing a civic crown above a shield bearing a bishop's mitre above diagonal bands of gold and green representing the 'riggs' (ridges) of medieval husbandry. Across the centre was a pattern of blue and silver wavy lines to represent the Kelvin and the Forth and Clyde Canal. Sadly, burghal status lasted for only eleven years before Bishopbriggs was swallowed up in the local government reorganisation that gave birth to Strathkelvin District, but it was a momentous decade that witnessed a further surge in housing as well as the creation of the splendid Sports Centre and the Churchill Way shopping centre.

West of the clubhouse of Keir golf course, there are two parallel footpaths, one running along the south bank of the Kelvin and the other some way to the south along the ridge of high ground, joining up with the minor road that marks the northern boundary of the Wilderness Plantation. Between the edge of this woodland and the top of the slope leading down to the Kelvin, further stretches of the Antonine Wall are quite distinct. At the eastern end of the wood are the remains of a Roman fortlet, while just beyond its western limit is the fifth fort in the chain, dominating the high ground above the present-day Balmuildy Bridge. Between the line of the wall and the river, near Buchley, is a cluster of huge, windowless buildings, their appearance made more sinister by their blackened walls. There are no signs to indicate their purpose, and one is left imagining that they are a relic of the Cold War or perhaps a mute reminder of some hush-hush operation from the Second World War. Whatever their original purpose, they are now used by the City of Glasgow for the rather more prosaic function of waste disposal and recycling the detritus of modern civilisation.

To the west, the Kelvin loops around a hill which has yielded abundant evidence of having been occupied as a Roman camp. Across the river can be seen the embankments of the former railway line running across the Haughs of Balmore, and just to bring the landscape up to date it is also traversed by two lines of electricity pylons. At the western end of Balmore Haughs is the hamlet of Bardowie, from which an unmarked road runs south to the dismantled railway line where there was once a station and from this point there is a footpath continuing the track down to the river. North of the former railway line the track is metalled, though it is very rough and full of huge potholes, but apart from that it is a very pleasant walk through what the Victorians liked to describe as sylvan glades. There are some large houses here, well set back from the road among the trees, but at the approach to the main road you will suddenly come across a late-Victorian red sandstone terrace that looks as if it were plucked out of Pollokshields and dropped down here in the middle of nowhere, the incongruity heightened by the poor state of what is euphemistically termed an 'unadopted' road. Bardowie formerly boasted a railway station, now long vanished, and there are neither shops nor pubs. Cross the main A807 from the private road and continue along a minor road running in a northeasterly direction and you pass Bardowie Loch on your left. The loch is about 80 acres in extent and on the far side of it, nestling among the trees, is Bardowie Castle. This crenellated pile of grey granite was occupied as a country seat until the early years of this century but is now in a semi-ruinous state.

Robinsfield, on the south side of the loch, was for many years the residence and studio of Robert Macaulay Stevenson (1854-1952). Destined to follow in his father's footsteps, he trained as an engineer but clearly he had little enthusiasm for the work. After a series of jobs in Glasgow he enrolled for evening classes at the Glasgow School of Design and later came under the influence of the Barbizon group of painters, but developed his own distinctive brand of Impressionism. His endless experiments with the effects of twilight on trees and landscapes led to him being dubbed 'The Moonlighter'. For a time, he lived at Montreuil-sur-Mer before settling at Bardowie where he produced some of his most evocative works. George Eyre-Todd, who visited him at Robinsfield in the early 1900s, later described the panoramas of the loch and the Campsies from Stevenson's windows in the entry on the artist in his *Who's Who in Glasgow* (1909). Apart from occasional sojourns in Kirkcudbright, a favourite haunt of the Glasgow Boys, Stevenson drew much of his inspiration from his surroundings in Strathkelvin, typified by his canvas entitled 'Near Bardowie, a Scottish

Pastoral'. He remained active right up till the end of his life at the venerable age of ninety-eight.

Baldernock Parish Church, showing the outside stairs and the unusual belfry

From Bardowie you can walk northwards to the quaint Baldernock Church at the crossroads, and thence all the way to Milngavie. This fine old parish church dates from the early eighteenth century and retains the outside stairs which were a characteristic of Scots kirks right back to the Reformation, as well as a curious belfry with exposed bell-rope. It has some literary claim to fame as the setting for Graham Moffat's comedy *Bunty Pulls the Strings*, set in the 1860s, which enjoyed a measure of popularity before the First World War and was a perennial favourite for amateur theatricals up to the 1950s. Nearby, on the banks of the Craigmaddie Burn, a tributary of the Allander, there is a water mill in full working order, although nowadays it is used to power a sawmill rather than for grinding flour. It is the sole surviving mill in Strathkelvin, yet the prevalence of place-names in the district shows that mills were once very thick on the ground.

Southwest of Bardowie, the Kelvin receives a major influx of water from the Allander Water which passes under a trio of bridges just south of the round-about where the A807 meets the A879. Rising in the Dumbarton Moor on the southern slopes of Auchineden and the Whangie, it runs in a southerly direction, joining forces with the Craigton Burn on the northwestern outskirts of Milngavie and then flowing through that town. The Allander is both accessible and a stream of great beauty from its origins among the heather to its meeting with the Kelvin, affording endless vistas of infinite variety, from babbling brook tumbling over the rocks, to a placid stream meandering between lush meadows or pleasant woodlands. Not surprisingly, therefore, it is a traditional favourite with ramblers and hill-walkers and from its confluence with the Audmurroch Burn, the West Highland Way runs southward along its east bank. Near its head-waters is Auchengillan, familiar to Scouts of the west of Scotland as a campsite, and just to the north is the Queen's View, named in honour of Queen Victoria, from which one gets panoramic views of the mountains to the north and west. On the banks of the Allander past Carbeth can be seen the huts where three gen-erations of Glasgow's working classes have enjoyed a breath of fresh air and a welcome respite from the City's factories and offices. From time to time there is a move to have them ejected and the huts demolished but proletarian solidarity is well organised and the 'hutters' have so far successfully resisted. The huts are a legacy of the Depression years. Some of the original campers later went off to fight in the Spanish Civil War, and it is really to the memory of those who fell in the first great fight against fascism that the statue of La Pasionaria, on the north bank of the Clyde in the centre of Glasgow, is dedicated.

Between the Allander and its tributary, the Craigton Burn, are several golf courses. By contrast, on the west side of the A809 is a stretch of open moorland beyond High Craigton where model aircraft enthusiasts put their machines through their paces, performing the most amazing feats of aerobatics by remote control.

The footpath along the Allander passes through a heavily wooded defile known locally as the Khyber Pass, carrying the minor road across Craigallian Bridge from Craigton to Mugdock. The narrow road twists and winds on either bank of the Allander. You have a choice of route here, with a good path north-ward to Craigallian Loch and thence to Cuilt Brae, or the road that leads to Craigend Castle. This nineteenth-century structure about a mile north of the Allander is notable only for having been the temporary home of Glasgow Zoo before it moved to its present location south of the City. Nowadays most people drive up the steep winding road, but for ramblers there are various paths through the woods, offering a shortcut to the top of the gorge where one can pause to recover one's breath and take in the panoramic views.

Nearby is Mugdock Castle, an ancient seat of the Grahams. Although the part which was largely rebuilt in 1875 has been restored as a visitor centre for Mugdock Country Park, the original square grey keep is in a ruinous state. It dates from the late thirteenth century when it was the stronghold of Sir Patrick Graham who fell in battle at Dunbar in 1296. His kinsman was Sir John Graham, Wallace's gallant lieutenant who lost his life at the battle of Falkirk in 1298. The greatest of all the Grahams was the Marquess of Montrose, the Covenanter who became a Cavalier and lost his head in 1650. The highs and lows, the lightness and shade of his brilliant but ultimately ill-starred career, have made him a popular figure in historical romance.

In *In and Around Milngavie* (1908), John Shearer waxed lyrical about Mugdock and the beautiful wooded walks around the Corporation Waterworks. 'In point of natural beauty,' he wrote, 'it is safe to say that St Mungo does not possess, with the exception of Rouken Glen and the estate of Ardkinglass, a finer sylvan retreat than that of the Waterworks... Among the more popular paths, there is the Lovers' Walk, which in summer resembles the promenade at a coast town, with the wide expanse of water on one side and the rugged hillside on the other.' The cluster of cottages at Mugdock were all that remained of a village which, centuries ago, was a burgh in its own right, complete with a weekly market, and it is recorded that the citizens of Mugdock looked down on their neighbours in the clachan of Milngavie.

Mugdock is a very popular attraction for walkers and mountain bikers, affording magnificent views across the City of Glasgow to the south and the mountains to the north. Along the ridge can be seen the remains of a wartime anti-aircraft gun battery operated by girls of the ATS under the command of officers of the Royal Artillery. Some years after the war I was with a group of boys exploring the gun emplacements when we found a peach tree laden with fruit against one wall, a perfect sun-trap. Many years later I discovered that one of my colleagues in London had been a major in the Royal Artillery and had commanded the Mugdock AA battery. When I told him the story about the

Gavin's Mill on the Allander, Milngavie

peaches, he smiled broadly and told me that it was he who had planted a seedling, grown from a peach stone. In more recent years I have been back to that spot many times, but all traces of the peach tree have vanished, just as the remains of the gun battery are themselves rapidly disappearing with the passage of time.

To the south are the Mugdock and Craigmaddie reservoirs which feed the Glasgow water supply. The Allander runs all the way through Milngavie and then continues past the town cross, where a bridge provides good vistas up and down stream. Milngavie (pronounced 'Milguy'), as its name suggests, was a place which made good use of water-power. The town takes it name from Gavin's Mill which still exists, although its massive water wheel is now static and the mill itself has been tastefully converted into artists' studios and a cafeteria. Elsewhere in and around the town there are interesting vestiges of the water-power on which the prosperity of Milngavie was based, including a sluice gate with a balustraded parapet and parts of a water-mill which was actually designed by James Watt, presumably before he diversified into steam-power.

The development of Milngavie parallels that of Lennoxtown and Milton of Campsie where a ready abundance of water attracted various occupations associated with textiles. Inevitably these industries, such as calico printing, paper manufacture, bleaching and dyeworks, had a distressing tendency to pollute the Allander and thus the Kelvin itself. Today it is a residential town, mainly for people working in nearby Glasgow, and the Allander has been cleaned up and revived. Along the banks of the Allander and the Craigton Burn there are now pleasant woods, parklands and golf courses that reflect the nature of Milngavie as a dormitory town. The Allander twists round the railway station, terminus of the branch line connecting the town to Glasgow 10 kilometres (6 miles) away. There is a footpath skirting the south side of Dougalston Loch, whose outfall runs into the Allander behind the Sports Centre.

Adjoining the railway line near here was a very short stretch of monorail track from which was suspended the Bennie Railplane. The brainchild of George Bennie, a partner in the shipbuilding firm of Steel and Bennie, it was constructed in the 1930s and was intended as a breakthrough in passenger transport, but through lack of funding never got beyond the prototype stage. The outbreak of the Second World War put paid to further development, but for some years thereafter it remained in *situ*, its streamlined silver hull a source of wonderment to passers-by. Eventually the site was required for redevelopment so the Railplane was taken down and its gantry demolished. It has now been preserved in Glasgow's Museum of Transport. Undoubtedly Bennie was ahead of his time, for monorails are now in operation in many parts of the world – though not in the land of their birth.

Shortly before the Allander joins the Kelvin there is a roundabout where the A807 from Milngavie to Torrance meets the A879 (Balmore Road), running due south to the Glasgow suburbs of Lambhill and Milton, and the B8049 from Bearsden. On the north side of the roundabout is an old building, formerly the Allander Toll-house and a relic of the eighteenth century when the roads were managed by turnpike trusts. Southwest of the toll-house lies Douglas Park golf course leading to the regional council buildings, but closer to the river lies New Kilpatrick cemetery which has the unique distinction of having a Roman fort at its centre. Along the line of the Antonine Wall to the west is the aptly named Roman Road (with the adjacent Roman Avenue, Roman Drive and Roman Gardens for good measure). Between Roman Road and Roman Court lies the site of a Roman bath-house. East of the cemetery, the Antonine Wall turns and twists round Summerston and at one point runs almost due south for about two kilometres before it remembers what it is supposed to be doing and turns sharp left to head in an easterly direction once more. Trying to follow the line of the wall at this point is confused by the remains of the old railway embankment which, after Bardowie, turns to the southwest and eventually peters out at the edge of Balmore Road. There is a point at which the dying embankment crosses the Roman wall, bounded by the main road on one side and the Kelvin on the other.

The Kelvin flows due west to its confluence with the Allander but then continues the course set by that tributary and heads in a southerly direction for more than a kilometre. The confluence, in fact, marks the most northerly boundary of the City of Glasgow, and though this is still open farmland it seems likely that in the not too distant future housing will occupy this 'greenfield site'. In the loop formed by the Allander and the Kelvin lies Summerston which gives its name to some cottages and a nearby farm, but ominously it is also the name of an already vast and sprawling housing scheme about three kilometres to the south, on the edge of the City.

Shortly before the Kelvin reaches Balmore Road it turns to the west again and on its southern bank lies the site of Balmuildy Fort. A few metres west is Balmuildy Bridge, carrying the road across the river. The bridge, erected in the nineteenth century, underwent extensive widening and strengthening at the beginning of 2000.

The stretch of the Kelvin from Balmore to Balmuildy has a tolerable footpath on both banks, and an excellent track along the south bank past the bridge. Much of the surrounding countryside is arable, although west of Balmuildy the chief activity appears to be poultry farming. Just past the bridge, on the north bank of the river, is a large pond or lochan draining the higher ground farther north and west towards Kelvin View. The river meanders placidly for about three kilometres through this flat terrain before it is joined by a small stream on the north bank, significant only in so far as it marks the northwestern boundary of the city. Just outside this lies Killermont golf course, with an elongated copse of mixed woodland attractively lining the riverbank. Through this woodland runs a footpath which passes the clubhouse, then follows the line of the river westward to the bridge at Maryhill Road. On the opposite bank of the river, there is a church recreation ground and a riding academy. The golf course and the recreation ground, in fact, mark the end of the Kelvin's rural course; from this point onwards the Kelvin crosses the City boundary for good. From here until it enters the Clyde, the Kelvin is an urban river, even if it connects a string of parks and stretches of riverbank that provide a welcome 'lung' for Glasgow, bolstering its traditional image of 'the dear, green place'.

Thomas Muir

Thomas Muir

A name which recurs in these pages is Thomas Muir, whose paternal grandfather was the 'bonnet laird' of Hayston and Birdston, the Kirkintilloch poet William Muir being a cousin. Thomas was born in Glasgow on 4 August 1765, the son of James Muir, a hop merchant and grocer who made a fortune which enabled him to purchase the estate of Hunters Hill in the ancestral parish of Cadder. He built a mansion which he called Huntershill House on the outskirts of Bishopbriggs. Son Thomas was a child prodigy who matriculated at Glasgow University at the tender age of ten, studied divinity and graduated Master of Arts at the age of fourteen. He then went to Edinburgh University to read law and was called to the bar in 1787. Early the following year he began practising in Edinburgh, at first specialising in commercial litigation and conveyancing, but he had marked forensic abilities and delighted in the cut and thrust of the courtroom. From the outset he also had a well-developed social conscience, and long before there was a proper system of legal aid for poor defendants he was always willing to take on such cases, especially when he felt that individuals had been wrongly accused of serious crimes.

At the remarkably early age of twenty-one he was appointed an elder of Cadder and every Sunday, when he was back home, he would walk from Huntershill to the parish church. In 1790 the elders locked horns with the heritors (those landed proprietors who had the right to select a new minister). The elders represented the congregation which favoured Archibald Provan who had assisted in the district and was very popular with parishioners; but the heritors ignored this and, under the baneful influence of James Dunlop of Garnkirk, a wealthy coal-owner and ironmaster, they rigged the election in favour of their own man. The congregation refused to accept this blatantly corrupt situation and appointed young Muir to investigate the suspect qualifications of Dunlop's supporters. Dunlop vociferously objected, and the matter went to the Court of Session. Here, of course, Muir was in his element and trounced the opposition. Provan was elected and the congregation was triumphant. Muir was hailed as a champion of democratic principles, but he had also made some deadly enemies.

The outbreak of revolution in France in July 1789 had been greeted euphorically in Britain which generally viewed the *ancien régime* with distaste. Developments across the Channel were watched with the keenest interest, and as France, in the early stages of the Revolution, seemed to be heading for a true democracy in which the king was retained as nominal head of state, there was a widespread clamour for sweeping change in Britain also. Reform was the buzzword, as people looked back to the Glorious Revolution of 1689 and wondered what had happened to all those high-flown sentiments in the Bill of Rights. In particular, the corrupt and thor-oughly unrepresentative nature of the House of Commons became the target of the reformers. In 1792 the playwright Richard Brinsley Sheridan helped to found the Society of the Friends of the People and branches sprang up all over the country. In July that year Muir took a leading role in establishing a branch in Edinburgh and the following October he was the prime mover of a similar organisation in Glasgow known as the Associated Friends of the Constitution and of the People which aimed to reform Parliament, slash the defence budget, democratise local government and ecclesiastical elections, as well as make the public more politically aware. These were all noble sentiments at which no one would cavil nowadays, but the government of William Pitt was increasingly apprehensive, especially as the Revolution in France began to take an increasingly ugly turn. There was a genuine fear that the disease of Jacobinism would spread to the British Isles, and a frightened government began to take repressive mea-sures against the advocates of reform.

For several months Muir stomped the country, making speeches and helping to organise other local committees. One such was formed at Milton of Campsie as a result of a stirring speech by Muir to the calico workers at Kincaidfield. In the same period, late in 1792, he also addressed vast crowds at Paisley, Kirkintilloch and Lennoxtown. His most recent biographer, Christina Bewley, makes the valid point that Muir's tireless efforts to reach out to the artisans and labourers laid the foundations of those workingmen's political clubs which later provided the power base for the radicalism of the nineteenth century, thereby establishing the strongly socialist character of Scotland which has endured to this day. The importance of Thomas Muir in the political transformation of Scotland cannot be overestimated.

The core of Muir's message was that every man should have the right to vote, regardless of wealth, property or social standing. Plans were laid for a petition to Parliament on the matter of universal suffrage, but they were severely set back by the deterioration in Anglo-French relations with the trial and imprisonment of the King and Queen. Soon after Louis XVI and Marie Antoinette went to the guillotine in January 1793, war broke out between Britain and France, and any talk of reform was regarded as high treason. Some weeks earlier, however, when the country was in a ferment and rioting had broken out in many districts, the government took swift action against the dissidents. One of the first to fall victim to this repression was the encyclopedist and pioneer balloonist James Tytler, arrested in November 1792 for publishing a seditious handbill, in fact an advertisement for a meeting of the Friends of the People the following month.

On 2 January 1793 Thomas Muir was on his way from Glasgow to Edinburgh to attend Tytler's trial when he himself was apprehended at Holytown by a messenger-at-arms named Williamson in whose custody he completed the journey. Muir was charged with sedition, but released on bail to appear before the court the following month. He immediately set off for London and travelled thence to Paris with the intention of interceding on behalf of King Louis but his errand of mercy came too late to save the luckless monarch from the scaffold. The outbreak of war a few days later trapped Muir in France. Unable to return to Edinburgh to stand trial on the due date, he was pronounced an outlaw on 25 February, his enemies maintaining that he had fled the country to escape justice, and by this act he had revealed his guilt. Eventually, however, he managed to board an American ship bound for Dublin. He spent some time there, becoming a member of the Society of United Irishmen and was fêted by the reformers of the Irish capital. In July he sailed to Scotland with the avowed intention of standing trial, but on landing at Stranraer he was promptly arrested by a Customs official and after a spell in the local gaol he was conducted by Williamson, via Dumfries, to Edinburgh. The sorry spectacle of the leading reformer being escorted in chains through the village of Gatehouse of Fleet was witnessed by none other than Robert Burns who was so moved that he composed 'Scots Wha Hae' that very day, and scratched the lines on a window of the inn at Gatehouse in memory of the occasion.

Muir was brought to trial on 30 August before the Lord Justice Clerk, Lord Braxfield, and four Lords Commissioners of Justiciary. The fifteen members of the jury consisted of nine landed gentlemen, three merchants, two bankers and a bookseller. In the indictment, Muir was charged with creating disaffection by means of seditious speeches and harangues. Muir, who had established quite a reputation as a defence counsel, opted to defend himself; but though he succeeded in demolishing the Revd James Lapslie, the main witness for the prosecution, the packed jury brought in a guilty verdict, and Lord Braxfield handed down a sentence of fourteen years' transportation to Botany Bay. This was not only outrageously harsh, but also virtually a death sentence, for the chances of surviving that length of time in the brutal conditions of the penal colony were very slim.

Muir survived the rigours of the terrible voyage in the prison-ship and settled down to serve his sentence, but in 1796 influential friends in America organised a rescue mission and Muir and some companions made good their escape. Their vessel took them to Nootka in Alaska, whence Muir travelled south on a Spanish ship bound for California where he hoped to journey overland to Philadelphia and meet George Washington. The Spaniards suspected him of being a spy and. sent him under guard to Vera Cruz in Mexico and thence to Havana in Cuba where he was again imprisoned for several months awaiting a ship to Spain. As this vessel approached Cadiz, it was attacked by a British warship. Muir, fearing recapture by the British, fought alongside the Spaniards but was badly wounded in the face and lost his left eye. The wounded Scot was taken ashore to receive medical treatment and spent some time in the local hospital recovering. The Spanish authorities, however, would have imprisoned him but he was released on the personal intercession of Napoleon who invited him to France where he was hailed as a hero of democracy. He was made a citizen of the French Republic and spent the last year of his life in relative tranquillity. Just as royalist *émigrés* had fled from France to Britain, so many political dissidents from the British Isles had gathered in Paris. Although virtually penniless and dogged by ill health, Muir worked tirelessly on behalf of this expatriate community and even helped to organise the abortive invasion of Ireland in 1798. By now a committed republican, he hoped that this would be but the prelude to the establishment of independent republics in Ireland, Scotland and even England itself. Worn out by his exertions and suffering the after-effects of his wounds, he died in January 1799 at the early age of thirty-three.

Sadly, no proper memorial has ever been erected to Thomas Muir, although in 1844, when Chartism was at its zenith, a monument was erected by friends of Parliamentary reform in the Calton burial ground in Edinburgh, in honour of Muir and his fellow exiles, Thomas Fyshe Palmer, William Skirving, Maurice Margarot and Joseph Gerrald. The memorial bears Muir's final words at his trial: 'I have devoted myself to the cause of the People; it is a good cause; it shall finally triumph.' Huntershill House in Bishopbriggs now houses the Thomas Muir Museum.

CHAPTER FIVE

Killermont to Kelvindale

In medieval times the lands in what is now the northwestern district of Glasgow belonged to the Church and provided a lucrative income for the archdiocese. After the Reformation, the estate of Garscube came into the possession of the Campbell family. It passed to a Dunbartonshire branch in 1687 and thereafter formed part of the estates of the Campbells of Succoth. Half a century later the fortunes of these Campbells went into orbit as a result of their connection with the founding of the Royal Bank of Scotland in 1727. Sir Ilay Campbell became the first chairman of the bank and, as such, his bewigged portrait can be seen on the obverse of the banknotes to this day. He was elevated to the peerage as Lord Ilay and later succeeded his kinsman, becoming third Duke of Argyll.

Scotland already had a banking system, the Bank of Scotland having been founded in 1695, but the rival establishment came about in rather unusual circumstances. One of the spin-offs from the Union in 1707 was that a sum of money, amounting to £398,065 and known as the Equivalent, was put aside in order that Scotland could take its fair share of certain fiscal liabilities of Great Britain. In 1719 an Act of Parliament placed a ceiling on the Equivalent, namely the figure at which it then stood. This created a surplus of £24,855 for the existing creditors who thereupon formed the Equivalent Company and cast about for some worthwhile project in which to invest the money. Eventually they were granted a charter, on 31 May 1727, enabling them to establish the Royal Bank of Scotland. This was one in the eye to the Bank of Scotland, and as if to rub salt in the wound the new bank proceeded to issue banknotes bearing the portrait of the reigning monarch, King George II. There were political overtones; the Bank of Scotland was suspected of Jacobite leanings while the new bank was staunchly Whig and loyal to the Hanoverian dynasty. This led to the Battle of the Banks, the Old Bank and the New Bank, as they were popularly known, resorting to all manner of skulduggery and chicanery to do each other down, but the Royal Bank had a virtual monopoly of the government business in Scotland and this ensured its success. The list of directors and senior officials was almost a roll call of the Campbell lords and lairds.

The Campbells of Succoth might be relatively low in this pecking order, but inevitably they benefited from their clan connections. A grandson of the original purchaser of the Garscube estates was Archibald Campbell whose son Ilay, born in 1734, is apostrophised in two of Burns's poems, 'The Author's Earnest Cry and Prayer' and 'Extempore in the Court of Session'. He became a prominent member of the legal establishment, entered Parliament in 1784 as member for the Glasgow burghs, and became Lord President of the Council in 1789. He took a major role in the supervision of the construction of the westward section of the Forth and Clyde Canal when work was resumed in 1786. He was noted for the brilliance of his intellect and the dullness of his voice. He was Lord Rector of Glasgow University in 1799-1801 and was created first Baronet in 1808. His son Archibald, second baronet, became a judge of the Court of Session. His butler, Robb, helped to establish the 'kiss and tell' tradition of domestic servants ever since by publishing a memoir about his master and mistress which sheds an interesting light on life at Garscube. Sir Archibald commissioned the celebrated architect William Burn to design a mansion worthy of his wealth and position and Garscube House, completed in 1827, was the result. According to Robb, Sir Archibald and Lady Campbell spent the winter months in Edinburgh during the sittings of the court, but returned to Glasgow at the beginning of March to escape the sharp east winds of the capital. This annual peregrination was a major upheaval, which Robb described in some detail. The Campbells travelled by road in their large, personal coach, followed by two hay wagons loaded down with luggage and furniture, while the servants took the cheapest mode of public transport then available, a passage-boat towed by horses on the Forth and Clyde Canal.

Garscube House, built in 1827 to a design by the celebrated architect William Burn

Robb described how her ladyship was a keen gardener, spending most after-noons with the outdoor staff, planting and weeding. Sir Archibald, on the other hand, was a bon viveur who meticulously supervised the daily dinner menu. A considerable gourmet, he had a penchant for turtle soup. The turtles procured from Glasgow merchants were kept alive in one of the bathrooms and fed on lettuce until they were ready for the pot. Some idea of his wealth can be obtained from the inventory of his personal estate, published after his death in 1846. He had formed a major collection of oil paintings and a formidable library of rare books and silver, but it was the size of his wine cellar that excited the greatest comment, for it was found to contain 202 dozen bottles of sherry, 42 dozen bot-tles of Madeira and 103 dozen bottles of claret, though fewer than two dozen bottles each of whisky or brandy.

A later baronet of the same name played a prominent part in the creation of Westerton, Scotland's first garden suburb. Following the example of Titus Salt in laying out the garden suburb of Saltaire near Manchester, and the creation of Welwyn Garden City at the turn of the century, Glasgow Corporation began to give serious consideration to the creation of satellite towns beyond the City's boundaries. By 1911 the proposals had been narrowed down to two, Giffnock on the south side and Garscube in the north. Eventually the latter was chosen for this pioneering essay in social engineering, and for this purpose Sir Archibald Campbell provided the lands on the western side of his estate. The scheme, under the name of Westerton, was formally inaugurated on 21 April 1913, and the first houses were in occupation by the time the First World War erupted. Nowadays the growth of housing spreading out from Glasgow has engulfed this area and it has become part of Bearsden, although as late as the 1920s Westerton retained its separate identity. Even now, the core of this suburb reveals its gar-den character.

The Corporation of the City of Glasgow acquired 72 acres of the Garscube estate in 1921, from which was created Dawsholm Park, while the University purchased the mansion and the rest of the estate in order to create the Department of Veterinary Science based on the home farm which fronts on to Switchback Road. The mansion itself was converted into flats for University staff but it had to be demolished in 1954 when it was found to be riddled with dry rot. Ten years later the Wolfson Hall of Residence was erected on the site, and named in honour of Sir Isaac Wolfson, founder of Great Universal Stores and a major benefactor to the University. The core structure, built in 1961-5 to designs by the Building Design Partnership of Preston, is in grey brick with con-trasting white weatherboarding – not the best choice for a climate that is notori-ously damp. Residential wings were added at various times up to 1969, produc-ing a rather bewildering conglomeration of buildings on several different levels.

The grounds on the east bank of the Kelvin have been beautifully landscaped in recent years to accommodate a wide range of buildings connected with the West of Scotland Science Park. This was a joint venture of Glasgow and Strathclyde Universities, the Scottish Development Agency and Glasgow District Council, undertaken from 1983 onwards and still growing. On the western side of Maryhill Road is the Kelvin Campus, radiating to the north and west of Wolfson Hall, and comprising three strings of single-storey buildings discreetly located amid woodlands and shrubbery. The area on the east side of Maryhill Road lying south of the river is the location of the Todd Campus, named in honour of another Glasgow man, Alexander Robertus Todd, first Baron Todd of Trumpington, who was awarded the Nobel Prize for Chemistry in 1957 for his research on enzymes. William Gillespie & Partners designed the twin structures in warm red brick with contrasting grey steel roofs and grey-tinted glass set into the gently undulating landscape.

The Kelvin forms a wide loop as it passes through the campus grounds. Apart from a wide choice of footpaths in the campus grounds, there is a long driveway from Maryhill Road that passes in front of Wolfson Hall and runs diagonally across the campus to a bridge over the Kelvin, providing access to the Veterinary buildings on the west bank. On the southwestern side of this loop, fronting on to Switchback Road, is the University Veterinary Hospital. The unpretentious red-brick building was designed by Gillespie, Kidd & Coia and erected in 1957-58, while the Wellcome Laboratories adjoining, designed by W.N.W. Ramsay, were built in 1959-60. The Veterinary School, by the Building Design Partnership, however, is a more imaginative structure with an eye-catching copper roof. There are footpaths along both banks of the river, that on the west bank being very much higher than the east bank and both heavily wooded. Just past the Veterinary Hospital there is a footbridge connecting the paths on both banks and a few hundred metres farther downstream there is a weir, the first that we encounter on the river. Most of the University buildings are of relatively recent origin, and in previous generations Garscube Estate was used for all kinds of public gatherings and sporting events. I vividly recall taking part in a Scout rally back in the early 1950s when HRH the Duke of Gloucester came to inspect us and I was selected to give him a demonstration of cooking damper and twist, the Scout equivalents of unleavened bread.

Doubtless other events of much greater importance were also staged there. Back in June 1929, for example, George Eyre-Todd, the poet, novelist and encyclopedist of Glasgow, organised the Pageant of the West, which one newspaper dismissed with the laconic words, 'a brave show, marred by a week of wet weather'.

The footbridge provides a convenient access, from the Maryhill Road side, to Dawsholm Park, formed in the 1920s from the 72 acres acquired by the Corporation. The spelling is the phonetic form, the more genteel version being Dalsholm (pure Norse for 'wood vale'). Both spellings are to be found on old maps of the district, but while the park follows the colloquial form, the Dalsholm version was used for the paper-mill, at one time the largest industrial concern in this area, and this is perpetuated in the name of the road which runs between Maryhill Road and Cleveden Road in Kelvindale.

The Kelvin at Dawsholm Park, looking upstream

Dawsholm Park itself is hemmed in between the Kelvin on the north and the Forth and Clyde Canal on the south, with the Switchback Road on the western side and Dalsholm Road on the east. On the far side of the latter road is Dawsholm Industrial Estate, now given over to a wide variety of light industrial concerns but formerly the location of the Dalsholm Paper Mills, commenced about 1750 by James Macarthur and Company. This operation was always much smaller than its counterpart at Kelvindale, and specialised in high quality paper made from linen rags. The story goes that only the old shirts worn by Irish navvies would produce the best quality rag paper, much esteemed for deckle-edged writing paper as well as weighty ledgers. Apart from the pulping, most of the processes in this mill were carried on by hand, but in 1880 papermaking machinery was installed and fine quality wove papers were then manufactured. Production of machine-made paper increased steadily until the First World War, then fell back slightly before increasing sharply from 1947 onwards, when the firm went over almost entirely to the manufacture of wrapping paper, made from waste paper and wood pulp. The firm became a private limited company in 1890 but was taken over in 1934 and later formed part of the Associated Paper Group. Even at its height, this firm only employed about seventy hands.

At the northeast side of the park there is a string of reservoirs. At one time they were employed as the storage basin for logs used in the production of wood pulp. I have been told that, up to the Second World War, it was customary to roll logs down the Kelvin to the paper-mills, but latterly they were brought to the factories by more humdrum road transport. Today, many of the original mill buildings are mouldering in decay, covered with moss or festooned with vegetation and rapidly blending in with the surrounding terrain. Dawsholm Park is not noted for its formal landscapes, but rather it has been allowed to remain largely unspoiled and is still a rather pleasant 'wooded vale' as its name implies. Significantly it was one of the last places in the Glasgow area where red squirrels could be seen; but nowadays it is overrun with the larger, more aggressive grey variety.

The lands of Dawsholm were incorporated into the City of Glasgow in 1912, the momentous year that witnessed the absorption of the burghs of Govan and Partick along with portions of Lanarkshire, Renfrewshire and Dunbartonshire. The accretion of some 6,208 acres and a population of 226,335 brought the population of Glasgow as a whole above the million mark for the first time.

On the east bank of the river there are still vestiges of masonry indicating the mill lades which temporarily diverted water to power mills. South of the railway line, this area was notable for bleachfields, dyeworks and later calico printworks, all of which were derived from the cotton industry. By the early years of the nineteenth century there were over a hundred cotton mills in the Glasgow area and while some of the larger mills (such as the vast complex in Tradeston) had their own facilities for finishing cloth, a great deal of this work was carried on in smaller establishments, many of which were located along the banks of the Kelvin. Originally the bleaching of cloth depended on broad fields on the riverbanks, relying on sunlight, but the discovery of chemical bleaches by Charles Tennant of St Rollox in the 1790s revolutionised this business, which flourished for seven decades. The collapse of the Western Bank in 1857 hit many of the bleachworks hard, and the outbreak of the American Civil War a few years later dramatically cut off supplies of raw cotton, precipitating a sharp decline from which Glasgow's textile industries never recovered.

As in the Campsie villages that sprang up on the banks of the Glazert, the pattern of textile works was gradually transformed, from bleachfields, to bleach and dyeworks, and latterly to printfields. Calico printing in this district was initiated by William Stirling in the middle of the eighteenth century, and although he moved his operations from Dawsholm to a much larger and more convenient location in the Vale of Leven about 1770, other firms continued to operate in this area for many years. The original printworks were demolished in 1872 to provide the site for gasworks, and in turn, they have been demolished in more recent years. The Maryhill Printworks was established on the east bank of the river in the 1830s, on a site between the railway line and the aqueduct, but nowadays part of the parklands between the river and Lochgilp Street. This factory, operated by Messrs Reid and Whiteman, was hard hit by the violent strikes that erupted throughout the calico industry in 1834. Originally block-printing was done by hand and was a very skilled job to ensure accurate registration. Consequently calico printers were among the highest paid employees in the textile trades, but their status was eventually undermined by the adoption of steam-powered printing presses which could do the same work more accurately and infinitely faster. Alongside the printworks was a weaving factory employing upwards of two hundred handloom weavers, but by the middle of the century they had become redundant, when steam-powered looms were installed at a purpose-built factory in Wyndford. In turn, this textile mill gave way in the 1890s to the Castle Brewery which, in more recent years, was demolished to make way for Maryhill police station (immortalised in the *Taggart* television series).

The development of the northwestern corner of Glasgow, bounded by the Kelvin, owes much to the brothers George and Thomas Hutcheson, lawyers and notaries public, who flourished in the reign of King James VI. The bachelor brothers, whose statues, sculpted by James Colquhoun in 1649, can be seen to this day on the facade of Hutchesons' Hospital in Ingram Street, Glasgow, each clad in ruff, doublet and hose, amassed a fortune, some of which they ploughed back into good works, such as the aforementioned hospital, as well as the grammar schools for boys and girls which rank among Glasgow's foremost education institutions to this day. But they also shrewdly invested in property, acquiring lands south of the Clyde (now the district of Hutchesonstown) as well as estates north of the City.

The brothers hailed from Lambhill, south of Balmuildy, and in 1600 George purchased the lands of Gairbraid. He died in 1639 and brother Thomas two years later, and their worldly goods passed to their sister's son, Ninian Hill. Ninian's son Hew rebuilt the farmhouse of Laigh Gairbraid in 1688, which, with additions in the early eighteenth century, was a substantial two-storey structure with extensive outbuildings. An estate plan by Charles Ross, dated 1759, shows Laigh Gairbraid with its Laigh Park, Cow Park and East Park. At that time, the area was still completely rural, although the establishment of the turnpike road from Glasgow to Garscube in 1753 promised to open up this district to enterprise. Thirty years later the farmhouse was demolished to make way for a mansion and for a number of years Gairbraid House reflected the new-found wealth and position of its occupants, Robert Graham of Dalsholm and his wife Mary Hill. She was born at Gairbraid in 1730 and eventually fell heir to the Gairbraid estates on the death of her father Hew Hill. In her thirties and still unmarried, the heiress seemed doomed to end her days an old maid, when along came dashing Robert Graham, eight years her senior, and swept her off her feet. They were wed in 1763, a union that would last more than forty years till his death in 1804. Mary outlived him by five years.

'Captain' Graham was a colourful character who had gone to sea at an early age, and had had the misfortune to be captured by Barbary corsairs and then sold into slavery in Algeria before securing his manumission. Returning to Glasgow, still a young man and very definitely on the make, he wooed and won the heiress and then tried his hand at various business ventures. For a time he speculated in collieries at Garscube and Gilshochill but enjoyed only moderate success. Although the local coal was of a high quality the mineworkings were prone to flooding and Graham could not afford the pumping machinery to dry them out. South of the Kelvin, opposite Killermont golf course, is Sandyflat from which Acre Road runs westwards to join Maryhill Road. South of Acre Road lies Maryhill Park, but between the park and the road is a patch of ground cryptically called Acre – not an allusion to the place in the Holy Land besieged by the Crusaders but simply indicating the acre of ground which Graham set aside for miners' rows in connection with his Garscube colliery. The coal-mine closed before this minuscule piece of town-planning could be realised, but out of sentiment, perhaps, Graham kept back this small piece of land when the rest of the estate on this side of the river was feued off to create Maryhill. Today, Graham's little acre is infinitely better known for other reasons, for it is the site of Acre House, a nineteenth-century mansion in the Italianate style which was acquired by Glasgow University for its department of Marine Technology and has been extensively refurbished and enlarged since the 1960s. Nearby are the Hydrodynamics Laboratory and the Astronomy Building, both designed by Keppie, Henderson & Partners and constructed in 1964-7. Both are buildings of the rather plain, no-nonsense variety, although the latter is immediately recognisable on account of its pepperpot observatory dome.

For a time, Robert Graham coasted along by dabbling in a calico printworks and then selling off the northerly portions of his wife's lands to the adjacent estates, but the corner was finally turned in 1788 when he successfully negotiated a deal with the promoters of the Forth and Clyde Canal to route their waterway across his wife's estate. It may be recalled that, by 1775, the canal had extended as far west as Stockingfield, no longer in existence but roughly at the east end of Ruchill golf course; Smeaton Street in Ruchill was named after John Smeaton, the civil engineer originally employed in building the canal. After a hiatus caused by a lack of funds, the promoters were persuaded by the merchants of Glasgow to continue the canal due south to Hamiltonhill (Possilpark), completed in 1777. Due to the chronic shortage of cash, the plan to drive the canal westward was shelved until 1784, when the government advanced the sum of £50,000 from the sale of forfeited Jacobite estates, and this enabled work on the westward section to start up in 1786 when Robert Whitworth, creator of the Kelvin drainage system east of Kilsyth, was commissioned to take the canal west from Stockingfield, to enter the Firth of Clyde at Bowling. The proposed course of the canal ran more or less due west from Stockingfield across the Gairbraid estates. Apart from the sum paid to the Grahams for this privilege, the construction of the canal and its aqueducts brought an immediate influx of workers, and where the canal ran industry was sure to follow very swiftly thereafter. By 1790 a dry dock had been cut at the side of the canal just west of the turnpike road. Like Kirkintilloch a generation earlier, this district really dates its development from that time. In the same year the entire length of the canal, from east to west, was opened to traffic on 28 July, the Glasgow branch was extended to Port Dundas and a junction with the Monkland Canal was completed.

Whitworth excelled the feat of Smeaton in building the Kirkintilloch aqueduct carrying the canal over the Luggie, when he constructed the great Kelvin aqueduct at Maryhill. Of the various contemporary accounts of this marvel of engineering, that provided by the Revd John Burns of the Barony Church seems to be the most accurate:

> The great bridge over Kelvin was begun in June 1787 and finished in April 1791. It is carried over a valley 400 feet long, and 65 deep. It consists of four very large arches of excellent masonry work; is in height about 83 feet from the bed of the river to the top of the bridge and is one of the most stupendous works of its kind perhaps in the world.

And Robert Denholm (1804) waxed lyrical when he described the extraordinary sight of 'square-rigged vessels navigating at a height of seventy-five feet above the level of the spectators'.

To the north of the aqueduct there are two bridges spanning the Kelvin. The more northerly one carries Cowal Road, open to motor traffic, between Maryhill Road and Dalsholm Road, but alongside, and to the south, is the bridge that links Bantaskin Street in Maryhill to Skaethorn Road in Kelvindale. It is now closed to vehicles by a line of bollards and this dead-end, screened by trees, has unfortunately become a convenient spot for joy-riders to abandon and set alight stolen cars whose burnt-out wreckage disfigures the landscape. The only saving grace of this bridge is that from its low parapet one gets an excellent view of the river in both directions. At this point, the river runs through a gorge. The current picks up speed as the Kelvin begins its descent to sea level; from this point onwards the river played its part in the development of the mills and printworks which depended heavily on water-power. After a period of post-industrial decay, most of the former mill and factory buildings have vanished and this stretch of the river has been attractively landscaped, with gardens, shrubbery and footpaths, mainly on the Maryhill side, for the heavily wooded west bank is very much higher and almost sheer in places. From the bridge there is a path running very steeply up the west bank towards Cleveden Place, but it is only for the fit and foolhardy. At this point you can see the entrance to one of the many railway tunnels that honeycomb the west bank of the Kelvin and testify to the low-level or subterranean lines that formerly criss-crossed the district. The massive stone pillars that carried this railway line from the tunnel across the Kelvin to Maryhill are still standing, although nowadays the only purpose they serve is to provide a convenient perch for the cormorants who have colonised the river. To see these birds patiently observing the river below and then swooping into its depths is one of the most heartening sights for someone who remembers when the river was virtually an open sewer, poisoned by effluent from countless industrial concerns. The cormorant is proof positive of the transformation of the Kelvin in recent years. Where there was once only the turgid sludge of chemical works and pulpmills there is now generally clear water. Of course, it can be a rich chocolate hue during spring spates, but in summer it is as crystal clear as it was before the Industrial Revolution.

The despoliation of the Kelvin was the downside of the great developments wrought in the closing years of the eighteenth century. Only a few metres from this bridge is the aqueduct carrying the canal, and from the towpath one gets not only the best view of the river but panoramic vistas of the surrounding district. To the east of the aqueduct is the series of five locks (locks 21 to 25) constructed by William Gibb and John Moir. Between locks 22 and 23 Whitworth planned a graving dock where 'Nature seems almost to have formed the proposed situation for such a purpose.' Incidentally, in allusion to lock 20, the highest on the canal system, that part of Maryhill which grew up around these locks came to be known as Wyndford. Although the canal was little used for passenger traffic once the railways were established it continued to be an important medium for the conveyance of freight from one side of Scotland to the other, until 1962 when it closed down. Mention has already been made of the Queens that operated excursion services between 1893 and 1939; in their heyday they ran all the way from Kirkintilloch to Maryhill. After the Second World War the only vessels to be seen at Maryhill were occasional cabin cruisers and yachts or coastal fishing vessels, though Aileen Smart, in *Villages of Glasgow* (1988), notes that in June 1952 the midget submarine XE IX passed through the locks on its voyage from the Clyde to the Forth. This stretch of the canal survived in better condition than the more inland areas, thanks in large measure to the efforts of the Forth and Clyde Canal Society, and a walk along the towpaths has long been appreciated as a pleasant outing for bird watchers. After four decades in limbo, however, the locks are undergoing renovation as part of the exciting Millennium Link. In the not too distant future, ramblers on the Kelvin pathways will be able to crane their necks once more and admire the spectacle of vessels under sail gliding along the aqueduct high above their heads.

On the strength of the original canal development Robert Graham and Mary Hill were able to afford their splendid mansion erected in 1789. Alexander Thomson, in his *Random Notes and Rambling Recollections of Maryhill* (1895) described Graham as 'a square man [who] built a square house: large and plain, without any architectural adornments'. A picture of this stolid pile appeared in *Old Country Houses of the Old Glasgow Gentry*. In 1793 the northern part of the estate was surveyed and divided into lots which were feued to a wealthy grocer, Robert Craig, who planned to create a new town between the northern limits of Glasgow and Dawsholm Bridge. As part of this land deal, Robert Graham insisted that the new town was to be named after his wife Mary Hill. Like so many of Graham's other dreams, the new town never amounted to anything in his own lifetime. By the time Mary died in 1809 Maryhill consisted of little more than the cluster of cottages around Whitworth's graving dock which was known alternatively simply as Drydock or, more pretentiously, as Kelvindock.

The graving dock was leased to Thomas Morrison who carried on a business as a ship-repairer, but his son-in-law, David Swan, diversified into shipbuilding after taking over in 1837 and this family enterprise continued till 1893. At first Swan concentrated on small wooden vessels such as passenger scows, but the development of iron foundries in the neighbourhood in the 1840s gave him a ready source of plates for the manufacture of iron barges. In 1857 (the year after he became the first provost of the burgh) Swan built the *Glasgow*, officially described as a 'screw lighter' but soon nicknamed a 'puffer' and thus initiating a long line of sturdy little cargo vessels which were once a common sight on the canal and the waters of the West Coast. Like their counterparts in Kirkintilloch, Swans not only built puffers but also larger vessels which were constructed in sections and then re-assembled when they reached the coast. Such sectional iron ships were also transported overland and were a popular means of navigating the great lakes of Africa and South America. For three decades after the Swan business terminated, puffers were constructed at Kelvindock by other companies, and the last vessel was launched in 1921. The dock continued to accommodate a boat-repair yard as late as 1962. The Swan family had their residence at Collina Cottage, south of the locks and once described as 'a superior cottage commanding a view of the whole of Maryhill'. It was demolished some years ago to make way for the high-rise apartment blocks at Collina Place on the high ground overlooking the Kelvin.

By 1826 Maryhill had grown sufficiently for the Church of Scotland to establish a small chapel of ease to serve the inhabitants; out of this eventually came Maryhill Old Parish Church. This was a plain, unpretentious building on the east side of Maryhill Road between Shiskine and Duart streets and is described in *The Buildings of Glasgow* (1990) as 'a simple harled two-storey box', its severe outline relieved only by a Venetian window on the east side. Reflecting the increasing size and importance of the district it served, in 1850 it was raised to the dignity of a parish church in its own right, separated from the Glasgow Barony parish. In 1893 the interior was stripped and completely refurbished, and a quarter of a century later Jeffrey Waddell added the pedimented and pilastered west front whose squat central door and window betray some Bauhaus influence. Although it fell into disuse in 1981, services being conducted thereafter in the nearby church hall, its kirkyard is well worth visiting, not only for the tombs of Maryhill's earliest inhabitants but also for the Trades Union Martyr Memorial Pillar, a cast-iron column surmounted by a draped Grecian urn which recalls one of the more violent incidents in the industrial disputes which affected the textile trades in the 1830s. It commemorates George Millar 'mortally stabbed at the age of Nineteen on the 24th of February 1834 by one of those put to the Calico Printing Trade for the purpose of destroying a Union of regular workmen, formed to protect their wages'. This monument was 'erected by his fellow-operatives'.

The first incumbent of the chapel of ease was the Revd Robert McNair Wilson who led most of the congregation away from the Church of Scotland in 1843 at the Great Disruption that created the Free Church. His place was taken by the Revd Robert Thomson Johnston who, seven years later, became minister of the newly created parish of Maryhill. Meanwhile the breakaway congregation built Maryhill Free Church at Sandbank Street in 1846-8 to a design by Charles Wilson. A steeple was added in 1859 but otherwise this pseudo-Gothic building was distinguished only by the hideousness of the pews installed in 1907. Five years later the Deil's kist o' whistles, an organ by Abbot & Smith of Leeds, was added. After the reunion with the Church of Scotland in 1929 it was renamed Maryhill High Church. Churches of several other denominations reflected the dramatic growth of the burgh and its diverse population, notably Gairbraid Church (United Presbyterian, 1871) and St George's (Episcopal, 1891). The large Catholic community was not too well served in the early years of the nineteenth century, and every Sunday morning the Catholics of Maryhill went in solemn procession down Gairbraid Street (now Maryhill Road) to St George's Cross and beyond, all the way to St Andrew's Cathedral in Clyde Street to attend Mass. It is recorded that the cavalcade was headed by a Highlander, Archie Darroch, playing the bagpipes. However, as Smart points out in *Villages of Glasgow*, a site was obtained in 1851 between Duncruin and Kilmun streets on which was erected the Church of the Immaculate Conception of the Blessed Virgin Mary, the first of its name in Scotland since the Reformation in 1560. This church was enlarged in 1900 when the Donegal Aisle was built, so-called on account of the many young men from that county who were then employed in the local gasworks. The church was devastated by a landmine on 14 March 1941 following a German air raid which left 107 people in Kilmun Street dead. St Mary's Primary School was later erected on the site, and a new church was erected in 1955-6 at Bonville, north of the railway station, between the Kelvin and Maryhill Road. Sadly, it had to be demolished in the 1980s on account of structural faults, but a new church is now in the course of construction on the same site. In the interim worshippers had the alternative of St Gregory's, erected in 1965. This church, located at the corner of Kelvindale Road and Kelvindale Gardens in Wyndford, has the church, hall and presbytery grouped around a formal garden in the manner of a medieval monastery.

After the deaths of Robert and Mary Graham their daughter Lilias continued to reside at Gairbraid House, until she died unmarried in 1836. The estate then passed to her nephew, John Dunlop who was much more pre-occupied with his Renfrewshire estates and seldom visited Gairbraid. On a visit to his maiden aunt in 1829 he noted with stern disapproval scenes of drunkenness at Kelvindock which impelled him, on returning to Greenock, to found the first temperance society in the British Isles. It is recorded that Aunt Lilias and her companion were the first to 'sign the pledge'. In November that year Lilias herself was instrumental in starting a Men's Temperance Society, under the chairmanship of the minister of the chapel of ease. The society got off to a good start: no fewer than ninety men signed the pledge at the inaugural meeting. Alcohol in its many forms was certainly a major problem in Maryhill, even at that early date, with an alehouse for every sixty inhabitants. Dunlop had a staunch ally in Richard Collins, proprietor of the Kelvindale Paper Mills.

Being quite realistic about it, the temperance society urged its members to abjure 'strong drink' or 'spiritous liquors', leaving them the option of wine, cider, ale and beer in its various forms, and it was not until the 1840s that the campaign for total abstinence from fermented liquors of all kinds got under way, the leading light at that time being Edward Morris, the ticketing agent of the canal company at their Port Dundas terminal. Unlike Kirkintilloch, however, Maryhill never went so far as to vote for Prohibition.

John Dunlop's brother William, known as 'Tiger' Dunlop, emigrated to Canada and built the road between Toronto and Goderich on Lake Huron, a feat of engineering almost as stupendous as the Forth and Clyde Canal itself. In memory of his ancestral home he named his Ontario estate Gairbraid. He was the very antithesis of his dour, Calvinistic brother and certainly did not share his zeal for temperance. His will contained the curious bequest: 'I leave my silver tankard to the eldest son of Old John, as the representative of the family. I would have left it to Old John himself, but he would have melted it down to make temperance medals, and that would have been a sacrilege. However, I have left him my big horn snuff-box; he can only make temperance spoons out of that.'

In his book on the old country houses (1870), John Guthrie Smith makes a sad comment on the state of Gairbraid House by that time:

The old house now stands naked and forlorn amidst a wilderness of 'free coups'; broken bottles and bricks, pools of dirty water, clotheslines fluttering with part-coloured rags and all the abominations of a new suburb. Instead of the singing of birds and the music of the soft flowing Kelvin, which of yore pleased and refreshed the passer-by, the air is now vocal with the discordant voices of rough men, scolding women and 'greeting bairns', with the clang of machinery and the hiss of the steam engine.

At the time of the first census (1841) the population of Maryhill had risen to 2,552 and it was still very much a country village. Soon afterwards, however, an ironworks was established and the construction of iron barges commenced at Kelvindock, hence the 'clang of machinery' noted so dolefully by Guthrie Smith. Apart from the canal, a waterway of a very different kind brought work to the district in the 1850s when the pipeline from Loch Katrine was constructed. By 1856, when it was raised to the status of a police burgh, Maryhill had a population in excess of six thousand. In the same year the Glasgow, Dumbarton and Helensburgh Railway provided work for a vast army of navvies, recruited mainly in the Highlands and Ireland, and many of them subsequently settled in the area. Glasgow and its environs was a boom area throughout most of the second half of the nineteenth century and the population of Maryhill rose dramatically. When the Helensburgh Railway opened a station at Maryhill Park in 1857 this had the effect of encouraging the spread of the town northwards from Kelvindock. After the work on the canal and the railway lines came the improvement in the main Maryhill Road and the laying of streets, sewers and street lighting in the burgh. There were even collieries, whose improved pumping machinery succeeded where Robert Graham had failed. In the second half of the nineteenth century many other industries sprang up in the Maryhill district, including paintworks, rubber works, oil works and glass bottle factories, all of which enjoyed a period of prosperity before going into decline in the course of the twentieth century. In spite of the hundred and one industries that developed in the district from the 1860s onwards, the manufacture of paper and related products continued to be the mainstay of the area, largely as a result of the Collins family.

In the nineteenth century Lochgilp Street was known as Kelvin Street. Together with Whitelaw, Reid (now Cowal) and Walker (now Glencloy) streets, this made up a square facing the river. A map of the area dating from the early nineteenth century proudly proclaims this to be the Town of Maryhill. To the south of this was an area designated on the map as the Botany Feus, although why it was thus named has never been convincingly explained. One theory is that it was named after Botany Bay in Australia, apparently alluding to the fact that many of the labourers who worked on the construction of the canal were convicts who, faced with the prospect of a canal gang or transportation to the ends of the earth, chose the former as the lesser of two evils. It makes a good story but unfortunately no evidence has ever been found to support it. Less plausible is the story that the area was so named by the calico printworkers who derisively likened their working conditions to life in the notorious penal colony. Whatever the truth, the name has not been preserved in any of the district's streets, and the expression 'Butney' has long since vanished from the local patois. By the 1860s this part of Maryhill was the most densely populated part of the burgh. A perusal of the 1861 census reveals that a high proportion of its inhabitants were either born in Ireland or the children of Irish parents. It was an area of drunkenness and lawlessness, though much of the latter consisted of vandalism, street brawls and generally mindless assaults on strangers rather than organised crime. The situation only began to improve after Maryhill became a police burgh in 1856, but for two decades Kelvin Street remained a 'no-go area' for the local constabulary.

A stone's throw away (quite literally), a rudimentary police station and lock-up was erected, and in this modest way the municipal buildings of Maryhill came into being. Things began to look up after 1869, the year in which Maryhill Barracks were inaugurated. Although the soldiers, frequenting the local pubs when off duty, undoubtedly exacerbated the situation at first, gradually the proximity of a well-disciplined force, which could be called out in aid of the civil power at a moment's notice began to have a calming effect. As Maryhill lost its reputation as a frontier town new industries flocked into the area. By 1876 there were over forty factories or mills in the district and in that year something was done at long last about erecting a Burgh Hall. Duncan MacNaughtan was commissioned to design the building which, sited on the hill with a commanding position overlooking Maryhill Road, was said to resemble a French hotel of the luxury class, with a very steep hipped roof and cupola, replete with architectural sculpture in the finest traditions of the French Renaissance. The removal of the cupola and the restyling of the roof in later years lessened its French appearance, although there are still many features of the interior decor that remind the visitor of the original concept. Sadly the stained-glass windows by Stephen Adams illustrating the twenty principal trades and industries of the burgh have been removed to the People's Palace on Glasgow Green. Maryhill ceased to be an independent burgh in 1891 and thereafter its fine municipal buildings declined in importance; but after many years of neglect they have now been restored and refurbished as public halls serving the community.

Of the other public buildings in Maryhill the most prominent is the public library, designed by James Rhind and erected between 1902 and 1905. Although dwarfed by the commercial buildings on either side and not as impressive as Rhind's other public commissions, it nevertheless exhibits the characteristics of his style, with an opulent facade dominated by the figure of a mother encouraging her children to read a book.

During the nineteenth century the schools in this district were invariably connected to one or other of the religious denominations and were funded and maintained by the churches. After Maryhill School Board was established in 1873, however, education was, to some extent, secularised, the Parish and Free Church schools amalgamating to form Maryhill Public School. It was moved to Gilshochill in 1884 and continued as Maryhill Primary School. Wyndford Primary and St. Gregory's Primary were erected on the same campus in 1963-4 to serve the Protestant and Catholic children of the Wyndford Estate, while secondary education is provided by John Paul Academy, inaugurated in 1980 and located in the new district of Summerston to the northeast of Maryhill. Beyond purely educational circles, John Paul Academy has one claim to fame: it is the current home of Maryhill Harriers, one of Scotland's oldest and best-known athletic clubs, founded in 1888. Wyndford and St Gregory's are prominent landmarks set atop a steep, heavily wooded hill rising above the Kelvin; from the riverbank they present the impression of gigantic building blocks.

Maryhill is well provided with sporting amenities which date from February 1861 when a bowling club was founded. A site was obtained on the north side of Duart Street near the railway station and the ground levelled and turfed so that it was ready for matches by the summer. Several clubhouses have stood on the site since August 1861, the most recent having been erected in the 1980s. The cottage at the rear, now used as the bowls house and directors' accommodation, was the original Penny School of the parish and later the church officer's residence. In recent years large, fully equipped recreation centres have been established on Duncruin Street, Gilshochill and alongside the former Burgh Hall in the very heart of Maryhill.

Firhill, alongside a canal basin on the east side of Maryhill Road, is the home of Partick Thistle Football Club, known to its supporters as the Jags. As its name suggests, this club originated some miles away in another part of Glasgow altogether, but it has always favoured grounds near the Kelvin. It started life in 1876, playing on a public pitch on the south bank of the Kelvin where the Kelvingrove Art Galleries and Museum now stand. When that site was redeveloped in 1888 the club moved to Jordanvale in Whiteinch but thereafter returned to Partick and played at Muirpark, Inchview and latterly Meadowside at the mouth of the Kelvin. When that site was acquired by Henderson's shipyard in 1909 the club obtained its present grounds at Firhill Road. A new stand was erected in 1927 on land acquired from the former Caledonian Railway Company. For many years this was obscured by the tenements of the surrounding streets but in more recent years their demolition has revealed the Firhill stadium in all its red-brick glory.

The First World War was a turning point for Maryhill. After a brief period of wartime boom, there was a long period of post-war depression. The heart was torn out of the original town when the congested slums around Kelvindock were swept away in one of the first great clearance projects of the 1930s. The closure of the canal in 1962 marked the *coup de grâce*, many of the older industries having vanished by that time. Remarkably, the population of Maryhill in 1961 was less than it had been in 1861; but in the past four decades there has been a remarkable transformation in the district. New housing, both council and private, on brownfield sites has led to the emergence of Maryhill as a dormitory district for the city centre. New roads have cut a broad swathe through the formerly densely populated tenements, but the most dramatic change of all has been the redevelopment of Maryhill Barracks to form the Wyndford Estate, complete with a large shopping centre.

The people of Glasgow had a healthy disregard for a military presence and preferred to keep military personnel at a safe distance. In the late eighteenth century the barracks in the Calton district on the southeast side of Glasgow accommodated a battalion of infantry while a squadron of cavalry, housed at Eglinton Street, could be called out quickly whenever demonstrations on Glasgow Green threatened to get out of hand. After the Napoleonic Wars, however, this accommodation was neglected or sold off and when trouble erupted in 1848, the Year of Revolutions, the remaining barracks could barely cope with a couple of infantry companies and a cavalry troop. Although the Chartist troubles passed off, eventually the upholders of law and order began agitating for much better security, especially as Glasgow and its environs were now growing so rapidly and attracting so many 'undesirable' elements in the process. Various sites were then considered for an entirely new barracks but rejected as unsuitable. Thus it was not until 1869 that the War Department purchased thirty acres on the Garrioch estate from Davidson of Ruchill. The cost of erecting the barracks was estimated at £100,000 but a dispute with the contractors held up work for two years. In 1873 the War Department purchased a further twenty-seven acres and solved the problem of construction by handing over the project to the Royal Engineers. Maryhill Barracks was completed in 1876 and provided accommodation for an infantry regiment, a cavalry squadron and a battery of field artillery.

The infantry barracks consisted of two- or three-storey blocks, including married quarters and barrack rooms for single men. Nearby was the officers' mess, then the cavalry and artillery barracks to the west of the infantry parade ground, together with stables and gun parks, a veterinary establishment, a sixty-bed hospital, chapel, gymnasium and defaulters' block with twenty-one cells. The Barracks were entered through an imposing main gate on Maryhill Road, beyond which was the guardroom and the parade ground. On the south side of the site, occupying about a third of the total area, was the training ground where generations of young soldiers (myself included) learned the skills of fieldcraft. The training area bordered on the Kelvin and I well recall an incident when the officer

Maryhill Barracks, home of the Highland Light Infantry

in charge of the training platoon decided that we were not charging around in a sufficiently realistic manner. He lined us up on the bank and then proceeded to lead us across. The platoon sergeant (a London Irishman and a superb cricketer) held back with the other NCOs while the recruits, in denim overalls and steel helmets, uncertainly followed the lieutenant. He was in summer 'shirt-sleeve order' but wore a kilt and carried an ash walking stick with which he gingerly prodded the riverbed ahead of him. One moment he was there, the water almost touching the hem of his kilt, but the next moment he was gone and only his tam-o'-shanter bonnet was floating on the surface! Mr M… had plunged into a deep hole and had to be hauled out by some of the more adventurous recruits. Apart from a thorough soaking he was none the worse of his baptism but there was never any attempt to repeat the exercise after that.

Although many different regiments were quartered at Maryhill during the first half-century of its existence, the barracks was latterly most intimately associated with the Highland Light Infantry which had its regimental depot there from 1920 onwards. The HLI inevitably attracted a couple of nicknames: Harry Lauder's Infants being only marginally less offensive than Hairy Legged Irishmen. Forty years ago, however, there was an element of truth in the latter, for the training company was divided into two platoons. While the National Service platoon was a mixed bag of conscripts drawn from all over the Glasgow area, the Regular platoon consisted almost entirely of recruits from the Irish Republic. At that time there was little opportunity for young Irishmen to follow a military career in their own country. Later on, however, the situation changed as the Irish Army expanded to meet the threat from the troubles in Northern Ireland and also became heavily committed to the UN peacekeeping forces. Many of the warrant officers and NCOs in the latter were, I understand, graduates of the old HLI which amalgamated with the Royal Scots Fusiliers in 1959 to form the Royal Highland Fusiliers. The HLI cap-badge depicted an elephant and the battle honour Assaye from the Indian campaign of 1803, enclosed in a bugle-horn, the emblem of the light infantry.

Two people were briefly associated with Maryhill Barracks, one at the outset of his career and the other at the end of it. After training at Sandhurst, David Niven was gazetted second lieutenant and posted to the HLI in 1929. He spent two years with the regiment before resigning his commission and going off to Hollywood, though, to his credit, he came back in 1939 and re-enlisted, eventually attaining the rank of lieutenant-colonel about the time of the Normandy landings. Niven's witty memoirs contain numerous self-deprecatory anecdotes about his time as a subaltern in the City of Glasgow Regiment. By contrast, Maryhill Barracks was also the temporary resting place of Rudolf Hess after his dramatic flight to Scotland in 1940. His plane crashed near Eaglesham and he was brought under guard to Glasgow and lodged in the detention block at the Barracks before being transferred to the Tower of London and, ultimately, solitary confinement in Spandau.

The year after the regimental amalgamation, the War Office closed the Barracks, which were subsequently demolished and the site redeveloped by Glasgow Corporation for the Wyndford housing scheme. All that remains today is the regimental guardroom and the barrack wall, and even that was under threat, when a project to widen Maryhill Road was under consideration. The erstwhile infantry parade ground that once resounded to the boots of square-bashing recruits has now been grassed over and makes a very pleasant park for the Wyndford Estate, with landscaped parkland and pathways down to the football pitches on the riverbank. Between 1960 and 1969 the housing scheme was created by the Scottish Special Housing Association as a blend of high-rise, medium-rise and walk-up flats accommodating about five thousand people. Surrounding the four high-rise blocks and thirteen medium-rise blocks are clusters of yellow-brick town houses and maisonettes. The retention of the old Barracks boundary wall was a happy decision as it gives Wyndford Estate a sense of solidarity which is often lacking in other housing schemes, while the tasteful landscaping of the little tree-lined squares, pedestrian walkways and streets (appropriately named after places in the Highlands, whence came the ancestors of so many of the residents) makes it a very pleasant place in which to live. The shopping centre to the north (by the architectural department of the Co-operative Wholesale Society) stands on what was once the Barracks railway station, later renamed Maryhill Central, which was demolished in 1966. This line ran in a southerly direction and crossed the Kelvin just beyond the western end of Garrioch Quadrant.

Today little remains to remind the passer-by of the military presence in this district. Northeast of Maryhill Park are Caldercuilt playing fields, while to the southeast, behind the Nurses' Home on Maryhill Road, is a quiet little cul-de-sac with an oval patch in the centre. This is the Prince of Wales Gardens, named in honour of the future King Edward VIII and Duke of Windsor, who visited Glasgow and inaugurated these gardens as a memorial to the servicemen who had fallen in the First World War. Around the gardens are the pebble-dash cottages built in 1920-2 for the veterans of that conflict. Near the former Barracks' gate is the Elephant and Bugle public house, named after the regimental badge and containing a number of interesting mementoes of the HLI. At the junction of Garrioch Road and Shakespeare Street is Walcheren Barracks, the rather striking blue-and-white-painted headquarters of the 52nd Lowland Volunteers, a Territorial Army unit whose name alludes to the successful assault on the German-held island off the Dutch coast by the 52nd Lowland Division in 1944. It is a matter for regret that space was not found in the redevelopment of the Maryhill Barracks site for a regimental museum. Instead, this is to be found near the Charing Cross end of Sauchiehall Street in the heart of Glasgow.

Across the road from Walcheren Barracks is Garrioch Drive, a short thoroughfare which runs along the east side of the Kelvin. At this point, the river runs through a deep gorge, and through the railings at the side of the drive you can look straight down at the riverbank a hundred feet below. There are gates at both ends of the drive giving access to the steep footpaths that zigzag across the slope. There is a slightly arched footbridge across the river, and, beyond, a flight of steps made from old railway sleepers, flanked by a pleasing arrangement of stout logs which leads up to a little park, in reality the most northwesterly appendage of the Botanic Gardens and forming part of the Kelvin Walkway. The last time I visited this little oasis of greenery at the northeastern tip of Kirklee, men from the Parks Department were hard at work clearing away the last of the trees which had been killed by Dutch Elm Disease. The steep hillside looks sadly naked without those mighty trees, but hopefully it will not be long before this area has been replanted.

On the east bank, the footpath runs along the riverbank under a cluster of bridges towering high above. A steep footpath leading to the exit at the west end of Garrioch Drive also provided access of a sort to the bridges, both of which are disused. The first is a road bridge which formerly connected Garrioch Quadrant to Kirklee, but now has Berlin-type walls at either end preventing egress. Alongside is a railway bridge, all that remains of a line which, in pre-Beeching times, ran from Partick to Possilpark. It seems a great pity that the road bridge, in particular, has not been restored and re-opened. The Kelvin, which has probably had more bridges in Glasgow than the Clyde, seems to have suffered disproportionately from the closure and demolition of these useful structures.

South of the canal where it crosses the Kelvin is the district now known as Kelvindale which always strikes me as a misnomer, for its characteristic feature is that it occupies a large hill round which the river curves on the eastern flanks. Kelvindale is a typical Twenties housing scheme of bungalows and semi-detached houses developed by Mactaggart & Mickel, distinguished from count-less others of the same vintage by the little shopping parade of red sandstone, completed in 1926 as a single entity, with tiny cupolas at either end to maintain symmetry. The district is dominated by Cleveden Road which runs diagonally from the canal on the northwestern side to Great Western Road on the south-eastern side. Although the development of the Kelvinside estate began in 1840 it was still open countryside until the 1870s, with little more than two or three large mansions set in extensive parkland as the only features. Balgray and West Balgray have long since vanished, and not even their names remain in any of the streets of Kelvindale. Beaconsfield (now Kelvinside House) is recalled in the crescent-shaped Beaconsfield Road which runs northeast from Great Western Road, while Bellshaugh near the river gave its name to Bellshaugh Road, Lane, Place and Gardens. As the name implies, Bell's Haugh was a stretch of low-lying land alongside the river, liable to flooding. Bellshaugh Road is the location of Queen Margaret Hall, the student residential buildings of Glasgow University designed by W.N.W. Ramsay in 1964 and now comprising several tower blocks.

Most of the development of this hill consists of concentric circles radiating from Cleveden Road, the housing on the upper slopes having been erected in the period following the First World War. On the southern and southeastern slopes, where the ground is more level, were erected some of the most sumptuous vil-las and mansions in Glasgow. For the aficionado of late-nineteenth century architecture this area is a veritable paradise, a riot of eclecticism. This part of the district is known as Kelvinside which has the doubtful reputation of passing into everyday language, especially if the word is pronounced 'Kelvinsayd'. According to the *Concise Scots Dictionary* (1985) this adjective denotes 'a very affected, over-refined pronunciation of Scottish English'. The analogy has overtones of Glasgow's *nouveau riche* moving out of the older parts of the City and settling in Kelvinside at the turn of the century, and having to refine their speech to suit their posh surroundings. This is also reflected in the street names of the district. Between the west side of Cleveden Road and Weymouth Drive which encircles the area, the names of English towns have been exclusively applied; but to the east of Cleveden Road many of the names have been inspired by the earldom of Crawford and Balcarres, though less imaginative are the names ending in 'field':

Endfield, Highfield, Stonefield, Bradfield and Hopefield, perhaps inspired by the original Beaconsfield Road which, of course, ultimately derived its name from a town in Buckinghamshire. Small wonder, therefore, that the upwardly mobile residents of this classy neighbourhood felt that they had a lot to live up to. Beaconsfield House, however, probably derived its name not from the town itself but from the Earl, former Prime Minister Benjamin Disraeli whose Buckinghamshire seat, Hughenden, lent its name to the playing fields of Hillhead High School and several street names in that vicinity, south of Great Western Road. Beaconsfield House was erected about 1874, the Italianate tower and Baronial extension being added in 1894. It seems to have acquired its present name of Kelvinside House about 1955 when it became a private school.

From the north end of Cleveden Road there is a bridge crossing the canal and linking up with Dalsholm Road. From the middle of Cleveden Road, near Kelvindale post office, Kelvindale Road runs in an easterly direction and eventually joins Maryhill Road, but it dips towards the river and crosses by a bridge. On the north side of Kelvindale Road, adjoining the river, there is new luxury housing on the site of one of the most famous industrial enterprises anywhere on the banks of the Kelvin.

In the aftermath of the Jacobite Rebellion of 1745-6 Edward Collins, an Englishman from either Shropshire or Suffolk (accounts vary) who is believed to have been involved in the uprising, settled in Glasgow. Although suspected of Jacobitism, Collins always maintained that he had been conscripted into the Hanoverian army under the Duke of Cumberland and fought on that side at the battle of Culloden. Whatever the truth of the matter, he never returned to England but preferred to remain in Scotland. Where he got his money from was as much a mystery as where he had come from; but in 1747 he established a paper-mill at Kelvindale, along the river below Dawsholm Bridge. Paper-making had been carried on in a desultory fashion on the banks of the Kelvin since 1690, but it was Edward Collins who injected new life into the industry. Even so, his enterprise had a shaky start because of the intermittent flow of the river at that period, and he soon moved his business to Dalmuir on the Clyde where the supply of water to power the mill was infinitely more dependable. The Dalmuir plant flourished, as Edward Collins and his son Richard diversified into bleachfields and the manufacture of logwood extract. The Dalmuir factory continued till 1857. In 1840, however, Edward Collins & Sons moved back to the district, establishing a paper-mill farther downstream on the west bank at Kelvindale, using steam-power rather than the uncertain river current to operate the pulping machinery. It is believed that William Collins, the printer and publisher, was somehow connected with the family of Edward Collins but the link has never been established.

As long ago as 1756 Edward Collins was awarded a medal by the Royal

Society of Edinburgh for 'the best printing paper' and thereafter the company was renowned for the superlative quality of its products. Two centuries later, it was still enjoying a worldwide reputation for highgloss and superfine calendered papers ideal for chromolithography and art printing, as well as a wide range of chart, music and cartridge papers as well as bond, cream laid and wove writing papers. An early speciality of the firm was blotting paper, manufactured from 1792, some years before this type of paper was widely accepted. Unlike the calico works in the Glazert Valley, this company had a remarkable record for stability and continuity, remaining in the hands of the Collins family, through seven generations, until 1948. It was a wholly privately-owned company until 1914 when, as a result of a disastrous fire two years previously, it went public in order to raise the capital needed for rebuilding and new plant and machinery. Six years later it was taken over by the Associated Paper Mills Limited but continued to operate under the Kelvindale name. As late as the 1960s the factory was employing more than four hundred hands, but it closed down in 1989.

Although the paperworks has now disappeared, several houses near Kelvindale Bridge, built to accommodate foremen's families, have survived and present an intriguing appearance, with their attractive contrast of white and red-brown brickwork.

CHAPTER SIX

Kelvinside

Although Kelvinside was the name applied to the whole area west of the Kelvin, between the Forth and Clyde Canal and Great Western Road, it is nowadays confined to the area south of Kelvindale Road. The district on the west bank of the river is now known as Kelvinside, while that on the east bank is North Kelvinside. These two districts could scarcely be more different; whereas upper-middle class Kelvinside contains some of Glasgow's most valuable residential properties, North Kelvinside is essentially a working-class district dominated by sandstone tenements and a wide range of light industrial concerns.

From the western end of the Kelvindale road bridge it is possible to follow the west bank of the river fairly closely along a lane which terminates near the junction of Balcarres Avenue and Winton Drive. Shortly before you come to the north end of Bellshaugh Gardens there is a footbridge giving access to the recreational grounds on the site of Maryhill Barracks. From the other end of Bellshaugh Gardens, it is possible to follow the course of the Kelvin as it curves in a more southerly direction. This stretch of open ground has been developed in recent years and continues into Wyndham Street, from which a short road runs off due north to the New Bridge across the Kelvin which then leads to Garrioch. This was still open countryside 130 years ago, the only building of note being Kirklee, a mansion which later lent its name to the district and a number of streets. This large villa stood on high ground overlooking the river, at a point where it was held in check by a dam, with lades running off to the east to serve some of the mills that formerly stood on the east bank. Just below the dam there was a ford which enabled pedestrians to pass from Kirklee to the strip of the Botanic Gardens on the east bank of the river and which gave its name to Ford Road, the short thoroughfare from Kirklee Road to the western entrance of the Gardens. The Kirklee area began attracting the attention of Glasgow's leading architects and builders in the 1870s and from then until the outbreak of the First World War this district was gradually filled with elegant villas set in extensive grounds of an acre or more, well wooded and landscaped. This part of Glasgow superficially remains much as it was a century ago, but look closer and you will see that some of these imposing structures have been converted into flats, while others are now private nursing homes, hotels or company headquarters, and relatively few now appear to be in private occupancy by a single family.

A singular feature of Kelvinside is that most of the street names appear to have been changed from their original designations. At the western extremity, on the north side of Great Western Road, West Balgray Road, which ran northwards in a curve towards West Balgray House, is now Beaconsfield Road, and where it curved back to rejoin Great Western Road farther east that portion is now the beginning of Cleveden Road, although in the 1870s it was known as Crossloan Road. In this case, the name was obviously changed to avoid confusion with a road of the same name in Govan. Changes of this sort became imperative in 1912 when Govan and other hitherto independent burghs were absorbed into Glasgow. Within the semi-circle there was Montgomerie Crescent and Montgomerie Drive, now renamed Cleveden Crescent and Winton Drive, although the original name has been retained for the elegant terrace on the northeast side, known as Montgomerie Quadrant. This terrace of three-storey houses stands out from its surroundings – as well it might for it was allegedly designed by Alexander Thomson and erected in 1882-6. As 'Greek' Thomson, the foremost Glasgow architect of his day, died in 1875, it is more likely that this remarkable terrace was designed by his brother (who continued the firm under the name of A. & G. Thomson), while it has even been suggested that James Sellars (who lived there) may have been the architect. These are matters for academic debate that need not influence our enjoyment of the beautiful sweep of the frontage or the finer architectural details and wrought ironwork. Winton Drive, running northeast from the junction of Beaconsfield and Cleveden roads, boasts an assortment of interesting late nineteenth-century houses, notably number 9, Winton House, which was designed by Robert Turnbull around 1880. The semi-detached villas farther on were erected at the turn of the century and were designed by Woodburn Sturrock. Cleveden Crescent was designed in 1876 by John Burnet as a symmetrical terrace of fourteen houses with pavilions at either end. In nearby Cleveden Drive, most of the handsome villas were erected between 1880 and 1900. There is a wealth of architectural ornament, not to mention some very fine stained-glass windows by Daniel Cottier, but the most impressive villa is Stoneleigh (number 48), designed by H.E. Clifford about 1900 for the Glasgow stockbroker, Joseph Turner, built in the style of a Tudor farmhouse. It was converted into an old people's home in the 1950s but its fine Arts and Crafts interior decor has been beautifully preserved.

East of Cleveden Road, Cleveden Drive continues towards Kirklee. On a roughly triangular site bounded by Cleveden Drive, Bellshaugh Road and Kirklee Road stands Kelvinside Academy which was most assuredly designed by James Sellars and built in 1877-9. There are conscious echoes of 'Greek' Thomson in its impressive neo-classical facade, although it may also have been inspired by the Royal High School of Edinburgh by Thomas Hamilton. It is dominated by the central doorway in the form of a Grecian temple, surrounded by Ionic pillars surmounted by a triangular metope. The classical atmosphere is heightened by the school emblem above the main entrance, in the form of a helmeted bust surrounded by a wreath of bay leaves. The central core of the building is flanked by colonnades and pavilions. Although the interior is relatively spartan, there are nice ornamental touches, such as the engraved windows depicting scenes from Homer. To complete the classical character, the helmeted bust is repeated in the boundary wall, with the school's Greek motto signifying 'always strive to be the best'. The school gates and railings represent wrought ironwork of the very finest quality, and the overall impression is of a seat of learning intended for the sons of Glasgow's wealthier families. Interestingly, Kelvinside Academy was founded in 1877 and existed in temporary premises for about a year while the school was being built; but it was sufficiently advanced for the pupils and staff to move in by the autumn term of 1878. It has remained an independent school ever since.

On the southern side of Kelvinside the obvious, if artificial, boundary is Great Western Road which was created as a turnpike road by Act of Parliament in 1836 to link St. George's Cross in Glasgow with Anniesland Toll. Through its entire length this road runs straight as a die and were it not for the curvature of the Earth it would be possible to stand at one end and look right down the full length. Despite the fact that it was never conceived as an entity, it has evolved into one of the finest suburban boulevards to be found anywhere in the British Isles. What is even more remarkable is that, although this great road traversed the estates of several landowners, the houses erected along it were invariably of the highest quality of design and construction. We shall be returning to this impressive thoroughfare later on, but suffice it to say here that from St George's Cross to Kelvinbridge it is lined by elegant tenements, and farther on there are the great terraces, the equal of anything to be found in London or Bath, with such aristocratic names as Belhaven, Devonshire, Lancaster, Lowther and Grosvenor to match. One of the few local names perpetuated in this stretch is Redlands Terrace, derived from an estate on the north side of the road, between Cleveden and Kirklee roads. Although the estate was broken up and portions sold off in the 1890s, Redlands House, erected in 1871, has survived to this day. It was built for James Mirrlees, the estate's proprietor (after whom Mirrlees Drive, opposite Kelvinside Academy, is named) by James Boucher and distinguished by its fine masonry and exuberant use of wrought ironwork. James Salmon added a studio at the rear and many other changes in 1922-3 when the mansion was converted into a women's private hospital.

Most of the really outstanding terraces on this section of Great Western Road are on the south side, marking the northern limits of Hillhead and Hyndland. At number 4 Devonshire Gardens, before his move to the even grander Great Western Terrace designed by 'Greek' Thomson, resided Sir William Burrell, the shipping magnate and magpie extraordinaire whose vast and varied collections of the applied and decorative arts are now on public view at the Burrell Collection in Pollok Park. The reason that the Collection is so far from the city centre was that Burrell insisted that the municipal authorities should find a site that was well away from the atmospheric pollution of Glasgow. Devonshire Terrace and Belhaven Terrace were both designed by James Thomson in his inimitable style. By contrast, the north side of the road is occupied by 'a self-conscious string of smug villas sporting an assortment of bay windows, columned porches and balustrades' as the compilers of the Glasgow volume in *The Buildings of Scotland* series acerbically describe it. The farther west they progress, the more opulent and extravagant they become. One of the really outstanding buildings is number 998 Great Western Road, built in 1877 to a design of James Boucher on behalf of James Marshall of the Saracen Iron Foundry in Glasgow's east end. Appropriately for the palace of one of the City's greatest iron founders, this Italian Renaissance mansion is replete with handsome ironwork. It was acquired by St Mungo's Academy and now forms their Centenary Club which has lovingly preserved the extraordinary interiors of preposterous opulence, with their sculptures and friezes, florid plasterwork, gilding and embossed leather wall panels. I doubt whether there is anything to match this anywhere else in Glasgow, or the rest of Scotland for that matter. Its neighbour, now the Homeopathic Hospital, is positively dowdy by comparison, although its rooftop tower is a delightful touch, and was the smoking room (well away from the rest of the house) in its heyday as a rich man's villa at the end of the nineteenth century.

Not surprisingly, both of the churches in Kelvinside bear lavish evidence of endowment by wealthy patrons. Belhaven-Westbourne Church, as its name suggests, was an amalgamation of the former Westbourne Free Church and Belhaven Church (the latter now defunct). Westbourne was built in 1880-1 to a design by John Honeyman in the style of the high Renaissance with borrowings from Sir Christopher Wren's St Paul's Cathedral. It seems to have every architectural feature known to man, but the mixture of styles is redeemed by the very quality of the workmanship. It boasts a number of fine stained-glass windows, by Douglas Strachan or Margaret Chilton. St. John Renfield is located at the top of Beaconsfield Road and despite its Gothic flourishes it was actually designed by James Taylor-Thomson and constructed in 1929-30. It, too, has a splendid window by Douglas Strachan, executed about 1932 as a memorial to Alexander Osbourne. A block westward are the playing fields for Kelvinside Academy, and farther west lies the Glasgow University Athletic Ground. Past the gasworks at the north end of these grounds is the canal again, and beyond it Dawsholm Park.

The southeast side of Kelvinside is the district now generally known as Kirklee, from the mansion which once occupied this estate and which was sold off about 1870 for development. All that remains of the first phase is a handsome terrace of seven houses now known as Kirklee Quadrant but which originally rejoiced in the name of Windsor Circus. Some time afterwards, Windsor Terrace was laid out parallel to Great Western Road, but when this district was incorporated into the City of Glasgow the names had to be changed to avoid confusion with the Windsor Terrace in the Woodside district. The southern curve of Windsor Circus was subsequently developed as Kirklee Circus whose entrance on Kirklee Road is guarded by a pair of double villas, also of 1870s vintage. Kirklee Circus is one of the hidden architectural gems of Glasgow; you could easily drive past the entrance without being aware of its existence, but pedestrians are more likely to spot it and enter out of curiosity. There is a tiny elliptical patch of communal gardens, a riot of greenery in the centre, dividing two rather narrow roadways which, on account of their slope and camber, were clearly never intended for the horseless carriage. It is possible, with difficulty and extreme care, to drive round this little circus but there is no through road, for the eastern end of the circus forms the western limit of the Botanic Gardens. It is one of the most picturesque little cul-de-sacs to be found anywhere, and I envy those fortunate enough to live there. It is the sort of highly desirable oasis in the city where houses sell by whisper rather than word of mouth and nothing so vulgar and unsightly as an estate agent's board ever sullies its beauty.

Beyond Kelvinside Academy is Kirklee Gardens, built in 1877-8 to designs by James Thomson. This terrace is unusual in having very broad houses, each having five-bay windows flanking a central door with long sidelights. There are two much taller houses at the south end, forming a pavilion, and it seems as if this feature was intended to be repeated at the north end, but the terrace appears to have been cut off before the project could be fully realised. South of the junction of Bellshaugh Road with Kirklee Road there is a terrace of nine house designed by John A. Campbell and built in 1900-9. The core of the terrace consists of four pairs of houses, with taller houses at each end decorated with elaborate gables and turrets in the best Scottish Renaissance tradition. Campbell adapted the same idiom to the houses, which he also designed in adjoining Mirrlees Drive.

Heading south on Kirklee Road towards Great Western Road, there is Kirklee Terrace on one's left. The house on the corner (15 Kirklee Terrace, with a side entrance at 2a Kirklee Road) has been divided into flats, hence the two street numbers. Originally a mid-nineteenth-century villa, and thus one of the oldest buildings in the neighbourhood, it was substantially altered and expanded by John J. Burnet at the turn of the century, when the Baronial tower and elaborate wrought-iron, glazed porch were added. It was for many years the residence and studio of the sculptor Benno Schotz, not something that the passer-by would know, for Kelvinside is not the sort of district where anything so vulgar as a wall plaque would ever be permitted. It is a district which, over the years, has attracted many painters, sculptors, architects, designers, artists, writers and, latterly, producers and scriptwriters associated with the BBC nearby. Not that Kelvinside can be regarded as an artists' colony by any means; there is no sense of community and it is a district where anonymity and a low profile are the watchwords.

Glaschu in Brythonic is said to mean 'the dear green place', allegedly first applied to Glasgow by its patron saint, Mungo or Kentigern, back in the sixth century. For many years this translation was regarded as ironic, although it is only fair to point out that, even at the height of its industrial power, Glasgow had more parks and open spaces in relation to its overall size than any other city in Europe. In 1910, for example, the city's Parks Department was responsible for 1,260 acres of parks and open spaces, and that figure would almost double within a decade. It is only within the past two decades, with the elimination of atmospheric pollution and industrial effluent, together with the massive programme to remove the accumulated grime of centuries from the City's buildings, that Glasgow has begun to live up to its historic reputation as the dear green place. Apart from the green belt along the Kelvin's banks which provide the City with a vital lung as well as giving its wildlife a safe corridor, two of Glasgow's most famous public parks lie along the river.

The first of these is the Botanic Gardens, which have a history that goes back very much further than their present location. The earliest garden, established specifically for the study of plants and their medicinal properties, was the Physic Garden, laid out in 1705 in the grounds of the original University in the High Street. From this developed the gardens which Sir William Hooker, Regius Professor of Botany at the University from 1820 to 1841, made world-famous through his extensive writings about its collection of plants from every part of the world. The Botanic Gardens were established in 1817 by Thomas Hopkirk and some friends, all keen amateur botanists, who enlisted the help of the University and leading merchants of the city to raise the money. Even the government contributed to the fund and granted a royal charter to the Institution. An 8-acre site (now Fitzroy Place near Sauchiehall Street) was purchased and Hopkirk donated his extensive private collection which formed the nucleus. Two decades later, however, atmospheric pollution in the city was so bad that the plants were suffering, so it was decided by the Royal Botanic Institution to move the gardens to a new site far removed from the City. A 7-hectare (18 acres) site was obtained in 1839 and over the ensuing three years the gardens were laid out and the plants transferred. Among these was the famous Weeping Ash, transplanted from the original Botanic Gardens in 1840 and still going strong. The Gardens were formally opened on 30 April 1842. Although the Botanic Gardens were not generally open to the public until 1891, the Royal Botanic Institution allowed admission of non-members on Saturdays, at a price of a shilling a head, and from time to time permitted the 'working classes' as well, the reduced charge of a penny a head being made. The Botanic Gardens were an important factor in encouraging high-quality residential development in the neighbourhood.

In 1863 Boucher & Cousland designed a magnificent glasshouse as a conservatory for John Kibble's country seat, Coulport House on Loch Long, and in 1871 he offered it to the Corporation of Glasgow as a sort of Crystal Palace on Clyde to be re-erected in Queens Park as a concert hall and art gallery. Instead, the Institution acquired it and erected it in the Botanic Gardens, subject to several major structural alterations, which included the enlargement of the dome and the addition of a vestibule. The grandly named Kibble Crystal Art Palace and Royal Conservatory (to give it its full title) ranks as one of the oldest and largest glass structures of its kind and is the Gardens' most notable landmark. It contains a staggering collection of tropical plants, including a huge banana palm whose fruit went to East Park Home and the Sick Children's Hospital at Yorkhill all through the dark days of the Second World War when less disadvantaged children never saw a banana for years on end. Amid the lush vegetation are eight highly erotic sculptures by Hamo Thornycroft, Goscombe John, Warrington Wood, Roscoe Mullins and others, which must have been a sore distraction to high-minded Victorian young ladies attending the musical soirées in the Palace. It continues to serve a dual function as a home for hothouse plants and as a cultural venue, albeit a rather unusual one; and in April and May 1993 it really came into its own, as one of the attractions of the World Orchid Conference when it took place in Glasgow.

By 1881 the Institution found itself in deep financial trouble and borrowed heavily from the Corporation of Glasgow. In fact, by 1887 the Institution was still so strapped for cash that it could no longer repay the interest on the loan from the Corporation, which was therefore obliged to take possession of the Gardens, even though they were outside the City boundary. The gardens continued as a private venture until 1891 when, as a result of the extension of the City that year to incorporate the burghs of Hillhead and Maryhill, they were thrown open to the public free of charge. This concession had been stipulated in the City of Glasgow Act passed that year to enable the City to absorb these burghs. The City increased the size of the Gardens in 1892-3 by 1.6 hectares (4 acres), incorporating the strip of ground on the north bank of the Kelvin. At the same time, the cast-iron footbridge (known familiarly as the Humpbacked Bridge) was erected at the eastern end of the park to provide easy access to the additional ground. A bridge was also installed at the western end, familiarly known as the Halfpenny Bridge because of the modest charge made to people crossing it. It was closed down and demolished in 1994 but at the time of writing there are proposals to replace it with a new bridge.

The Botanic Gardens in 1907

In 1900 a parcel of land at the Kirklee end was added, bringing the total area up to 10 hectares (25 acres). The very impressive wrought-iron gates at the main entrance were installed in 1894, and about a decade later the twin lodge houses in mock-Tudor cottage style replaced a pair of smaller lodges which dated from the early 1870s. The Manager's House (now the Visitor Centre) was built in 1840 and stands to the north of the Kibble Palace, while a range of smaller glasshouses were erected in 1883, replacing earlier 'Hot-houses' and an aviary. Later additions included the bandstand (demolished after vandalism in January 1965) and an ornamental pond near the main entrance. Between the pond and the Kibble Palace is a herbarium whose plants are raised for their medicinal properties. Incidentally, the sundial nearby is embedded in a grinding stone from the old flint-mill a few hundred metres downstream (see below). The Peter Walker Memorial Fountain, erected in 1906 by his widow Zoe McNaught Walker, is unusual in that it contains provision for dogs to slake their thirst as well as their masters. The Main Glasshouse is a cluster of hothouses which get progressively more torrid and consequently accommodate plants from the tropics and equatorial regions of the world. The last of the series is the Tropical Pond House which has some giant carp swimming languidly amid the water lilies and other aquatic plants.

Beyond these buildings are formal gardens and herbaceous borders. Of particular interest is the Chronological Border in which plants have been arranged according to their date of introduction to Britain. There are two exits to the

Gardens at the west end, the Kirklee Gate, near Great Western Road, and the Arboretum Gate which leads on to Ford Road. The Arboretum was only laid out in 1975 and serves as a monument to David Douglas (1798-1843), who collected many of the plants exhibited here. Beyond the Arboretum the path leads to the New Bridge across the river to link up with the Kelvin Walkway. The Gardens slope upward from Great Western Road, then fall away sharply on the edge of the Kelvin gorge. Steep paths zigzag through the woods to the path along the south bank of the river.

The Botanic Gardens is not just a park containing exotic trees and shrubs from every part of the world, but very much a living force in Glasgow. Just as the Visitors' Centre regularly hosts art exhibitions as well as the permanent displays regarding the flora and fauna of the park, so too the Kibble Palace is used for all manner of concerts and lectures, and the open spaces themselves are given over to a wide range of events, the high point being the West End Festival in June. The 'Botanics' have been the source of endless inspiration to poets and painters and now it even has its own resident poet. The sculptor Benno Schotz, who lived at Kirklee from 1950 till his death more than three decades later, has recorded how much the park meant to him. In his autobiography he describes how, one winter's day in 1950 not long after he and his family moved to Kirklee, he was walking beside the Kelvin in the gardens and noticed the exposed roots of a tree high on the inclined bank. The roots suggested reclining and intertwining figures, so he rushed home for his sketchbook to draw them. 'This was my first revelation that one can see more in a tree than just the bark and the wood it contains. Thus my search for figures in trees began.' On one occasion he spotted a small hedge and saw some interesting shapes among the trunks which yielded a sketch that might make a frieze. When he returned to the scene a few weeks later, however, he found that the hedge had been uprooted. Now its memory is preserved only in the sketch which Benno framed and hung in his sitting room.

At one time the Glasgow Central Low Level Railway, operated by the Caledonian Railway, passed under the Gardens or ran along the river bank; traces of the line as well as the tunnel entrances can still be discerned, especially in wintertime when they are not obscured so much by foliage. The Glasgow Central Railway was incorporated in 1888 but was taken over shortly afterwards by the Caledonian Railway. Its underground line ran from the Central Station westward underneath Argyle Street, then turned north to Stobcross and then westward again, with stations at Kelvinbridge, the Botanic Gardens and Kirklee. The line was of the standard gauge and 0-4-4 tank engines provided the locomotive power. It must have been a tremendous feat of engineering, for virtually the entire line ran through tunnels which had to be dug through the densely populated districts of Anderston and Stobcross, and great care was taken not to disrupt the traffic in the busy thoroughfares, only a few feet above the heads of the tunnellers. The line passed from Stobcross under Kelvingrove Park and briefly saw the light of day when it emerged at the junction of Park Road and Eldon Street. For a short distance it ran overgrown alongside the Kelvin, before disappearing into a tunnel near the Kelvinbridge Station. From there to the Botanic Gardens, there was a relatively steep incline. The next station on the line was actually well below ground level, but a staircase led up to the booking halls and waiting rooms at street level.

Near the main entrance of the park stood the Botanic Gardens Station, heavily disguised to blend in with its surroundings. Well, I suppose that that was the intention, but the result could hardly have been more startling. The building, inaugurated in 1896, was a long, low structure designed by James Miller, with a steeply pitched roof, flanked by small square half-timbered pavilions in mock-Tudor style at the ends, but what gave the station its unique character were the turrets at each end of the main roof, surmounted by railed galleries, gilded balls and weather vanes. The rear of the building, overlooking the Gardens, was much plainer, although not without some pleasing decorative touches, especially in the twin banks of windows with circular tops. The gilt sign proclaiming BOTANIC GARDENS STATION remained in place until the building was demolished, but after the station ceased to function as such the windows were either heavily barred or bricked up. The interior was rather sombre, the blue and white marble floors contrasting with the dark mahogany panelling.

Although the train service every fifteen minutes was mainly used by people commuting from Hillhead into the city centre, it was linked to the mainline services and Henry Brougham Morton, in his wonderfully evocative *Hillhead Album*, reminisced about the occasional sight of a horse cab drawing up at the entrance and depositing a passenger laden with luggage. Unlike the Glasgow Subway, the Central Low Level Line was never electrified, and passengers had to endure the disagreeable combination of smoke and steam before emerging into daylight at their destination, covered in smuts. Morton quotes Hamilton Ellis as commenting on 'these fuming burrows' which, unelectrified, had grown old in sin. By failing to move with the times, this line lost the battle against the trams and buses, which increasingly took over the commuter traffic. The stations at the Botanic Gardens and Kirklee closed on 6 February and 24 April 1939 respectively. Kelvinbridge survived much longer, closing down on 4 August 1952. Although passenger services were discontinued, the line remained in use for goods traffic until it closed altogether on 5 October 1964.

After the passenger service ceased the Botanic Gardens Station was closed and remained in limbo till about 1950, when it was converted into a cafe. The Silver Slipper was a favourite hangout for teenagers, especially boys from the two Academies and the girls from Laurelbank and Westbourne independent schools located in Hillhead, but it was destroyed by fire in 1970 and the site, subsequently levelled, was incorporated into the Gardens once more. The stretch of Great Western Road from the main entrance of the Gardens to Kirklee was a favourite promenade in late-Victorian and Edwardian times. The gate was the preferred meeting point for the many Highlanders who worked in Glasgow, and on a Sunday afternoon the air would resound with Gaelic greetings being exchanged. The stretch of Great Western Road fronting the Gardens was memorable also for the line of very elegant lamp standards which ran along the centre of the roadway and supported the wires for the tramcars that plied between Anniesland and Oatlands.

Kirklee Station, designed by Sir John Burnet, was situated just outside the western entrance to the Gardens at Ford Road. This was a more conventional stone building which, despite its substantial construction, was allowed to stand derelict for many years until vandals reduced it to such an eyesore that it was finally demolished in 1971. This stretch of the line has a curious connection with royalty. During the First World War, when industrial unrest on 'Red' Clydeside was at its height, King George V and Queen Mary paid a three-day visit to Glasgow and for security reasons used Kirklee Station as their headquarters. Every morning a large brown Daimler limousine with the royal arms affixed to its roof would drive up to the station to whisk Their Majesties off on another tour of the City, and in the evening it would return. The King and Queen would alight, pass through the station, and board the Royal Train which was then shunted into the tunnel under the Gardens for the night where it was closely guarded by a detachment of the Glasgow Highlanders (9th HLI). This seems an extraordinary arrangement, but it must be remembered that the government was afraid that a Bolshevik-style revolution was about to break out on Clydeside at any moment, and it must have required considerable courage for the King and Queen to put their lives at risk.

During the construction of Kirklee Station and the railway line approaching it, one of the best-loved features of the Gardens was destroyed. Old maps indicate that a well stood on this spot, actually a spring set amid a cluster of three laburnum trees which Glaswegians called pea trees on account of their seed pods. This site thus came to be known as the Pea-Tree Well and was a favourite haunt of young lovers. In time the name was corrupted to Pear-Tree Well, which was ludicrous as there were no pear trees nearby, and latterly it was known more prosaically as Three-Tree Well.

Across Queen Margaret Drive from the Botanic Gardens stands a cluster of buildings with a fascinating history. The nucleus was Northpark House built in 1869-70 for the brothers John and Matthew Bell, who amassed a fortune from their Glasgow Pottery in Stafford Street. The Bells produced a wide range of fine earthenware, both utilitarian hollow wares and decorative pieces such as vases and urns, and some of this is on display in glass cases in the older part of the building. The mansion was designed in the style of a Renaissance palazzo by John Thomas Rochead, completed by John Honeyman and later embellished by James Miller. This Italianate extravaganza was not long destined to be the retreat of the eccentric bachelor brothers; within a decade it had become the first seat of higher education for women anywhere in Scotland. In emulation of Girton, Newnham and Holloway in England, the Association for the Higher Education of Women was founded at Glasgow in 1877 and incorporated six years later as a college, named after Queen Margaret, the wife of Malcolm Canmore who made such an enormous contribution to the education and civilisation of Scotland in the eleventh century. Queen Victoria set her seal of approval on the institution when she visited the college in May 1888.

Seven years later John Keppie and his infinitely more famous partner Charles Rennie Mackintosh designed the Medical Building where two genera- tions of would-be lady doctors received their training. In the early years, these girls had classes from 6 a.m. to 9 a.m. because the lecturer, Hogarth Pringle, then had to attend to his day job at the Royal Infirmary and this was the only time he could fit them into his busy schedule. Eventually women students were allowed to attend classes alongside their male counterparts at the University on Gilmorehill so Queen Margaret College became redundant. It was then acquired by the British Broadcasting Corporation and has been their Scottish headquar- ters since 1938. Part of the old Medical Building was demolished and the rest substantially modified to meet broadcasting requirements, but sufficient remains to show the idiosyncratic touch of the great master of Scottish Art Nouveau, notably in the entrance gates.

The inaugural broadcast from the new Broadcasting House took place at 7.30 p.m. on Friday, 18 November 1938, the opening address being performed by Colonel Walter Elliot, the local MP. Strangely enough, Lord Reith, who had known this district so intimately from boyhood, was conspicuous by his absence on that august occasion. In the post-war period, with the great expansion in radio as well as the addition of television, the BBC building has spread in all directions so that it is a positive rabbit-warren of corridors and passages connecting studios, audito- ria and other facilities, with the result that the original Northpark House has been swamped and its distinctive character lost. The BBC complex now extends right along the north side of Hamilton Drive. Probably the best vantage point to appre- ciate the original building is from the opposite bank of the Kelvin.

If Kelvinside is bounded by the Kelvin and Great Western Road, then North Kelvinside is bounded by the river and the canal, or rather the Glasgow branch which winds all the way southeast to Port Dundas in the very heart of the City. Compared with the leafy avenues and large villas set well back in their ample grounds, the overall impression of North Kelvinside is one of densely packed streets, tenement blocks and factory buildings. It is hard to imagine that this district was open countryside until the last decade of the eighteenth century. The construction of the Glasgow branch of the canal brought industry and commerce in its wake and this coincided with the period of greatest use of the Kelvin to power a wide variety of mills. Even a century later, when the western side of this district was still undeveloped, the map is studded with ironstone pits, at Ruchill, Eastpark, Firhill and Napiershall; and nearby are the ironworks and foundries which rapidly crushed and smelted the ore. The area was also dotted with engine works and machine shops, chemical works and cotton mills. South of Wilton Street there are two short streets named Tillie and Henderson, which leads me to suppose that they were named in honour of the firm of Tillie & Henderson, the largest shirt-making company in Glasgow at the close of the nineteenth century (and memorable as one of Sir Thomas Lipton's earliest employers). Little now remains of the industries, large and small, located in this area at one time. As recently as 1990 the Glasgow volume of *The Buildings of Scotland* noted that an isolated example was the premises of the Kelvinbridge Artistic Stationery Works at 24-8 Herbert Street, erected by Thomson, Turnbull & Peacock in 1898, but even that has since disappeared.

Until the 1880s, however, most of this development lay on the eastern side of the New City Road, now the branch of Maryhill Road running south from Queen's Cross. At the cross, the eastern fork became Garscube Road and most of the tenement building from the middle of the nineteenth century onwards took place there. They were given such names as Burnbank Gardens, Wilton Gardens, Doune Gardens and Lothian Gardens among many others; indeed 'gardens' was the keyword in the developers' vocabulary. In some cases narrow strips of green with a few trees interspersed these streets to preserve the illusion, but a decade later all such pretence was thrown to the four winds. The first streets in this area to be laid out were Kelvinside Gardens and, to the south, the twin prongs of Kelvinside Terrace, North and South which extended eastwards, through Doune and Carlton terraces to Wilton Crescent and Wilton Street. The last named was actually quite a short street at the time, but in the course of further development in the 1880s it was widened and extended westward to join what is now Queen Margaret Drive. These tenements were conceived on a grand scale and although they became more densely packed the farther east they went, they were well built and also, where they fronted Maryhill Road, often graced with architectural flourishes. This area was hard hit when the Maryhill Corridor was created in the 1980s. Although the old three-storey tenements have given way to apartment blocks it is a blessing that these have been restricted to no more than eight floors, while a great deal of private development has resulted in a pleasing mixture of maisonettes and semi-detached housing.

When the Botanic Gardens were inaugurated in 1842, speculative builders were attracted to the area, and middle-class housing sprang up along the lofty heights overlooking the east bank of the Kelvin and extending eastwards to Maryhill Road. The first bridge constructed over the river in this vicinity was somewhat to the east of where the modern Queen Margaret Bridge now stands. The map of 1876 does not even dignify this bridge with a name, but it was popularly known as Walker's Bridge (after its promoter) and it carried the road from Hamilton Drive in Hillhead to Kelvinside Terrace West. Projections from the west end of Kelvinside Terrace North and South converged a hundred metres westward at the junction of Kelvin Drive and Kelvinside Avenue (now Queen Margaret Drive). Kelvin Drive, developed in 1865, ran along the top of the escarpment high above the river and curved in a northerly direction to terminate at Garrioch Cottage. The area bounded by the river on almost three sides was laid out on a grid plan to create Derby Crescent (now Botanic Crescent), Montgomery Street (now Clouston Street) and Kelbourne Street, running east and west. Kelbourne Street actually marks the line of the Kelburn or Kelvin Burn, a stream that has long since been built over and now serves as a drain exiting into the river beyond the west end of Clouston Street. The streets running at right angles were originally named Gower and Albany but after the admission of Govan in 1912 they were renamed Sanda and Mingarry respectively. Further development, north and east, resulted in streets named after William Shakespeare and his wife Anne Hathaway, while Hotspur and Northumberland allude to the medieval warrior family of Percy.

The houses in this area are a mixture of late nineteenth-century styles, although a notable feature of those fronting on to the river is their large bay windows. Kelvin Drive, in particular, has some very attractive features including rather exotic wrought-iron balconies, while, on the corner, is a distinguished Italianate villa of about 1860, complete with a tower overlooking the river.

In the 1890s the track leading to Garrioch Cottage was transformed into Garrioch Road and extended all the way north to join Maryhill Road near the site of the new shopping centre. In the 1870s the land south of Garrioch Cottage was laid out as a cricket ground, bounded on the west by a belt of trees above the river bank. The cricket pitch has long since been built over, but there is still a substantial park to the south of it, bounded by Clouston and Kelbourne Streets. This area was developed at the turn of the century when the red sandstone tenement blocks were erected and the triangle of Garrioch Quadrant, Drive and Crescent was created to take fullest advantage of the commanding position high above the Kelvin. In quite recent times there have been a number of small private developments, either in-filling or the redevelopment of brownfield sites, and some of these are worth a second look. Craigen Court off Shakespeare Street is particularly commendable for the way it blends so well with the refurbished tenements nearby, yet providing a nice contrast in the imaginative use of different building materials.

Across Maryhill Road at the top of Avenuepark Street is East Park Homes for Infirm Children. This philanthropic project was inaugurated by William Mitchell in 1874. East Park was then an isolated hamlet of only six houses midway between Maryhill and Springbank and the Home was created by linking two of these cottages and gradually extending and adding to the original structure. There seems to be some controversy regarding the present building which some authorities aver still shows evidence of the original Eastpark Cottage and Chapelside which formed the nucleus, while others maintain that the oldest part of the conglomeration, with its little tower and matching spire, dates back no further than 1888. The Home was considerably expanded on several occasions between 1932 and 1947 by John Fairweather & Son. In her *Villages of Glasgow*, Aileen Smart notes that both of the original cottages were previously occupied, at one time or another, by David Caughie who became master at the first model school opened by the Glasgow Infant School Society in the Drygate in 1827 and was subsequently a lecturer at the Free Church teacher training college in the Cowcaddens. The Home was established to care for children maimed by the diseases of malnutrition, such as tuberculosis and rickets, but these ailments are largely a thing of the past, and nowadays it is mainly concerned with the care of the mentally handicapped. For more than a century and a quarter the Home has been the focus of a great deal of charitable activity involving not only the people of Maryhill and North Kelvinside but many organisations, such as churches and youth groups, much farther afield although the highlight for the youngsters is the annual outing organised by the Glasgow Taxi Owners' Association.

From the north side of Kelvindale Bridge it is possible to follow the riverbank, skirting the football grounds and recreation centre of the Wyndford Estate, but then the heights on the east bank become too steep to traverse with safety so a detour is required, up to Contin Place and thus into Garrioch Drive, well worth it for the stunning views over the Kelvin to the south. Garrioch Drive runs into Garrioch Road and from there a footpath descends to the riverside and that strip of the Botanic Gardens which is north of the Kelvin. Apart from the New Bridge which leads from Wyndham Street across the gorge to Garrioch Drive there is Kirklee Bridge, some way to the east, which links Kirklee Road and the west end of Clouston Street. From the parapet of this bridge one gets fine views of the river which, at this point, lies well below. This beautiful red sandstone bridge was constructed in 1899-1901 by William and Charles Wilson. It is generally regarded as Glasgow's finest stone bridge and, as far as civil engineering can be regarded as florid, it represents the acme of Victorian ebullience. The balustrades and Ionic columns are of polished pink granite, while a nice touch is provided by the roundels carved with the civic arms.

In the parkland far below you can get right down to the water's edge. Half a century ago this was a trap for the blackest and most viscous sludge from the mills upstream but today there are even stretches of sandy beach and the water is so clear that you can see the pebbles on the bottom. Footbridges at either end of this strip of park gave access to the main part of the Botanic Gardens, but there is also a footpath which continues along the north bank of the Kelvin, and runs under Queen Margaret Bridge. This replaced an earlier but much narrower structure of 1870 some way to the east and was built in 1926-9 to a design by Thomas P.M. Somers, the City Engineer. It consists of a large reinforced concrete span of 41 metres (135 ft) carrying the road high above the river. The utilitarian nature of this bridge is softened by decorative touches and the deft use of red Corncockle sandstone and polished Peterhead granite on the parapets and balustrades. The width between the parapets has been described as a generous 24 metres (80 ft), although, with the volume of traffic which the bridge now has to contend with, connecting the Maryhill Corridor to Great Western and Byres Roads, Somers is to be commended for his foresight.

Footbridge over the Kelvin, Botanic Gardens

The footbridge at the eastern end of the Botanic Gardens was erected about 1890 and has attractive cast-iron railings. A footpath on the north bank runs westward, past a children's play area to what was formerly an Old Men's Shelter, one of several erected by the Parks Department all over Glasgow. These buildings offered a retreat for senior citizens where they could play draughts and dominoes. They even organised championships between teams drawn from the various OMS, but nowadays old men prefer to snooze in front of the telly. Most of these red-brick structures have long since disappeared, but the one in the Botanic Gardens has survived and now forms the permanent headquarters of the Friends of the River Kelvin, where they foregather for the monthly clean-up of the river. Nearby stood the footbridge, which replaced the old ford to Kirklee. Originally, this consisted of a wooden bridge erected early in the nineteenth century at the expense of Dr Thomas Latham and known as Three-Tree Well Bridge. David Boyce notes that this bridge collapsed mysteriously one night in the 1880s, although it is not shown on the 1876 map of Glasgow, which suggests that its destruction occurred some time previously. A more substantial replacement was a lattice-girder bridge with iron railings, erected in 1886. In more recent years, it was shamefully neglected and when it became unsafe its gates were merely locked to prevent passage. Finally, the floods of December 1994 washed it away altogether. It was known as the Halfpenny Bridge, on account of the charge levied by the owner of Kelvinside House to limit the use of the right of way across his land.

Beyond Queen Margaret Bridge, the footpath runs along the north bank close to the water's edge. Parallel to this and some way to the north is Queen Margaret Road and, towering above this, is Kelvinside Terrace with massive retaining walls. Halfway along there is a flight of sixty steps designed by 'Greek' Thomson, connecting the two roads and providing access to the original Queen Margaret Bridge, sometimes known as Walker's Bridge after John E. Walker, a prosperous coach-builder, who built it in order to give him easy access to the land on both sides of the river which he then owned. Walker's Bridge was demolished in 1970, and all that now remains to remind us of it are parts of the upright supports in the river bed and a squat columnar screen which was designed by Thomson, although oddly enough he had no hand in the design of the bridge itself.

A little way upstream from the Sixty Steps and the remains of the old bridge there was a weir at one time. Little of its masonry now remains but you can still trace the line of the lade that diverted the current towards Garriochmill some distance downstream of the old bridge and just about in line with the end of Hamilton Park Terrace, high up on the opposite bank. The flint-mill was probably one of the earliest industrial concerns that once lined the Kelvin, and its preservation seems to have been quite fortuitous. Not much is left, to be sure, but what there is of the bare walls forms a fitting tribute to the many other mills that once studded the river banks. Previously there was a barley-mill on this site, whose sale was advertised in the Glasgow newspapers in 1758. A view of this old mill, by then a picturesque ruin, was sketched by William Simpson in 1845. The following year it was demolished to make way for the flint-mill powered by a wood and iron undershot wheel, which has now disappeared. The flint-mill was operated by the Verreville Glassworks which used calcined flints in the manufacture of flint glass. The flints, imported from as far afield as France, were first burned in the nearby kiln to make them white and friable, and then they were ground to powder which, mixed with water, formed a thin gruel stored in long, shallow vats, which were then heated so that the mixture dried into slabs that could be cut up. As well as glass, the flint paste was utilised in the manufacture of ceramics, hollow wares and tiles. The flint-mill was still in use as late as 1934 when 'Peter Prowler' (James Cowan) wrote an interesting description of it, commenting on the massive heaps of flintstones, some as large as an orange or as small as a schoolboy's marbles.

The heavily wooded ground at the rear of the mill was formerly known as Berrydyke on account of the berries and nuts which local people gathered in the autumn. There is a story, oft retold, about a young soldier who fell down a disused mine-shaft in 1769 while gathering nuts in the vicinity of the mill. Unable to climb out, he cried for help and when some children heard the sounds they fled in terror, thinking that it was the Devil moaning beneath their feet. Eventually the miller heard the soldier's cries and organised a rescue party, which with incredible clumsiness cracked one of the poor lad's ribs as they were hauling him out. He collapsed in a faint, to be revived by the miller's wife who plied him with milk fresh from her cow (laced with something more stimulating, one hopes). Some years later a girl fell into the same mineworkings; she was not only none the worse of her ordeal but married one of her rescuers. That old mine-shaft was apparently still a hazard to the unwary as late as the 1850s but was subsequently filled in.

As you stroll through this heavily wooded gorge, it is hard to imagine that you are actually in the middle of a bustling city. To my mind, this is what gives the Kelvin its very special charm. Here you will often see anglers and, if you are really lucky, even kingfishers providing a flash of bright blue as they dart and skim over the water's surface, while longtailed tits have been recorded in the vicinity of the flint-mill.

Downstream from the flint-mill there is another footbridge; as the east bank is quite impassable beyond this point, the high bank resembling a cliff, there is no other alternative but to cross to the other side of the river and continue along the beautifully wooded footpath. Presently you come to a point at which the Belmont Street Bridge crosses the gorge far above your head. Perched on the very lip of the gorge is Kelvin Stevenson Memorial Free Church whose great height seems to be accentuated as you crane your neck upward to get a good view of it. It was originally the Nathaniel Stevenson Memorial Church and was designed in 1898 by John James Stevenson, assisted by Henry Redfern. Although the foreshortened view of the church from river level is very dramatic, it is well

*Kelvin Stevenson Memorial Free
Church and Belmont Street bridge*

worth the detour to cross by the bridge and see the church at street level. It is a riot of different forms and styles, brilliantly topped by a crown steeple reminiscent of King's College, Aberdeen. There are touches of the Baroque and the Baronial but the main elements of the design are derived from Renaissance motifs, both fourteenth century English and fifteenth-century Scottish. Not surprisingly, the interior is just as bizarre and fanciful but in spite of the eclecticism it works very well. Apart from the stained-glass windows by Gordon Webster, the communion table and suite of elders' chairs, dating from 1939, are noteworthy because they were presented by Sir John (later Lord) Reith, first Chairman of the British Broadcasting Corporation, who worshipped here as a boy.

Belmont Street was laid out around 1865, with the picturesque Belmont Crescent on the west side, a semi-circular terrace designed by John Honeyman in 1869-70. Parts of Belmont Street have suffered subsidence caused by old mineworkings, but sufficient remains to show the splendour of this street in its heyday. On the east side of the street near the bridge there is a footpath from which excellent views of the river gorge can be obtained. This district has close associations with Sir William Smith, founder of the Boys' Brigade. Although he was born in Thurso, he came to Glasgow as a boy and lodged with relatives at 28 Hamilton Park Terrace, near the BBC building. When he married Amelia Sutherland in 1884 he and his bride moved to 18 Ann Street, and in 1891 they moved round the corner to a flat at 12 Hillsborough Terrace. This was the Smith residence until 1906 when they moved to 13 Belmont Crescent. Sir William was knighted in 1909 and died of a cerebral haemorrhage in May 1914. The house remained in his family's possession until his sons Stanley and Douglas presented it to Glasgow Academy as a boarders' residence.

Retracing your steps and continuing along the river bank, you get a fine view of the backs of the houses on South Woodside Road on the far side. In some cases the cliff falls absolutely sheer to the river. There is a stream, long forgotten and completely enclosed by generations of building work in the city streets, but here it briefly emerges from a large circular pipe to cascade into the Kelvin some way below. This is the Pinkston Burn, clearly marked on maps of 1654 and

1795. It was formed from two streams, one rising on the Wester Common (where Sighthill Cemetery now stands) and the other in the Cowcaddens district some way to the south. The northerly stream was the main one, and it is remembered today in such placenames as Pinkston Road and Pinkston Drive, while Fountainwell Road, running along the south side of the cemetery, alludes to the spring from which the burn emerged. The two streams ran together somewhere to the south of the present intersection of St George's Road with Garscube Road and crossed Woodside Muir to join the Kelvin. Just above the confluence stood Woodside Mill, erected by William Gillespie in 1784 as a cotton mill, but because of the uncertainty of the current this venture was not a success. Later the Pinkston Burn was reduced to a sewer carrying away a considerable amount of effluent from many factories in the northern part of Glasgow. In 1872 there was even a scheme to divert the course of this burn due south to enter the Clyde, but it was never implemented. Today, the conduit is mainly used to drain water off the streets.

High above on the west bank of the Kelvin are the fences marking the boundary of Glasgow Academy, the city's foremost independent school. Following a meeting of some of Glasgow's most prominent citizens in May 1845, a company was formed to promote the founding of an academy providing a sound classical education. As a result, money was raised and a site purchased. While construction was in progress the 1846/7 session of the Academy was held in two private houses in Renfield Street, but at the start of the new session in August 1847 staff and pupils moved to the new buildings located on the east side of Elmbank Street near Charing Cross. This building was sold to the Glasgow School Board in 1877 and thither the High School was relocated. Meanwhile the Academy moved farther westwards and acquired a site near Kelvinbridge. Formerly a rubbish dump, this land on the west bank of the Kelvin had been acquired by the Caledonian Cricket Club which expended a considerable sum in clearing, levelling and turfing the ground and erecting a fine clubhouse. Although cricket was not a sport generally associated with Glasgow this club built up an international reputation and was the only British club wealthy (or rash) enough to bring over the Canadian Lacrosse team. The gamble paid off and the club made a handsome profit on the venture, recalled nowadays in the name of Lacrosse Terrace which runs at right angles from Belmont Street and abuts the river. Sadly, the sale of their grounds led to the immediate demise of the Caledonian CC.

The Academy occupied a building designed by H. & D. Barclay, an architectural partnership which had built up a sound reputation by specialising in no-nonsense board schools. The Academy, in fact, represented a de luxe version, with a splendid neo-classical facade and features that would not have been out of place in the Acropolis, perhaps in a bid to upstage the rival Kelvinside Academy which was then under construction not far away. A two-storey building in the same Grecian style was designed by H. & D. Barclay in 1903 to accommodate the school's laboratories. and art studio. Farther north along Colebrooke Street stands the Centenary Memorial Building, marking the Academy's hundredth birthday in an eminently practical manner. Despite this valuable extension, it has still been necessary to acquire some of the terraced housing on the other side of the street, mainly to accommodate the junior classes. A house in Lansdowne Crescent on the opposite bank of the Kelvin was acquired about 1910 to accommodate boarders, and later on houses in Belmont Crescent were taken over for the same purpose. A memorial to the former pupils who gave their lives.in the First World War was designed by A.N. Paterson and erected in 1924 on the wall on the corner of Great Western Road and Colebrooke Street. This was a mere token, for most of the money raised to provide a fitting memorial to those who had served in the war was administered by the Glasgow Academy Memorial Trust with the aim of maintaining the school as wholly independent.

The Academy had to compete not only with the newly created Kelvinside Academy but also the High School in Elmbank Street and, from 1885, Hillhead High School, created by Govan School Board to provide higher education on the north side of the Clyde; but the Academy has always held its own, and is regarded as the premier school of Glasgow's West End. It was singularly fortunate in having rectors (head teachers) of outstanding ability. The board of governors had the happy knack of recruiting promising young headmasters still relatively early in their careers and hanging on to them. Only four rectors ran the Academy in its first century, and this gave stability to the teaching staff. The Academy swiftly established a reputation as the school to attend, and as a result the roll-call of former pupils who went on to achieve fame and fortune is impressive. They range from the playwrights J.M. Barrie and James Bridie (O.H. Mavor) to the pioneer aviator Jim Mollison, the film star Jack Buchanan and Lord Reith of BBC fame.

As you stroll along the riverbank towards Kelvin Bridge you will see the algae-covered masonry of the dam which blocked the river, but long since breached and now doing little to impede the flow. Shortly after this point you pass under Kelvin Bridge and either continue along the river by a path over a footbridge, or ascend the flight of steps on the Otago Street side. There is also a footpath on the other bank of the Kelvin, approached by going through the archway under the bridge on the eastern side.

On the east bank, although there is no continuous footpath all along the river, you can walk along North and South Woodside Roads from which there are occasional glimpses of the Kelvin between the houses. There was a paper-mill, one of the earliest in Glasgow, located at Woodside, but all trace of it has long since vanished. At the corner of North Woodside Road and Great Western

Road stands Lansdowne Church, arguably the most impressive Gothic Revival church in Glasgow. Designed by John Honeyman, it was erected in 1862-3 for the United Presbyterians with many fine sculptural details by John Mossman. Situated high above the east bank of the Kelvin, it presents a very dramatic spectacle, with its slender tower and spire rising to a height of 66.5 metres (218 ft) above ground level. This prominent landmark was the subject of a fine watercolour by William Simpson, at one time hung in the People's Palace. The interior of the church is equally splendid, with many unusual features, including windows by Alfred and Gordon Webster, a bas-relief portrait of the Revd John Eadie by Mossman and the war memorial executed by Evelyn Beale in 1923. A short distance

The elegant Lansdowne Church in Great Western Road

farther along Great Western Road is St Mary's Episcopal Cathedral, erected in 1871-4 as a parish church, the spire by John Oldrid Scott being added in 1893. Inevitably the close proximity of these extraordinary edifices has invited comparison, in which Lansdowne Church has tended to fare better. To quote from the buildings volume on Glasgow: 'the robustly overscaled tower has none of the soaring verticality of that near neighbour', while the interior is dismissed as 'grand though predictable and uninspired'. The pulpit and font, with their matching colonnettes, were designed by John Oldrid's more famous brother Giles Gilbert Scott.

CHAPTER SEVEN

Hillhead and Woodside

Although the locality known as Kelvinbridge takes its name from one of the bridges over the Kelvin, that bridge is actually known as the Great Western Bridge. This part of Glasgow was not only open countryside till the beginning of the nineteenth century, but was also very sparsely populated, being dominated by a series of large country estates. Richardson's map of Glasgow (1795) provides a good overview of what this area was like at the time, the hachuring on both banks of the river vividly illustrating the precipitous nature of the gorge through which it flowed. In contrast to the paper and snuff mills farther upstream, this stretch was unsullied by industry of any kind. It was heavily wooded, as reflected in the names of Woodside and Southwoodside on the east bank of the river. The west bank was only sparsely clothed with trees and an otherwise blank map was relieved only by the isolated mansions or farmhouses at Hillhead, Byres and Hindland (later maps sometimes adopted the forms Byars or Hyndland).

Up to 1840 the road from Glasgow ran only as far as the river bank at Woodside, and anyone wishing to travel farther west would have had to make a considerable detour to the south in order to cross the Kelvin lower down at Partick. In 1836 legislation was enacted that permitted the construction of the Great Western Turnpike, and four years later the first high-level bridge to span the Kelvin gorge was constructed. The principal promoter of the road and bridge scheme was James Gibson (1800-62), scion of an ancient family of rentallers, that is to say tenants of the pre-Reformation archbishopric of Glasgow. He was descended from Andrew Gibson of Hillhead, maltster of Overnewton in the middle of the seventeenth century who was, in turn, the younger son of John Gibson of Clayslaps (now part of Kelvingrove Park). Another brother was Walter Gibson of Balshagray, one of the leading merchants of the seventeenth century and Provost of Glasgow in 1688-9, being the last to hold that eminent position by virtue of his appointment to office by the Archbishop. Ecclesiastical control of municipal appointments was swept away, along with the Episcopal form of church government, at the Glorious Revolution of 1689 and thereafter the provosts, and later lords provost, of Glasgow were elected by some relatively democratic method.

Today the Gibsons are remembered only in the name of the street that links Woodlands Road to Hillhead Street and thence to Kelvin Way, but James Gibson was the man who had the imagination and the energy to push the City westward.

He was a widower when he met and courted Elizabeth Smith. They were married in 1835 and the following year her father David Smith of Westbank was appointed to survey the route of the Great Western Road. The Gibsons are buried in the kirkyard of Govan Parish Church, far away on the south side of the Clyde, but it should be remembered that the parish of Govan once extended across that river and encompassed Partick and Hillhead. There is a watercolour by A. MacGeorge of North Woodside from the Kelvin Bridge, sketched in August 1869, showing how rural this area still was. In the foreground, cattle graze quietly in a water meadow and, beyond the bend of the river, the mansions of Woodside can be seen nestling among the trees. It is an idyllic scene that is hard to imagine nowadays, so built up has this area become.

The other name which survives today only in street names is Hamilton, as in Hamilton Drive and Hamilton Park Avenue on the banks of the Kelvin east of Broadcasting House. In 1799 John Hamilton purchased the small estate of Northpark, built a mansion and brought his young bride Helen Bogle thither the following year. A son of the manse (his father eventually became Moderator of the General Assembly), John Hamilton was one of Glasgow's leading merchants and was thrice elected Lord Provost. Great Hamilton Street (now part of London Road in Glasgow's East End) was named in his honour. Hamilton's Northpark House stood some way to the east of the Northpark mansion built later on by the Bell brothers and was where Ruskin Terrace, on Great Western Road, now stands, but it gave its name to this entire area between the turnpike road and the Kelvin. Provost Hamilton died in 1829, long before the coming of the turnpike road. His wife predeceased him, dying at Northpark in 1825. She belonged to the Bogles of Shettleston, another of the City's leading mercantile families, and her nephew Robert Bogle purchased the estate of Gilmorehill about 1800, which would later become the site of Glasgow University. Soon after the erection of Northpark, several other mansions were erected by well-to-do families on the banks of the Kelvin including Westbank (where Westbank Quadrant is now located), Ashefield (at the corner of Gibson and Otago streets), Janefield Cottage and Rose Cottage. In the 1840s large villas were erected and their names, Laurelbank, Lilybank, Oakfield and Hillhead, have been perpetuated in many of the street names of the district. Lilybank was at one time the residence of David MacBrayne, the coastal shipping magnate. William Govan built Laurelbank in 1842 as a double villa, which was occupied by himself and his eldest son until 1850, when the elder Govan moved to another double villa which he named South Park. Laurelbank eventually became the well-known girls' independent school which later extended to nearby Belmont Church, built in 1893-4 to a design by James Miller. Lilybank House, near the top of the hill, where Bute Gardens turned right to meet Great George Street, was designed about 1850 by Alexander 'Greek' Thomson. In the 1870s it was purchased by a Mrs Elder and converted into a hostel for young ladies attending Queen Margaret College, later renamed Queen Margaret Hall; it continued as a residence for female students until it was demolished in the 1960s during the extensive expansion of the University buildings.

The Bogles, Gibsons, Govans and Hamiltons were interrelated through several generations, part of the mercantile oligarchy that ran Glasgow and the surrounding districts for centuries. They appear to have joined forces to have the first, low-level, bridge erected over the Kelvin in the early years of the nineteenth century to take the place of Hillhead Ford. This simple stone structure of four arches was just wide enough to permit the passage of a single cart, and it crossed the river just below the mill dam, running from bank to bank at right angles. When the high-level bridge was constructed in 1840, it crossed over the top of the old bridge at an oblique angle in order that there should be no deviation in the straight line of the road. For many years thereafter the two bridges peacefully co-existed, the lower one being mainly used by pedestrians although the unmetalled track on the west bank only led to Holme Cottage, roughly where the northeast side of Glasgow Academy now stands. As the district developed in the 1860s substantial changes were wrought to the old bridge, which was extended at both ends, but at right angles to the original line, so that it conveyed the impression of zigzagging under its larger brother. On the east bank the parapet of the old bridge continued under the first arch of the high-level bridge and led to the footpath running northwards along the east bank of the Kelvin. At one time there was a modest charge for crossing the bridge, hence the tollkeeper's cottage and weighbridge apparatus at the eastern end, but a two-storey building was later erected behind it, its steeply pitched roof barely peeking above the low parapet of the high-level bridge. Turnpike toll charges were abolished in May 1883. The old bridge remained in use until 1890 when both it and the high-level bridge of 1840 were replaced by a single bridge built in 1889-91 by Morrison & Mason with iron and steel construction by Sir William Arrol (better remembered for the Forth Bridge, Tower Bridge in London and the Elizabeth Bridge over the Danube in Budapest). Glasgow City Council's art collection contains a watercolour by William Simpson entitled 'Old Bridge on the Kelvin at the Great Western Road', painted in 1888 and of immense interest not only for its fine view of Lansdowne Church but also the cluster of stone-masons in the foreground surrounded by piles of timber and blocks of stone in preparation for the task of demolition and reconstruction (Simpson's painting is reproduced on the cover of this book).

If you drive along Great Western Road you will cross this bridge without realising it, but to appreciate what a tremendous feat of engineering it must have been you have to descend by the flights of steps on the south side at either end and walk through the park below. Then you can begin to realise just how impressive it is. It consists basically of two enormous cast-iron arches, the spandrels containing cast-iron escutcheons of the arms of Glasgow on one side and the arms of the former burgh of Hillhead on the other. Hillhead became a burgh in 1869 but it was not until July 1871 that something was done about getting a suitable coat of arms. It is not recorded when, or how, the arms were eventually chosen but the Lion Rampant and French motto *Je Maintiendrai* ('I shall maintain') are identical to that of the Dutch royal family of Orange-Nassau. The parapets are of polished red granite and include several entablatures, one of which has engraved details of the construction and completion of the bridge. Sadly, the others have been left blank and encourage billposters to plaster their notices all over them. The roadway was laid on riveted steel girders, apparently left over after the construction of the Forth Bridge. On both parapets there are pedestals carrying ornamental lights, refurbished in 1994 as a joint venture of the Scottish Development Agency and the European Community.

On the eastern side of the bridge, the flight of steps descends to the park on the riverbank and also provides access to the Kelvinbridge Subway station. Glasgow led the way in the matter of providing a wide variety of different modes of public transport. In the 1890s its tramway system was a matter for justifiable civic pride, being one of the best and most extensive in Europe and carrying a fifth of all the tramway passengers of the United Kingdom. By the end of the century trams ran along Great Western Road at frequent intervals, carrying passengers for as little as a halfpenny for a single stage. Horse traction was gradually phased out in 1901-2 when the lines were electrified. A major development came in 1896 when the Glasgow Subway Railway Company inaugurated its underground railway whose fifteen stations, arranged in a circle, served the central and western parts of the City. Three of these stations were located in the vicinity of the Kelvin and the first of these which falls to be noticed was situated at the eastern end of Kelvinbridge and was known by that name. This system exists to this day, although there is a world of difference between the modern, electric system and the very primitive method of locomotion by rope haulage, which endured until 1935. Compared with the London Underground, the Glasgow Subway seems like a child's toy, yet it has been surprisingly effective ever since it was taken over by the Corporation and electrified. Remarkably, the original late-Victorian rolling stock was retained, being modified for electric, instead of gripper, traction. The pity is that no serious attempt was ever made to extend it to other parts of the City, although proposals were mooted from time to time. Its name was officially changed to the Underground after the Corporation took it over, but old habits die hard and Glaswegians continue to refer to it as the Subway, a distinction which it shares with the metropolitan rapid-transit systems of the United States. Half a century ago Kelvinbridge Subway station was a rather poky affair on the south side of Great Western Road at the east end of the bridge; past the ticket booth one descended by a rather rickety passenger hoist to the platform with lines on either side. In the 1970s, the system was closed down for extensive refurbishment and when it reopened Kelvinbridge had been utterly transformed. Now the station is approached by an escalator, which takes you down to the platform at river level, with a separate staircase to an exit on Woodside Road.

The area south of the station along the east bank of the Kelvin was formerly a railway goods yard, but following the closure of this line in 1964 the site was acquired by the Corporation and landscaped to provide a large car-park in association with the 'park and ride' scheme whereby one can park a car and take the Subway into the city centre. When this scheme started there was a charge of a shilling (5p) for two hours' parking, but you could park all day for twice that sum. It is regrettable that instead of closing the Central Low Level line the opportunity was not taken to merge it with the Subway. Ironically, when the Subway promoters were surveying the route west from Kelvinbridge they hoped to drive their tunnel straight along under Great Western Road but were prevented from so doing because the Low Level tunnel was already in place. Consequently the Subway had to be diverted to the south on its journey to Hillhead, and this entailed tunnelling at the deepest point of the line (47.7 metres or 155 feet below street level). While Kelvinbridge boasted one of the widest stations on the line, Hillhead had the shortest, with a platform only 25 metres (82 ft) long. The Low Level railway tunnels are still in place, so that it would be feasible to reopen them and extend a branch line from the Subway to the Botanic Gardens, Kirklee and beyond. The tunnel entrances at the side of the little park are now blocked by massive steel doors.

The flight of stairs at the southwestern end of the bridge led originally to the old Low Level station, long since demolished. Today, this area has been beautifully laid out as a little park, with a simple footbridge across the Kelvin and it is possible to follow the course of the river, past the car-park to the road bridge at Gibson Street. The stairs lead down to Caledonian Crescent, past a low-level restaurant and a colossal carved wooden fish, to the park. Beyond this end of the bridge is Otago Street and on the corner stands the imposing Caledonian Mansions, designed in 1895 by James Miller as a mixture of office and residential accommodation. Architecturally amusing, the red sandstone buildings are a skilful blend of several different forms and styles, although the influence of the Arts and Crafts Movement and Art Nouveau seems to have been uppermost. At the rear of the building is a balcony on the first-floor level affording excellent views across the Kelvin and the car-park. The Mansions, named after the Caledonian Railway, were designed in conjunction with the Low Level railway station, access to which was also afforded by the cobbled lane at the side, leading to the booking hall. Originally called Smith Street, Otago Street follows the curve of the river as far as its junction with Glasgow Street and then, after a slight kink, straightens up and runs almost due south, crossing Gibson Street and petering out where the river bends, to join up with Westbank Quadrant, a short row of tenements overlooking the river. At the side of the street, just above the river, is Otago Lane where there was a smithy until the late 1920s. Most of the local horses were shod there. At the north end of Otago Street there are two large industrial edifices, erected in 1887-97, which are best viewed from the park where their pattern of red and yellow brickwork can best be appreciated. Running west from Otago Street are Glasgow Street, a short street which ends at Hillhead Street, then Great George Street which runs all the way up the hill and down the other side to terminate at Byres Road, and then Gibson Street which likewise ends at Hillhead Street beside the University Library. These streets, laid out on a grid plan, are occupied by elegant tenements, but here and there they are interspersed by two-storey villas. This pleasant backwater is an area long associated with the University, a mixture of residences of the teaching staff and houses offering student accommodation. Explore these streets and you will come across antique shops and antiquarian bookshops.

Caledonian Mansions, Kelvinbridge

Colonel Charles Hepburn, the instigator and sponsor of Henry Brougham Morton's *Hillhead Album* (1973), was born in 1891 in Bothwell Place where Caledonian Mansions were erected a few years later. In the book, Hepburn contributed a chapter entitled 'Backward Glances', written in his eightieth year, and furnishing invaluable reminiscences about the people and shopkeepers who occupied this area. Hepburn's father, one of the first merchants to establish his business in Hillhead as the City moved westward, was a cabinet-maker and had his furniture showroom at Kelvin House on the corner of Otago Street. When Hepburn was a small boy the basement and ground floor flat in Bothwell Place were used as stables for the horses of the Corporation trams, but later

on the basement horse stalls became lock-up garages. 'The stables were approached from the back of the building by a cobbled track, known as the Bishops' Road that led to the stepping stones which the Bishops had used for centuries to cross the Kelvin on their way to and from the Cathedral when their summer residence was at Partick Castle,' comments Hepburn, and indeed, the line of the old ford can still be seen when you look over the north side of Kelvinbridge. Hepburn adds the interesting information that Caledonian Mansions were originally intended as an annexe to the Caledonian Railway's Central Hotel, but never actually used for this purpose, although this explains the unusual appearance of the building.

When he was two years old Hepburn moved with his family to a house at the corner of Great George Street and Otago Street called Parkview, because, at that time, it enjoyed an unimpeded view of Kelvingrove Park before the tenements on Gibson Street were erected. This area was still relatively undeveloped before the First World War and Semple's Dairy on the south side of what is now Otago Street grazed their cows on the slopes leading down to the Kelvin. Next to the dairy stood Henderson's stables which not only catered to the tramway horses but also provided broughams for doctors and the steeds for the Queen's Own Royal Glasgow Yeomanry, a crack cavalry regiment which provided mounted escorts whenever royalty visited the City. It was an elite body and even the troopers were prominent gentlemen, while the major commandant was none other than the Duke of Hamilton and most of the officers were aristocrats. The Yeomanry saw action during the Boer War but were transformed into infantry to serve on the Western Front in the First World War. Later they became part of the Territorial Army as the 64th Anti-Tank Regiment of the Royal Artillery.

Hepburn could recall the time before the area north of Otago Street was developed, when there was nothing between Sardinia Terrace (now Cecil Street) and Byres Road and this hill (from which Hillhead takes its name) was a great favourite of boys from all over Glasgow as a toboggan run in wintertime. Near the top of the hill was located Hillhead High School, opened by Govan Parish School Board on 13 April 1885 to provide secondary education to children in this part of the parish. Hepburn was a pupil at this school, as was Robert Service, the Bard of the Yukon who devoted a chapter of his autobiography to what he described as 'the Dream School' (in contrast to his first place of education which he termed 'the Drab School', in Church Street, Partick). Both Hepburn and Service have left accounts of the first headmaster, Edward Ellice Macdonald, who was drowned while sea-bathing at Cullen in 1912.

The school was built in 1883-5 to a design by H & D. Barclay. In 1908 an attic floor was added by Samuel Preston to accommodate an art studio and chemistry laboratory. As the population of the district rose, the school could not cope with the large influx of pupils and after the First World War the Corporation planned a new senior secondary school on a site in Oakfield Avenue on the eastern slope of the hill. This was designed by Edward Grigg Wylie, winner of a competition in 1921, but ten years elapsed before the school was completed and ready for occupation on a site formerly occupied by a villa known as Thornville House. It must have seemed far ahead of its time, with its bright red brickwork, Art Deco central block and open-plan corridors. From 1931 onwards the original building became the primary school, known originally as Hillhead Elementary School and now as Hillhead Primary School, although in my time there (1945-8) we wore the same uniform as the 'big' school and used its gymnasium. Stanley Baxter, a distinguished former pupil, once described Hillhead High School as ideally suited to the plains of India, but it was singularly out of place on one of the highest points of Glasgow where the open corridors were scoured by winds straight off the Urals and where snowdrifts piled up in wintertime. In recent years these open corridors have been partially enclosed.

The oldest buildings now extant in this part of Hillhead were erected about 1850 when the first house in Ann Street was built for William Govan and named South Park House. In the 1920s it was acquired by Lord Maclay and converted into a hall of residence for female students. Now part of the University complex, it gave its name to Southpark Avenue by which Ann Street is now known. Oakfield Terrace followed in 1855 and Granby Terrace was laid out a year later by William Clarke who had his own house there. In the second half of the nineteenth century this became, for a time, the most select neighbourhood in the Glasgow area, and it is significant that a number of the most prominent architects of the period had their houses there. James Miller (1860-1947) who designed Caledonian Mansions, as well as the railway stations at the Botanic Gardens and Kelvinbridge, lived for many years at 3 Hillhead Gardens (now 19 Hillhead Street). John Keppie (1862-1945) lived at 42 Hamilton Park Terrace from 1880 till 1904 and latterly lived with his two sisters at number 16. Sir John James Burnet (1857-1938), though better known for his work in London, was also born in Hillhead and designed the Kirklee railway station, as well as making notable additions to his family home at 80 Oakfield Avenue. Fra Newbery (1853-1946), principal of the Glasgow School of Art from 1885 to 1917 and one of the most influential figures in the development of the applied and decorative arts at the turn of the century, lived at 2 Queen Margaret Crescent from 1886 to 1893 and then moved round the corner to 6 Buckingham Terrace on the north side of Great Western Road where he lived for upwards of twenty years. His last Glasgow residence was 9 North Park Terrace (now 51 Hamilton Drive) opposite Broadcasting House, where he lived from 1913 to 1918.

Undoubtedly the most famous architect to live in this district was Charles Rennie Mackintosh (1868-1928) who moved thither in 1906 with his wife Margaret Macdonald. They occupied the end-of-terrace house at 6 Florentine Terrace (78 Southpark Avenue) until 1914 when they left Scotland, never to return. During their eight years' residence they reworked the interior in their inimitable style. Latterly it was purchased by the University and used as a professor's residence and I vividly recall being confronted with the Mackintosh style of interior design for the first time when I accompanied my girlfriend while baby-sitting for the family of Professor Frederick Rimmer, back in the 1950s. Sadly, the University demolished this building in 1963 to make way for the University Library and Hunterian Art Gallery, but as a compromise the latter incorporates the Mackintosh House, a recreation of the old Mackintosh residence incorporating (with considerable artistic licence) features from some of his more famous interior designs.

The part of Oakfield Avenue adjoining Great Western Road was erected in 1859 and Southpark Terrace was built in 1862. At 14 Southpark Terrace resided Dr William Francis Somerville who embarked on a second career when he retired from general practice, becoming President of the Society for the Conversion of the Jews. One of its missionaries was the Revd William Wingate who laboured long and hard to convert the Jews of Hungary, and it is ironical to recall that his grandson, General Orde Wingate, became a convert to Judaism and would undoubtedly have headed the Israeli Defence Force had he not been killed shortly before the end of the Second World War.

Hepburn recounts an amusing anecdote about Somerville soliciting a couple of guineas from his friend, Dr Hawthorn, to further the conversion of the Jews. Hawthorn replied saying that he could not spare any cash, but if Somerville cared to send him a couple of Jews he would do his best to convert them. Not surprisingly Somerville's Society made little headway, but he had rather more success with the Girls' Guildry which he founded in 1900. This movement, organised under the auspices of the Church of Scotland, later amalgamated with the Girls' Brigade, the female counterpart of the Boys' Brigade, which was founded by another resident of Hillhead, William Smith, who lived between 1892 and 1906 at 12 Hillsborough Terrace, later renamed Bruce Street and later still Bower Street. Some years earlier, however, Smith and his young bride had set up house at 4 Ann Street, the houses at that end of what is now Southpark Avenue having been erected in 1874. It was here that the youth movement which William Smith had founded in 1883 was reorganised and given a proper constitution on 26 January 1885 when the Council of the Boys' Brigade was established. This worldwide movement had its humble beginnings on the other side of the Kelvin, and is described later in this chapter.

Between Kelvinbridge and the top of Byres Road, opposite the main gates of the Botanic Gardens, the stretch of Great Western Road on the south side was once a serious rival to the fashionable shopping thoroughfares of Buchanan and Sauchiehall streets, its heyday being the early years of the twentieth century and symbolised to this day in the very striking building at the corner of Bank Street. Erected in 1886 for Cooper's, Glasgow's most select grocery business, it was designed by Robert Duncan in the French Renaissance style, with an elaborate clock-tower above the grand entrance with its pillared portico, as much of a landmark on this long straight road as Lansdowne Church in the opposite direction.

Alas, Cooper's is no more, although the building itself has survived and been converted to other uses. The vast ground floor area was the grocery department, but there was an ornate spiral staircase which led to the household emporium on an upper floor. The building evokes memories of the elaborate system of pneumatic tubes which carried cash from the various counters to the cashier's box, of the heady aroma of freshly roasted and ground coffee from an enormous brass contraption which was the showpiece of the side window, and of the rich assortment of broken biscuits sold at a penny a bag to schoolboys from nearby Hillhead High who preferred this cheap alternative to the meals served up in the school refectory.

Henry Brougham Morton has provided his own very detailed description of the shops along this stretch of Great Western Road as he recalled them from the period before the First World War. With the exception of Cooper's, they had all long since disappeared by the 1950s, but it is interesting to note that they included a mixture of arts and crafts shops, a high-class drapers and a confectioners, not unlike the range of shops and boutiques to be found here today. One of the architectural curiosities on the north side of the road, opposite the end of Cecil Street, was Walter Hubbard's bakery and restaurant, a splendid Art Deco building designed by James Lindsay in 1929, its contrasting patterns of glazed terracotta tiles recalling the Jazz Age. Unusually for this part of the road, it is a low building, its lack of height apparently dictated by fears of subsidence from mineworkings (which have, in fact, wrought havoc with other buildings in the locality in recent years). The bakery, which generations of boys and girls from Hillhead High School patronised – the school's initials, HHS, also stood for Hubbard's Hard Scones – no longer exists. Latterly it was taken over by the City Bakeries and closed in December 1970, although the building has been tastefully converted into a public house. Perhaps Hubbard's bakery had some influence on the design of the Hillhead Savings Bank, across the road at the west side of Otago Street, for it was designed in 1941-2 by Eric Sutherland in the same Art Deco idiom, although that angular style was more redolent of the Twenties. It is a single-storey building and out of keeping with the impressive corner sites elsewhere along this stretch of Great Western Road.

Beyond the intersection of Oakfield Avenue on the south side and Hamilton Park Avenue on the north side, the character of Great Western Road changes from tenement buildings above the pavement to spacious terraces set well back from the main road and separated from it by banks of gardens and belts of trees screening their private roadways. On the left-hand side as you head westwards there is a row of flat-roofed shops, above and behind which stands Alfred Terrace, but on the other side of Great Western Road there is the magnificent sweep of Ruskin Terrace and then Buckingham Terrace beyond, stretching to the junction with Queen Margaret Drive. As noted in the previous chapter, this pattern of broad tree-lined terraces continues for a considerable distance along Great Western Road, past the southern fringes of Kelvinside. This excellent example of integrated planning is to the credit of the Kelvinside Estate Company, headed by Matthew Montgomerie, John Park Fleming and J.B. Neilson, which acquired the land in 1840. They were determined to create the finest residential district in the Glasgow area and to this end commissioned one of London's foremost architects, Decimus Burton, to lay out the estate, which explains why this stretch of the road is reminiscent of the Nash Terrace in Regent's Park and the Calverley Estate at Tunbridge Wells, on which Burton had previously worked.

Belgrave Terrace, by Thomas Gildard and R.H.M. Macfarlane, was built in 1856, with the same arrangement of a banked garden abutting the main road and a private service road behind. Ruskin Terrace, across the road, was originally called St James's Terrace but was renamed in honour of the celebrated art critic John Ruskin. Opposite Buckingham Terrace, Alfred Terrace was created about 1870 and in its original form was set back from the main road, with a banked garden and a carriage driveway, but John Burnet drastically altered it in 1892 when the driveway was removed and the terrace was relaid along the tops of the shops on the road frontage, with a parapet of balustrades and a flight of steps to the street level at either end.

At the corner of Great Western Road and Byres Road, opposite the main gates of the Botanic Gardens, stood Kelvinside Parish Church, now the Bible Training Institute. It was designed by John James Stevenson in 1862 and substantially altered in 1886 when the organ loft was installed. The church was erected over old mineworkings which required iron piles to be driven deep into the bedrock to provide the necessary foundations. The church is topped off by a tall campanile tower with a pyramidal spire, a prominent landmark which appropriately marks the outer limit of our perambulations along the banks of the Kelvin. Byres Road, running in a southwesterly direction from this point, marks the western extent of this survey and continues all the way to Partick Cross on Dumbarton Road, described in a later chapter.

Within that part of Hillhead bounded by Great Western Road, Byres Road, University Avenue and Bank Street, there are a few other places of note. The red and yellow tenements in Kersland Street, running between Great George Street and Great Western Road, were erected between 1880 and 1905. In one of these Percy Pilcher, lecturer in naval architecture at the University, resided with his sister in the 1890s. In 1892 he became interested in the problem of aerofoil surfaces and he and his sister built a series of model gliders as a prelude to full-scale contraptions which were, in effect, the prototype of the modern hang-glider. On one occasion Pilcher tested a glider by hurling himself off the high bank overlooking the Kelvin and gliding down to land approximately where the

Kelvingrove Museum now stands. Later he took his gliders out to Cardross in Dunbartonshire where, in 1895, he made his first sustained flight. Successive gliders became more elaborate but at Market Harborough, Leicestershire in 1899, while attempting a flight in a machine powered by a small petrol engine, the aircraft stalled and plummeted to the ground, killing Pilcher at the early age of thirty-three. Had he lived, he would assuredly have beaten the Wright Brothers who achieved their first powered flight four years later.

In Cranworth Street, one block east of Byres Road at its top end, is the Western Baths, a private swimming club designed by Clarke & Bell and erected in 1876 in a curious blend of Palladian and Venetian Gothic, replete with ornamental ironwork. At first it prospered, but then ran into difficulties; due to ancient mineworkings part of the building subsided and the floor of the pool cracked. The promoters were unable to raise the funds necessary for the repairs and the company went into liquidation in January 1884. The company was reformed in 1886 and the baths eventually reopened the following October. In his autobiography, Robert Service graphically describes how as a small boy, in the early summer of 1886, he crept through a hole in a basement window and explored the semi-derelict building, only to stumble across the decomposing corpse of a tramp in what had once been the cooling room.

On Byres Road itself the most prominent building was Hillhead Burgh Halls, demolished in 1972 to make way for the public library designed by Rogerson & Spence. The development of this district really only got under way after the last of the Gibson family sold his estate to his lawyer, John Wilkie, in 1855. Wilkie lived in Hillhead House, a mansion which stood at the crown of the hill, at the top of what is now Great George Street. Most of the development of the area dates from this period. By 1869, when the population had risen to 3,654, Hillhead was elevated in status to become a police burgh, law and order being enforced by a force of nineteen constables, three sergeants and an inspector. At the rear of the Burgh Halls was the police station and lock-up; although this part of the building had long ceased to fulfil this function the heavily barred windows above the cobbled courtyard survived until demolition in 1972. Alongside were the stables and sheds of the burgh fire brigade. It is interesting to note that the Burgh Halls were erected in 1872 at a cost of £13,000, whereas the public library erected on the same site exactly a century later cost over £300,000.

From 1869 till September 1891 when it was absorbed by the City of Glasgow, Hillhead was known as the Model Burgh. The burgh minute books reveal that, almost from the outset, the argument raged over whether to join Glasgow or resist amalgamation, but in the end the former course was inevitable. The fact that the entire area had by 1891 become so built up rendered the continuation of Hillhead as a separate entity quite anomalous. Looking at the area today it is impossible to detect any difference in the character of the buildings along Byres Road, and this was accentuated by the fact that while Kelvinside Parish Church lay within the boundaries of Hillhead, Hillhead Parish Church was on the west side of Byres Road in the adjoining parish of Kelvinside. This extraordinary building, designed by James Sellars in 1876, appears to be a cross between the Sainte Chapelle in Paris and St Finbar's Cathedral in Cork. When it was built, it must have created a very dramatic impression, being then set in open countryside, but the erection of tenements in the surrounding streets in the late nineteenth century has lessened the effect. To confuse matters even further, this district south of Great Western Road and west of Byres Road is now known as Dowanhill. Strictly speaking, however, the burgh boundary, west of Byres Road, extended along Ruthven Lane, up the back of Victoria Terrace (now Victoria Crescent Road), then ran due west, along Prince Albert Road and Lancaster Gate as far as Hyndland Road, then ran northwards to rejoin Great Western Road near the boating pond. The boundary in Ruthven Lane meant that Hillhead was a virtually 'dry' burgh. While there were plenty of pubs to the south in Partick, Hillhead had only one licensed hostelry and that was the Curlers' Tavern on the east side of Byres Road, allegedly the oldest building west of the Kelvin. There is an apocryphal tale that there was a hostelry on this site by the late seventeenth century and that it was once frequented by King Charles II who granted it a seven-day licence in perpetuity, although there is no actual record of the Merry Monarch having ever visited Glasgow. The pub takes its name from the fact that there was once a curling pond nearby. More to the point is the splendid mural by Alasdair Gray portraying some of the tavern's habitués, including Hugh MacDiarmid.

Nearby is the entrance to Hillhead Underground station, which, before redevelopment in the 1970s, was a neo-classical building with a triangular metope flanked by balustrades. The entrance had cast-iron pillars crowned with wrought-ironwork acanthus leaves in the best traditions of 'Greek' Thomson and had a large sign SUBWAY on three sides, long after the official title had been changed to Underground. Ashton Lane, a cobbled alley running behind Byres Road, has gone up in the world since it was merely a back lane and now boasts more cafes and restaurants to the square metre than any other street in Glasgow – unless it is Ruthven Lane, on the other side of the road.

Hillhead had the distinction of two cinemas; not that there was anything distinguished in that, but what was remarkable was that both of them survived the drastic decline in cinema-going, mainly because the large student population of the district continued to patronise them long after most people preferred staying at home to watch television. The older cinema was the Hillhead Picture House (later the Hillhead Salon) in Vinicombe Street, designed by Brand & Lithgow and opened in 1913. Its elaborate plasterwork was redolent of the Art Nouveau style then fashionable. It managed to survive the slump in cinema-going by concentrating on 'cult' movies and revivals of classic films, but after a prolonged campaign to keep it going it finally closed its doors in 1991. At the corner of Ashton Lane and Byres Road stands the Grosvenor Cinema which made its debut on 3 May 1921 with 'Helen of the Four Gates' and 'Eastward Ho'. Greatly altered in recent years, this cinema is still flourishing.

The area to the south of Great Western Road on the east bank of the Kelvin is variously known as South Woodside or Woodlands, testifying to the fact that it was once heavily wooded. By the 1830s, however, industry was beginning to spread to this area. Some way back from the river, on this side of the road, was Woodside Quarry which provided much of the building material for the road and its bridges. Between the quarry (whose presence today is revealed only in the steepness of the streets as they dip towards the end of Woodlands Road) and the river there developed Woodside Village around a cluster of paper-mills. The dam on the north side of Kelvinbridge diverted the current into a series of mill lades which served these mills before rejoining the main course of the river just before the Gibson Street bridge. As you traverse the rear of the car-park look over the wall and you will see traces of the old mill lades in the masonry below.

East of the river and more or less parallel to it is Park Road linking Great Western Road and Eldon Street which continues westward to the bridge over the Kelvin at Gibson Street. Park Road has become quite a mecca for the antique hunter in recent years, with a number of shops that range from the strictly antique to the more interesting Aladdin's caves of bygones, junk and unconsidered trifles left over from yesteryear. From the top of the road one gets a good view across the Kelvin to the houses on the slopes of Hillhead and the University at the southern end. The tenements on Park Road were developed in the 1890s and towards the south end there is a block believed to be by Horatio Bromhead with interesting borrowings from 'Greek' Thomson. Alongside is a block of sheltered housing erected in 1987 by the Kelvingrove Housing Association, designed by Graham McWiggan and much admired by aficionados of fine modern architecture. To the east of Park Road, Eldon Street forms a triangle with the beginning of Woodlands Road. Within the triangle on the corner of Eldon Street is St Silas Episcopal Church designed by John Honeyman in 1864 and decorated with architectural sculpture by Thomas Earp and interesting stained-glass windows installed in the 1880s. The interior has a memorial tablet to Archibald Campbell of Blythswood who owned most of the land between the Kelvin and the City centre.

Occupying the rest of the triangle is the complex of sandstone buildings which still bear a carved inscription signifying that they constituted Woodside School (later Woodlands Public School). The land was acquired by Glasgow School Board in 1880 from the Streets Improvement Trust and by the end of that year the workers' cottages known as Kelvin Row were demolished and the site cleared. The building, designed by Robert Dalglish, was erected in 1881-2 and opened for the autumn term in August 1882. Making the most of the triangular location, it was executed in the Italian Renaissance style, inspired by a school which Dalglish had seen in Florence. A suitably Italianate extension was erected on the western side in 1896 on ground formerly occupied by Blythswood Cottage. Pressure of space as the number of pupils on the roll soared to 1,600 led to the acquisition in 1910 of the Albany Annexe, which had formerly been a college for training pupil-teachers. In 1925 the Annexe was taken from the school to become a clinic, but after the Second World War it was returned to the school and continues to this day as the Woodside Annexe. It ceased to be a school in 1972, when Woodside School was moved to a brand new complex in Berkeley Street and the old school building has now been tastefully converted into the Hogshead Restaurant. Oddly enough, Woodside School has now been renamed the Berkeley Street Campus of Hillhead High School. The most distinguished former pupil of Woodside School is Sir David McNee, formerly Chief Constable of Glasgow and later Commissioner of the Metropolitan Police.

Farther along Woodlands Road is Woodlands Methodist Church designed by David Barclay in 1909 when the Methodists relocated from Cathedral Street. Its rather austere interior is relieved only by some attractive majolica tiling in the Art Nouveau style. At the junction of Woodlands Road with Park Road is also the beginning of West Princes Street, which runs parallel to, and a block south of, Great Western Road, whose once-elegant tenements, developed in the 1850s, have had rather mixed fortunes in recent years. This street runs all the way east to St George's Road, south of St George's Cross and includes Queen's Terrace and Queen's Crescent which were designed by John Bryce in 1840. Sadly, these beautiful Georgian terraces have been allowed to become rather dilapidated although there are now moves to restore them. So, too, the houses along West Princes Street have suffered neglect in the past.

Woodlands Road, running in a southeasterly direction before turning east towards Charing Cross, was formerly called South Woodside Road before joining Eldon Street to continue as Woodlands Road. North of Willowbank Crescent, where Willowbank Primary School stands, was formerly the site of the Willowbank Bowling Club but the ground was taken over in 1896 for the school designed by Alexander Petrie, and the Willowbank Bowling Club then relocated in Dowanhill. This club traced its origins back to Glasgow's first bowling green, created in the Candleriggs in the city centre as long ago as 1695. In 1816 it moved to a site on the west side of Renfield Street and then, in 1832, obtained ground at Willow Bank on the corner of Bath and Douglas streets. It was only at this juncture that the club adopted the name Willowbank, but ten years later it moved again, to a site in Elmbank Street, which had to be vacated in 1859 when the land was required for the High School. In May 1859 it inaugurated a new green in what is now Woodlands Road. When the site was required for Willowbank School the club moved to Hillhead, purchasing the site at the junction of Dowanside Road and Victoria Crescent Road where it has been ever since, but retaining the Willowbank name.

A second club, known as Burnbank Bowling Club, started in 1865 on a site provided by Colonel Campbell of Blythswood, but in 1889 the lease expired and as the land was now required for housing, the club obtained ground at Herbert's Woodlands Farm which subsequently became the Burnbank Bowling Club, formally opened in May 1890. At one time, there was a German Church at the northwest corner of the grounds but this was demolished in 1919 and the ground annexed to the bowling club.

The Cradle of the Youth Movements

It is an extraordinary fact that both of the world's great youth movements had their origins in this district. It was on 4 October 1883 that William Smith organised the first meeting of the Boys' Brigade in the Woodside Mission Hall of the Free Church. Twenty-eight boys mustered under Captain Smith and his two lieutenants, the brothers J.R. and J.B. Hill. Smith, who hailed from Caithness but had come to work in Glasgow, was an enthusiastic member of the Volunteers (forerunners of the Territorial Army) and rose to the rank of colonel commandant of the First Lanark Rifle Volunteers. He was also a keen churchman and was concerned at the number of boys he saw loitering on street corners or getting into mischief. Combining his military and church interests, he came up with the idea of creating a body, organised on military lines but affiliated to the Church. The result was the Boys' Brigade which soon caught the imagination of the boys in Glasgow. Within eighteen months five companies had been formed, and it was then that Smith gave the embryo movement its definitive constitution, rules and uniform which was modelled on the British army fashion of the period, hence the pillbox hats worn by boys and glengarry bonnets of the officers.

William Smith, founder of the Boy's Brigade

The movement spread rapidly to other parts of Scotland and then to England and Ireland and eventually to all parts of the world where the Scottish churches operated. There was even a flourishing Chinese brigade in Shanghai before the Second World War. Smith was knighted for his services to youth in 1909 and died five years later.

In 1903 the Boys' Brigade staged a giant rally in Glasgow and invited the hero of Mafeking, Sir Robert Baden-Powell, to come and inspect them. Baden-Powell was so impressed by what he saw that he began formulating his ideas on scouting, originally intended to provide adventure training for the Boys' Brigade. However, after his experimental camp at Brownsea Island in 1907, scouting developed along separate lines. During the summer of 1907 boys from the cadet corps attached to the four schools (Glasgow Academy, Kelvinside Academy, Hillhead High School and Glasgow High School) approached Captain Robert E. Young, their adjutant, about starting some kind of weekly meeting at which Baden-Powell's principles of scouting could be taught. Captain Young agreed, and selected four squads of eight boys, one from each school, who met one evening a week from September 1907 onwards at Young's house in Athole Gardens, Hillhead. When this soon proved to be inadequate Young rented a flat at 6 Strathallan Gardens (now Caledon Street, off Highburgh Road). In this manner the First Glasgow Scout Troop came into being, and has long been recognised as the world's premier scout group. In May 1909 the 1st and 5th Glasgow joined forces to obtain more suitable premises at 8 Alfred Terrace, then reforming as A and B companies (former 1st Glasgow) and C Company (5th Glasgow). By 1919, the adjoining property at 7 Alfred Terrace was taken over as the 1st Glasgow Scout Group continued to expand. In 1944 the Group purchased 'Northcote', a large detached villa at 4 Victoria Circus near Kirklee and later erected a large hall in its grounds. Eventually the Group ran to four troops (A to D) as well as cub scouts, and continues to play a prominent role in the development of world scouting. 'Boss' Young, as he was affectionately known to three generations of scouts and cubs, was born in August 1877 and died on 7 February 1940, being Group scoutmaster from its inception until his death.

CHAPTER EIGHT

Woodlands and Kelvingrove

The bridge over the Kelvin linking Gibson Street and Eldon Street forms a convenient approach to one of the loveliest parts of Glasgow, Kelvingrove. The bridge itself was erected in 1895 by Formans & McCall, the cost being shared by the City of Glasgow and the burgh of Partick which then included the west bank, although the Caledonian Railway also had a hand in it, as the bridge replaced the much lower Woodlands Road Bridge of 1853 and was necessitated by the development of the railway line. Like its predecessor at Great Western Road, this bridge was constructed of cast iron, with a main arch of 21 metres (70 ft) reinforced by seven riveted steel girders. Although the ratepayers of Partick shouldered part of the cost of construction it seems surprising that only the civic arms of Glasgow decorate the spandrels. At the southwest end of the bridge is a gate leading into Kelvingrove Park and just beyond is the Park Campus of Glasgow Caledonian University which is in the process of being created around the nucleus of Queen's College, the old College of Domestic Science which for almost a century was affectionately known as the Dough School. The original red sandstone structure was designed by Cowan & Watson and built in 1905. The fortress-like building is relieved by some attractive sculptural detail in the Renaissance style. Extensions in 1950 and 1976, to the west and rear, considerably altered the outline of the college, and the complex of additional buildings in very recent years has further changed its overall appearance.

At the junction of Park Drive and Woodlands Road stands the bronze statue by Tony Morrow and Nick Gillon celebrating one of Glasgow's best-loved institutions, the Lobby Dosser strip cartoon by Bud Neil (1911-70). The stranger to Glasgow may be surprised to note that the horse in this equestrian group has only two legs, but that was, indeed, the salient feature of El Fideldo, the trusty steed of Lobby Dosser, the Sheriff of Calton Creek. The long-running cartoon chronicled the valiant attempts of the sheriff to outwit and convict Rank Bajin, shown in handcuffs in the statue group. To anyone not brought up in Glasgow the humour of this cartoon (like so much else of Neil's work) would be wellnigh incomprehensible. Even the sheriff's name signifies somebody of no fixed abode who habitually dossed in the lobby or stairwell of a tenement. The sheriff had a brother, named Dunny Dosser, a reference to the underground cellars and passageways in the old tenement buildings and derived from the word dungeon. Rank Bajin was a phonetic rendering of the Glasgow dialect for 'rank bad one', which loses a lot in the translation. In the cartoon, the Texas Rangers were invariably drawn as footballers in the well-known strip of the Glasgow team. Bud Neil launched Lobby Dosser on an unsuspecting world in 1949, the strip appearing in the *Evening Times*. Previously Neil had drawn individual cartoons which captured the humour and patois of the tenements, but Lobby Dosser rapidly became a classic, with a number of volumes as spin-offs. It is a matter for regret that the lovable characters never made the transition to the screen as animated films, but perhaps the humour they conveyed would not have been understood beyond a ten-mile radius of Glasgow Cross. In the late 1980s a campaign developed to erect a statue to the memory of Bud Neil and the press organised a fund which enabled the work to go ahead. The world's only two-legged horse statue was ceremonially unveiled on 1 May

Statue of Bud Neil's legendary character, Lobby Dosser, in Woodlands Road

1992. Despite being so accessible (it stands on a low square plinth) it has mercifully escaped the attention of vandals, but such conduct would be regarded as tantamount to sacrilege. Across Woodlands Road stands the Halt Bar which is appropriately adorned with reproductions of the cartoons and information on the artist and his work. Enquire within, and slake your thirst at the same time.

Turn right at the statue and walk up Woodlands Gate. Cliff Road on the right runs down the slope to rejoin Woodlands Road, but as you progress up the hill you come to the junction with Lynedoch Place. You are now approaching one of the crowning glories of Glasgow's architecture (the others are all around this stretch of the Kelvin). Turn left into Lynedoch Place and at the corner of Park Circus Place stands a tall tower in the West of England Perpendicular style, all that now remains of the Park Church, designed by John Thomas Rochead and erected in 1856-8 – a dismal reminder of the campaign back in 1968 to save this beautiful church from demolition to make way for an ugly office block serving the Bank of Scotland. The resulting excrescence is a blot on the landscape. At the end of Lynedoch Place, on the corner with Lynedoch Street, stands another of Glasgow's distinctive landmarks, the former Trinity College with its three towers. It was designed by Charles Wilson and erected in 1856-7 as the theological college of the Free Church of Scotland. Of the three towers, the most westerly is the tallest and most distinctive, being reminiscent of the square towers found in medieval hilltop towns in Lombardy. The lesser towers are a reminder of the Trinity College Church, destroyed by fire in 1903 and subsequently restored for use as the college library. In between, is a two-storey structure linking the towers. Superficially, the building looks much as it would have done a century ago, but what you see nowadays is merely a shell, the interior having been converted since 1985 into flats. Lynedoch Street still preserves the original granite setts in the roadway, which unfortunately do little to impede the traffic which now uses the hill as a glorified parking lot.

The truth is that the concentric circle of elegant mansions that crown Woodlands Hill, once the town houses of Glasgow's most prosperous merchants, are now for the most part divided up into office accommodation, hence the clutter of cars during the daytime. At the pinnacle is the flattened oval of Park Circus, with projections east and west in the form of Park Circus Place and Park Gate, leading to the outer circle of Park Quadrant (the continuation of Lynedoch Place) and Park Terrace with their magnificent vistas over Kelvingrove Park. Park Terrace leads on to Woodlands Terrace which joins up with Lynedoch Place. A spectacular granite staircase leads from the hilltop to Park Gardens and thence to Sauchiehall Street. The layout of Woodlands Hill is best appreciated from the air, providing an excellent view of the terraces and buildings rising like tiers of a gigantic cake, with the Park Church and Trinity College towers as the ornamental topping. Only then can one begin to realise what a magnificent achievement the clever use of the natural features was, especially in the dramatic utilisation of the great rocky outcrop overlooking the Park. Looking at the curvilinear symmetry of the terraces and their gently sloping links one would be forgiven for imagining that the whole scheme was the concept of a single genius. In fact the development of the hill was as haphazard and piecemeal as any other in Glasgow and one can only suppose that the different architects who had a hand in it over a period of many years were somehow inspired to pull together, in spirit if not in fact.

McPhun's map of Glasgow and suburbs, published about 1846, shows just how fragmentary and disjointed was the development of the area at that early period. In the previous decade the Edinburgh architect George Smith laid out a ground plan for the flatter ground on the southern slopes of the hill abutting on Sauchiehall Street, although only the houses along Woodlands Crescent, Clairmont Gardens and Woodside Place had then been erected and the east end of Royal Crescent. Two houses at the east end of Claremont (*sic*) Terrace had also been built and a solitary house halfway along Park Terrace, some of which were designed by John Baird, but the boom in hilltop development really only got underway in the 1850s, following the award to Joseph Paxton of the commission to lay out Kelvingrove Park. At one time the summit of Woodlands Hill had been earmarked as a potential location for the University, but instead the City fathers decided that it should be given over to residential development of the highest quality. For this purpose, therefore, they recruited Charles Wilson who rose to the challenge of a lifetime and designed Park Terrace and Park Quadrant which are truly elegant landmarks in their own right.

There are several ways of approaching the Hill, best on foot, and allowing plenty of time to explore side streets and lanes as well as the principal terraces to savour their charms. One approach, by way of Lobby Dosser, has already been mentioned. Another, almost as bizarre, is to start at Charing Cross, walking up from Sauchiehall Street to Woodside Crescent past the Cameron Memorial Fountain, Glasgow's answer to the Leaning Tower of Pisa. This drinking fountain (now dry) has a decided tilt to one side, probably as a result of those ubiquitous mineworkings. It used not to be so obvious, but the demolition of older buildings to the rear of it and their replacement in 1981 by Fountain House, a severely geometric glazed structure which the compilers of the Glasgow book on buildings pithily dismiss as having 'the appearance of an incomplete Rubik's cube discarded in frustration', has served to accentuate the lopsided appearance of the fountain. Designed by George Clarke and William Bell, it was erected in 1896 in memory of Charles Cameron, MP, whose profile appears on a bronze roundel sculpted by George Tinworth (employed as a modeller by Doulton). The fountain itself is a Doulton glazed terracotta extravaganza on a base of polished pink granite. Mid-nineteenth-century maps, incidentally, show the main thoroughfare running east as Saughyhall Street, but running west it was called Sauchyhall Road, while the district itself was called Sauchie Hall; obviously the orthography of Glasgow place-names was in a state of flux at the time.

As you ascend the slope you pass Woodside Place, dating from 1838 and marked by attractive Doric porticoes. Joseph, Lord Lister, the pioneer of antiseptic surgery, lived here in the 1860s and a plaque on the wall of number 17 records the fact. Originally Woodside Crescent curved round to the east, but the first five houses were demolished during the extensive road-widening of the 1960s in connection with the M8 motorway. At the top it curves to the left to run into Woodside Terrace, begun by George Smith in 1835 and completed seven years later. You can see the gradual development of Smith's penchant for Grecian doorways as you walk along this elegant terrace. The western end of the terrace curves downwards to join Elderslie Street, running due north and south. West of Elderslie Street (originally India Place) are matching terraces, Clairmont Gardens and Claremont Terrace which terminate in Clifton Street. On the west side of this short street stands the Christian Science Church, formerly the Queen's Rooms, which Charles Wilson designed in 1857. The exterior is of particular interest on account of the bas-relief roundels by John Mossman depicting historic personalities in the arts, science and literature. Interestingly, the facade is elaborately inscribed in giant lettering proclaiming that it was 'erected by David Bell of Blackhall, merchant in Glasgow, MDCCCLVII, Charles Wilson

Mqr (?) Architect, Mossman Sculptor, W.T. Edmiston, Wright, William York, Builder'. With suitable humility, however, Wilson deferred to David Hamilton (1768-1843) whose profile occupies the medallion representative of Architecture. Conceived as a classical temple with overtones of the Italian Renaissance, the building was for many years used as a concert hall and assembly rooms. About 1939 it was acquired by the Christian Scientists who planned to convert it into a church but the Second World War intervened and it was not until 1948 that the conversion was completed.

Why the French language should have been used to name the short tenement terrace between Clairmont Gardens and Royal Terrace remains a mystery, for La Belle Place was designed by Wilson in his best Italian Renaissance style and La Bella Piazza would have been more appropriate. Royal Terrace of 1845 nicely rounds off the series of terraces running along the southern base of the hill. Heading up Clifton Street you pass the west end of Claremont Terrace and Beresford House on the corner. This was one of those isolated houses erected before the rest of the surrounding terrace, and was designed by John Baird in 1842 with attractive classical ironwork balconies. The rest of the terrace was developed about five years later. Across Clifton Street, running westward is Park Gardens, a short terrace by Charles Wilson in the mid-1850s, at the end of which is one of the entrances to the Park. Running upwards at right angles are the massive triple-tiered steps leading to Park Street South and giving pedestrian access to Park Terrace and Park Circus. There are also steps of more modest proportions from the top of Clifton Street to Woodlands Terrace. To the west, at the foot of the steps leading to the upper terrace, is an enormous granite retaining wall which encloses Park Gardens Lane, intended as the mews for the terrace and retaining many original features to this day. This architectural curiosity is enhanced by the interesting conversion of the first two mews at the eastern end by John James Burnet in 1906 to form a house distinguished by walls of tiles in contrasting stripes. All of these terraces have lanes at the rear, and these too are well worth exploring if only for the interesting views of the backs of these great houses and their assorted outbuildings.

From this level run the three flights of colossal stairways which ascend to Park Terrace and Woodlands Terrace and lead into Park Street South, all part of Charles Wilson's grand design for the crown of the hill. The enormous plinths at the sides were intended for statuary and it is a pity that this part of the plan was never implemented. The granite staircase is the magnificent climax and well worth the climb up all those steps, although to appreciate the boldness of the overall concept you really have to cross the valley of the Kelvin and stand in front of the University on Gilmorehill, from which vantage point you get a panoramic view of the Terrace and the Quadrant, with the assorted ecclesiastical towers in the background. Another place to get a good view of what is undeniably one of Glasgow's architectural masterpieces is the pedestrian walkway near the motorway, used to dramatic effect in the opening sequence of the immensely popular television crime series *Taggart*. Incidentally, although the Botanic Gardens featured extensively in the very first episode, entitled 'Killer', Kelvingrove appeared in the second episode, entitled 'Dead Ringer', while 'Death Call' was set in Park Terrace and several episodes, from 'Double Jeopardy' to 'Flesh and Blood', were located in and around the University.

A truly panoramic prospect is also obtained from the car-park at the western end of Garnethill, not much altered (apart from the intervening motorway, far below, of course) from the view sketched by Muirhead Bone entitled 'Park Hill' which appears in *Glasgow in 1901* alongside a description of the scene which the passer-by at the beginning of the last century would have encountered:

> Over a wide valley where he sees a river wind, headlands and cliff of stone rise from the night on either hand, approach and recede again. Now trees appear screening the terraces, and through them he notes the waiting carriages, warm lights shining through open doors that mean the West End the whole world over. He is arrested by an almost antique beauty in the mysterious vacant face of a grey terrace on a hill - lit by lamps that the trees in a park screen from his view.

From the top of the stairs at Park Street South turn left and walk along Park Terrace. Balustrades on the sidewalk enable one to look over the craggy bluff at the western end of the hill, affording fantastic views across the broad sweep of Kelvingrove Park to the University, the Art Galleries and the Kelvin Hall. Farther away there is the giant crane, now a memorial to the long-gone glories of Clyde shipbuilding, the glass tower of the Moat House and the Scottish Exhibition and Conference Centre with Sir Norman Foster's Clyde Auditorium irreverently nicknamed the Armadillo, Glasgow's riposte to the Sydney Opera House. At sunset on a day after rain the view from this spot is truly breathtaking, with the hills of Renfrewshire silhouetted against the fiery horizon. I have often wondered what it must be like to live in one of these beautiful terrace houses with their lofty windows and wrought-iron balconies. These stunning vistas must surely have inspired poets and painters, yet when these buildings were in private occupation they seem mainly to have been inhabited by the City's merchants, worthy but dull burghers intent on amassing their fortunes.

Back in the late 1940s, when I was a boy, my father was the church elder for this district and on one occasion I accompanied him when he was personally delivering communion cards to his parishioners. In the immediate post-war period, some of these grand houses were still in private owner occupation. I have a dim recollection of two elderly ladies living in solitary splendour and a medical man of some kind who conducted a private clinic, but there were others. Architecture and interior design meant absolutely nothing to me then, but I have a vivid memory of enormous drawing rooms with huge bay windows overlooking the Park, and my father commenting that you could easily fit one of those new-fangled prefabs into one of them. Some years ago Scottish Television had a drama series entitled *The House on the Hill*, tracing the fictional history of one of these houses through successive generations of tenants from the 1850s to the 1930s.

Within the outer circle of flamboyant French Renaissance buildings with their great mansard roofs are the more restrained terraces which form Park Circus and its connecting streets, designed by Wilson and mainly constructed in 1857-8, although the house which is universally regarded as the finest of them all is number 22, built by James Boucher in 1872-4, a decade after Wilson's death but faithfully following his plans and therefore a fitting memorial to one of the greatest architects in a city which has had more than its fair share of architectural geniuses. Williamson, Riches and Higgs, in the Glasgow volume of *The Buildings of Scotland*, wax lyrical about this building in a description running to twenty lines. No expense was spared when Boucher fitted out the interior, from 'the arcaded ground-floor corridor' to the 'astonishing upper hall with Corinthian columns and galleries' culminating in the glazed dome with ironwork from the Saracen Foundry. James Salmon and Gaff Gillespie added the brilliant Art Nouveau billiard room and a domed anteroom, both richly embellished with embossed wallpapers. There are magnificent carved panels by Derwent Wood and a delightful cast-iron conservatory at the rear whose entrancing description merits a four-line description in its own right. The authors also note that at number 19 nearby, now occupied by the Franciscan Sisters, Jack Coia converted a former operating theatre into a small oratory for the Archbishop of Glasgow, decorated with the Stations of the Cross by William Crosbie. I wonder if this was the house occupied by the medical man I mentioned earlier. He took great delight in showing off some of his medical gadgetry to my father but I forget what it was supposed to do. Just inside Park Gate, at number 3 Park Circus, is the Scottish German Centre (Goethe Institut); at the other end of the spectrum Glasgow's youth hostel occupies 7 and 8 Park Terrace, the two houses offering 32 bedrooms totalling 156 beds. Other buildings in this prestigious locality, once occupied by the families of shipbuilders, ironfounders, mine-owners, distillers and textile manufacturers, are now student halls of residence (such as Kelvin Lodge at 9 Park Circus), private nursing homes, consular offices and, above all, company headquarters, although it is heartening to note how many of these are architectural partnerships. In the centre of the Circus is the small park which was laid out for the exclusive use of the residents; miraculously it is still there, the temptation to convert it into a car-park having been resisted. During the course of 2000, numbers 9-12 Woodlands Terrace were in course of conversion by Speyroc to form Woodland House, consisting of nine luxury flats, so that there is still some vestige of private owner occupation on the hill.

All round the crown of the hill is the escarpment, shallow and gentle at the east end but rising progressively towards the western side and culminating in the steep outcrop jutting from the terrace opposite Park Gate. This marks the highest point of Kelvingrove Park, steep paths running north and south from this point. Originally called the West End Park, at 34 hectares (85 acres) this is by no means the largest of the City's many parks but it is easily the most spectacular, especially when viewed from this bluff. It was formed mainly from the two estates of Woodlands and Kelvingrove which together amounted to about 66 acres. Kelvingrove, the more southerly of these estates, had long been a favourite haunt of young couples, coming out on Sunday afternoons from Glasgow into what was then open countryside. Even in the early years of the nineteenth century this attraction was sufficiently well known to inspire the song 'Kelvingrove' composed by Thomas Lyle, a Glasgow surgeon, published by 1829 when it appeared in a chapbook of popular ballads.

Let us haste to Kelvingrove, bonnie lassie, O,
Thro' its mazes let us rove, bonnie lassie, O,
Where the rose in all her pride,
Paints the hollow dingle side,
Where the midnight fairies glide, bonnie lassie, O.

It also appears in William Bentley's collection, *Kelvin Grove and Other Poems*, published in 1843, and remained a firm favourite of the concert platform for well over a century thereafter.

The West End, or Kelvingrove, Park in 1868

To the nucleus of Woodlands and Kelvingrove was added the lands of Clayslaps, Overnewton and Kelvinbank amounting to a further nineteen acres. The idea for a park in this pleasant valley of the Kelvin appears to have originated with the architect Charles Wilson who put such a proposal to the Corporation in 1851, and on his recommendation the City purchased the land the following year. At a subsequent date, however, Sir Joseph Paxton, fresh from his triumphs in creating the Crystal Palace for the Great Exhibition of 1851, was commissioned to devise a plan for landscaping the grounds and this he submitted to the municipal authorities in 1854. There is some doubt as to the exact extent of Paxton's involvement, for work on the footpaths, gardens and belts of trees had actually commenced in 1853, probably to Wilson's design. Wilson's project envisaged the erection of a winter garden but this was never carried out. He also proposed the creation of an ornamental lake on the east bank of the river near Kelvingrove House, but this was shelved, and when the pond was eventually created in 1872 it was radically different. Nevertheless Wilson, with the assistance of the surveyor Thomas Kyle, was mainly responsible for the actual development of the Park in its formative period.

Central to Wilson's plan was the broad sweep of the Pleasure Gardens, radiating westwards from the end of Park Gate, with a carriageway running from the entrance on Eldon Street and sweeping round the base of the hill to the exit at La Belle Place. There was also a shorter carriageway which looped upwards near the Eldon Street entrance to follow the line of the escarpment and terminate at the end of Park Gardens, with access to Park Gate at the middle point. Between these concentric carriageways the grounds were crisscrossed by footpaths which traversed the slopes between copses of trees and shrubbery, among which statuary was placed at strategic intervals. A promenade in these gardens was intended to provide exercise and uplift the spirit, with endlessly changing vistas across the valley in all directions, and aesthetic enjoyment from the statues and allegorical groups. In the roughly triangular area, between the lower carriageway and the river, the flatter ground eventually provided scope for a wide range of sporting amenities.

The best place to get an overall view of the Park is from the end of Park Gate. On this magnificent vantage point stands the great equestrian bronze statue of Field Marshal Earl Roberts of Kandahar, sculpted by Harry Bates originally for the Maidan at Calcutta in 1898, but a second cast from the same moulds formed the basis of the Glasgow monument unveiled by Lady Roberts on 21 August 1916. 'Bobs' is shown in field service dress and pith helmet, reining in his steed as he gazes towards the Khyber Pass on the North West frontier. In his *Hillhead Album*, Henry Brougham Morton whimsically adds that he is actually gazing in the direction of Glasgow's very own Khyber Pass, his nickname for the back of Kirklee railway station which rather fancifully reminded him of a fortified outpost guarding the gateway to India from the Pathans. Below the statue four pillars support a classical pediment beneath which are the allegorical figures of Victory and War, backed by a bronze frieze of a battle scene. Below the frieze, at the rear of the group, is a large tablet inscribed with the names of the campaigns, from the Indian Mutiny to the Boer War, in which Lord Roberts fought and an unusual feature is the enlarged bronze replicas of the Field Marshal's medals and decorations, including the Victoria Cross which he won during the Mutiny.

Underneath the row of medals is a six-line extract from a rousing speech which he made at Glasgow on 6 May 1913 during a propaganda tour on behalf of the National Service League which he founded in 1911. Roberts viewed the rise of German militarism with alarm and accurately predicted that Britain might soon be embroiled in a great European conflict. To this end he campaigned tirelessly for the introduction of conscription in peacetime, and his words at Glasgow had a strangely prophetic ring: 'I seem to see the gleam in the near distance of the weapons and accoutrements of this Army of the future, this Citizen Army, the wonder of these islands and the pledge of the peace and of the continued greatness of this Empire.' The doughty old warrior was eighty-two when war came, but this did not stop him constantly badgering the War Office for a field command. Born at Cawnpore, India, in 1832, the son of a general in the Army of the Honourable East India Company, he had been commissioned in the Bengal Artillery at the age of nineteen and rose steadily through the ranks of the Indian Army till 1893. It is not surprising, therefore, that when the first troops of the Indian Expeditionary Force landed in France soon after the outbreak of war, the aged field marshal should cross the Channel to visit them in the trenches of the Western Front. It was during a tour of inspection in atrocious weather conditions that 'Bobs' contracted pneumonia, and he died in the military hospital at St Omer on 14 November 1914. The people of Glasgow were greatly affected by his death and the campaign to erect this monument received widespread support, although by the time it was actually unveiled the jingoism of 1913-14 had largely evaporated. The Roberts statue seems oddly at variance with the image of Red Clydeside so often projected to the outside world, but it is a reminder of a time when Glasgow, Second City of the Empire (and proud of it) was one of the great bastions of capitalism. From time to time the graffiti of CND and other pacificist movements have defaced the entablature but otherwise this monument to our imperial past has remained remarkably free from the attention of vandals.

Below the statue there were, at one time, two bronze Russian cannon captured during the Crimean War, but they have long since been removed. Nearby is the stump of a tree felled recently because of storm damage. The opportunity was taken to carve the dates of planting and destruction across the pattern of rings, and it is interesting to note that it was planted in 1830. The bank below the statue is very steep, yet the grass always seems so trim. I used to wonder how the

Parks Department kept the grass so tidy without the assistance of a herd of goats, but one day I watched two gardeners at work with Flymos. They stood on the edge of the slope and aimed their machines down the hill on the ends of ropes. When the lawnmowers reached the pathway at the foot of the slope they hauled on the ropes and started all over again, an extraordinary performance, which works remarkably well. Immediately below Lord Roberts, far underground, runs the tunnel that carried the old Caledonian Railway's Glasgow Central Line from Finnieston northwards to Kelvinbridge and beyond. Until relatively recent years the stretch of the line between the Eldon Street Bridge and Kelvinbridge was in plain sight, but with the closure of the line the goods yard has been converted into gardens and the car-park mentioned in the previous chapter. The tunnel entrance, now blocked off, can still be seen from the northeast side of the bridge, but most people using the Park are blissfully unaware that the railway line traversed it.

Almost due west from the Roberts Statue, down the slope and past belts of trees, is another statue with a martial flavour. It was designed and sculpted by William Birnie Rhind and erected in 1906 as a memorial to the men of the Highland Light Infantry who perished in the Boer War. On top of a rock perches a soldier in khaki and pith helmet, gazing defiantly across the Kelvin towards a colossal granite statue of Thomas Carlyle, erected in 1883 two years after his death. The head and upper body of the Sage of Chelsea rises mystically out of the rock in a style first popularised by Auguste Rodin in his figure of Victor Hugo in Paris. Between these two very different statues is the beautiful footbridge over the Kelvin, designed by the City Engineer, Alexander B. McDonald and erected by P. McKissock & Son in 1894-5. It replaced a timber bridge of 1868, designed by the City Architect, John Carrick and painted to simulate stonework. Originally McDonald's bridge was to have been named the Albert Bridge, in memory of the Prince Consort, but it soon reverted to its original name of the Prince of Wales Bridge in honour of his eldest son, the future King Edward VII, for whose visit to Glasgow in 1868 to lay the foundation stone of the University the original wooden bridge had been created specially, as part of the ceremonial route from the City to Gilmorehill. Although intended purely as a temporary structure it proved to be such a useful amenity that it was retained. Its majestic replacement has a single slightly curved arch of red sandstone, with balustrades of pink Peterhead granite and a plethora of ornament in keeping with its royal nature, although, as usual, the opportunity was taken to add some more examples of the municipal arms, an obligatory feature of so many of Glasgow's public works.

Past the Carlyle Statue, the path rises steeply to the exit on Kelvin Way. Nowadays, Kelvin Way runs straight as a die from the intersection of Gibson Street and Bank Street, southward to Sauchiehall Street and conveniently marks the western limit of Kelvingrove, although in fact the park spills over on to the other side on both banks of the Kelvin as it curves round the broad base of Gilmorehill. Work on laying out this beautiful tree-lined road began in 1914 but was suspended on account of the First World War and not actually completed until 1926. Today Kelvin Way provides a motor link between Sauchiehall Street and Great Western Road; at first its use by vehicles was restricted, and later a ten mile an hour speed limit was imposed, though nowadays it is treated like any other road in the City. Looking at it today, it is hard to imagine a time when this elegant thoroughfare did not exist, but in Edwardian times where the road reaches its central point, there was the Macfarlane Fountain and, a little to the north, the bandstand, both legacies from the 1901 International Exhibition. The bridge on Kelvin Way, of Locharbriggs red sandstone, was erected in 1913-14 to the design of Alexander McDonald by John Emery & Sons. It is almost as broad as it is long, with a single arch. Indeed, as you drive northwards along Kelvin Way you would not realise that you were crossing a bridge, were it not for the tall pedestals at all four corners of the span, surmounted by bronze allegorical groups sculpted by Paul Raphael Montford. Each group consists of two figures symbolising Peace and War, Philosophy and Inspiration, Navigation and Shipbuilding, and Commerce and Industry. Each pair is tastefully draped over a sandstone pillar, topped out by the heads of four dolphins symbolising naval might, and terminating in a decorative lamp standard.

Montford's statues were the victims of both world wars. Although he carried out his part of the bargain in 1914, it was not until six years later that the bridge was completed sufficiently for the pedestals and statuary to be installed. The bridge was damaged during an air raid in 1941; ironically the group symbolising War and Peace was badly damaged but it was Philosophy and Inspiration which was toppled off its pedestal and disappeared into the alluvial mud on the riverbank far below. About 1945, when my family moved from Govan to Dowanhill, I vividly recall exploring the riverbank and stubbing my toe on what I thought was a rock, but which on closer examination – to my abject horror – proved to be a human skull! I fled the scene in terror and it was some years later that I realised that what I had stumbled across was part of the sculpture of Philosophy who was shown contemplating a skull, like Hamlet with the skull of Yorick. Subsequently the group was restored to its pristine glory by Benno Schotz and replaced on its pedestal in 1954.

There are several entrances to Kelvingrove Park on the east side of Kelvin Way, one close to the northeast side of the road bridge. Farther along there is an entrance leading to the footbridge over the Kelvin, erected in 1964 by Ronald Walker & Company, the design by W.T. Docherty of that firm being apparently inspired by the style evolved by Robert Maillart in Switzerland in the inter-war period. It is a modest little bridge, set quite low above the water, with unpretentious uprights and a wooden handrail, a far cry from the masonry extravaganzas so characteristic of other Kelvin crossings. Close to Kelvin Way, heading north, is the present bandstand erected by the Parks Department in 1924, quite an elaborate structure as bandstands go and more in the nature of an open-fronted theatre, with Ionic pillars on either side of the proscenium and a tiled roof surmounted by a very fancy dome and a cross. Two ticket booths were erected the following year at the entrance to the auditorium and designed in red brick to match. Sadly it has recently been vandalised.

The magnificent Stewart Memorial Fountain in Kelvingrove Park, with schoolchildren's murals

Within the Park the most attractive feature is the duck pond with its little fountain and, behind, a heavily wooded islet much frequented by a wide assortment of waterfowl. A path from the southern end of the pond runs in an easterly direction to the entrance at the corner of La Belle Place, but barring its way is the great Stewart Memorial Fountain which forms one of the Park's outstanding features. It was erected in 1871-2 to a design by James Sellars, with sculpture by John Mossman and is arguably his masterpiece. It is a truly remarkable example of Scottish Gothic at its most flamboyant, with its flying buttresses, pillars, arches, mosaic roundels of the signs of the zodiac, heraldic shields and bronze bas-reliefs illustrating the epic feat of bringing the water from Loch Katrine to Glasgow, as well as portraying Robert Stewart of Murdostoun (1811-66), the Lord Provost in whose tenure of office the project came to fruition. Stewart was Lord Provost from November 1851 to November 1854 and much of that time seems to have been taken up in promoting the waterworks.

Until the middle of the nineteenth century Glasgow relied on various private companies of varying competence to supply its demands for water, although the wisdom of such a practice was severely criticised after a series of cholera out-breaks in the 1830s and 1840s. In 1853 the Glasgow Water Company came up with a project to tap Loch Lubnaig in the West Highlands and bring the water to Glasgow in giant pipes, but this scheme failed to get the necessary legislation through Parliament. Stewart took up the idea, however, and was the instigator of the proposal to tap Loch Katrine in the Trossachs, an area much romanticised by Sir Walter Scott. At first this plan was also rejected by the Commons but Stewart persevered and, though now out of the chief magistracy, he had the satisfaction of seeing the Act passed in 1855. Work on the conduits, pipes and aqueducts progressed rapidly thereafter, and Queen Victoria herself journeyed to Glasgow in order to turn on the tap on 14 October 1859. The water scheme had set the City back by a cool million pounds, but it was a very wise investment which, within twenty years, was supplying almost thirty-seven million gallons of water every day to the rapidly growing City. And Stewart was doubly justified when the great cholera epidemic of 1866 which swept the country claimed only fifty-five victims in Glasgow. This was bad enough, but an insignificant trifle compared with the almost twelve thousand lives lost in Glasgow in the terrible epidemics of 1832-3, 1849-50 and 1853-4, before the advent of clean water.

It was against these grim statistics that the achievement of Robert Stewart has to be measured, and explains why, in the years immediately following his death at the relatively early age of fifty-four, the proposal to erect a suitable memorial won such universal approval. This veritable *tour de force* is splendidly topped by a larger-than-life bronze statue of the Lady of the Lake. Much admired in late-Victorian times, the memorial fountain was sadly neglected in later years; perhaps Charles Oakley's attitude towards it was not untypical of the period when he wrote *The Second City* (1946) and described it as 'that really dread-ful piece of work' which, in its heyday, 'would seem to have been looked on with less horror than today'. After decades of neglect and vandalism, however, it was restored by Page & Park in 1988 as Glasgow's year as European City of Culture became imminent. Sadly, by the time Glasgow basked in the limelight again as UK City of Architecture and Design (1999) the fountain had had to be boarded up once more to keep the vandals at bay. It was no consolation that the protec-tive hoardings were brightly decorated with murals by the City's schoolchildren.

Individual statues in the Park have fared rather better. To the northeast of the fountain is the Kennedy Monument, the rather pompous name for a very attractive piece of sculpture by Auguste-Nicolas Cain from a sketch by Rosa Bonheur in the best Animalier tradition. The bronze group shows a Royal Bengal tigress bringing a peacock as a tasty morsel to her cubs and it is mounted on a pedestal by John Mossman. It was presented to Glasgow by John S. Kennedy who had left his native city and made his fortune in New York. There is another cast of Cain's group in New York's Central Park, likewise presented by Kennedy to his adoptive city.

South of the Stewart Fountain is an area which has been developed in quite recent years as an adventure playground with imaginative climbing frames and all manner of trackways and obstacles for skateboarding and rollerblades. Interspersed are attractive flowerbeds and areas planted with heaths which provide a splash of colour even in the depths of winter. Proceeding south along Kelvin Way past the bridge, you pass the pavilion erected in 1924 to serve the bowling greens and tennis courts. The short Gray Street which runs along the east side of the tennis courts leads at right angles to Parkgrove Terrace which joins up with Royal Terrace and forms the southern boundary of the Park. These terraces are intersected by Kelvingrove Street which ends at the Park's most impressive entrance, the highly elaborate wrought-iron gates which were erected in 1897, the year of Queen Victoria's Diamond Jubilee. Originally the gates were topped by a row of gas-lamps, but these have long since vanished. The railway tunnel, parts of which are believed to be still intact, runs south of the park under Kelvingrove Street. Inside this Park entrance a path runs due east towards La Belle Place, past playing fields and the Children's Shelter, erected by the Parks Department in 1913.

In *Glasgow in 1901*, James Hamilton Muir (actually a triumvirate comprising the brothers James and Muirhead Bone with their friend Hamilton) waxed lyrical when writing of the West End Park as it was then known. No other park in Glasgow approached it for 'situation and popularity of character':

> It touches almost every kind of district in the city; the University and Park Terrace look across it from different points to Overnewton and Finnieston. As it is central, it is also a thoroughfare. Its gates are never shut, and all kinds of people pass through, and yet by day it has no great life of its own. Students pass through it in droves on their way to the University, and business men go through it of a morning on their way to their offices, but for the rest it is mostly given over to disabled workmen, who sun themselves in the summer-house and spin little tame discussions that lead to nothing. Sometimes old whales and barnacles that once were in the coasting trade join them, and tell of salvage services which, if the tow-rope had held, would have made shipowners of the narrators. On the high ground at the flagstaff you may see nursemaids with valuable babies from Park Terrace, but they do not venture often into the plains.

It is amazing how much this scene has altered in a century. Superficially the Park is much as it was in 1901, even if Kelvin Way was still some time in the future, but what has changed radically are the faces in the landscape. To be sure, there are still students passing to and fro, although the much more flexible nature of the class timetables means that you will see students in the Park at any time of day, studying, sunbathing or courting, for Kelvingrove with its tree-lined neuks and shrubbery was always a favourite spot for young lovers. Despite warnings about the risks of skin cancer, the southwesterly slopes are littered with semi-nude bodies in summer, soaking up the sunshine. It is a sad commentary on our times that the disabled workmen of yesteryear are more likely to have given way to the unwaged of today or the house-husband exercising the weans while his wife goes out to work. And I wonder just how long ago the last nursemaid perambulated in the park with her valuable babies from the Hill.

When these three very talented young men wrote their little book, Glasgow was preparing to stage the second of the great International Exhibitions. The book was probably in the press as the Exhibition opened, for the only reference to it was an open letter to the editor of a newspaper, making the plea that whatever surplus accrued at the end should be put to good use by the erection of some permanent tearooms and other recreational facilities in the park which, they felt sure, would be an attractive alternative to the public houses of the neighbourhood. This plea was sparked off by the recollection that the profit made by the first Exhibition had not been ploughed back in the Park itself, although, to be fair, the money was employed to build the Art Gallery and Museum at Kelvingrove, the great red sandstone pile between the Kelvin and Dumbarton Road described in Chapter 10.

Considering its commercial and industrial importance in the closing decades of the nineteenth century, Glasgow lagged behind other British cities in parading its achievements through the medium of a great Exhibition. London, of course, led the way with the Great Exhibitions of 1851 and 1862, the prototypes of later world fairs at which the more civilised nations vied with each other. Paris was early in the race, with its great Expositions of 1855 and 1867. Later came Vienna (1873) and Philadelphia (1876) celebrating the centennial of American independence. This was upstaged by Paris again (1878), marking the recovery of France after the disastrous war of 1870-1. By the 1880s the concept of the world fair had even stretched as far as Melbourne and Sydney. Nearer home, London staged its third exhibition and Edinburgh organised its National Exhibition (both in 1886), followed by Manchester's Royal Jubilee Exhibition honouring Queen Victoria's Golden Jubilee. All of these shows enjoyed enormous success and spurred Glasgow on to surpass them at the earliest opportunity. Like Paris a decade earlier, Glasgow felt the need to justify itself and let the world realise that the spectacular collapse of the City of Glasgow Bank in 1878 had been a mere hiccup. Proof of the City's remarkable resilience was seen in the splendour of its Municipal Chambers, commenced in 1883, and when Queen Victoria agreed to come back to the City in 1888 to inaugurate the building on its completion, this was all the incentive required to make it a double event, with the greatest exhibition ever organised within the British Isles up to that time.

According to the prospectus the aim of the Exhibition was 'to promote and foster Science and Art, by exciting the inventive genius of our people' and 'to stimulate commercial enterprise by inviting all nations to exhibit their products both in the raw and finished state'. One up on the old rival Edinburgh, Glasgow grandly styled its show as an International Exhibition. Significantly, from the outset, the promoters aimed to use the Exhibition as a means of raising the money to fund a museum and art gallery as well as a school of art. Civic pride manifested itself in the creation of one of the finest municipal art collections anywhere in the world. By 1870 it had outgrown the McLellan Galleries in Sauchiehall Street, and it was then that the City had purchased Kelvingrove House (which stood approximately where the roller skating rink is located). This fine Georgian mansion was built in 1782 to a design by Robert Adam for Patrick Colquhoun (1745-1820), one of the half-dozen greatest businessmen Glasgow ever produced, and occupied by him in the very year in which he became Lord Provost and a few months before he founded the Chamber of Commerce. This building which, by all accounts, was one of the great ornaments of Glasgow, was marred by the unsightly extension erected in 1876 to accommodate the rapidly burgeoning art collection, and it would be partly demolished in 1901 to provide additional space for the second of Glasgow's International Exhibitions.

Its inadequacies as an art gallery were painfully obvious by the 1880s and provided the immediate incentive for the Exhibition which opened on 8 May 1888. In every respect it dwarfed its predecessors, being three times the size of the London Exhibitions of 1851 and 1862 and slightly larger than the Centennial Exposition in Philadelphia. Only the Paris Exhibition of 1878 exceeded it in area, and that had incurred a very substantial loss. There was a feeling that anything over fifty acres was risky; yet Glasgow's first Exhibition occupied a site in excess of sixty acres. The bare statistics reveal that by charging a shilling a head (half-price for children) an attendance figure of 5,748,379 (rather more than the London attendance in 1886) netted a profit of £41,700.

James Sellars was the principal architect employed in the design and layout of the various pavilions, halls and public facilities. All of them were conceived as purely temporary structures, excellent use being made of the techniques of cast-iron and steel frames, although gaily painted wood rather than acres of glass (as in Paxton's Crystal Palace) gave the Exhibition a much more colourful appearance overall. The show was dominated by the Main Building, much larger than Manchester's and described in the Exhibition guide as 'gorgeous and striking'. This vast structure, resembling one of the larger German railway stations of the period, occupied the length of Sandyford Street (now the west end of Sauchiehall Street), with a square annexe for heavy engineering and machinery tacked on at the west end. Behind the Main Building and the Kelvin were the South Band Stand, the working dairy and the outdoor exhibits which lined the river bank, as well as the grandiose Doulton Fountain which was later transferred to Glasgow Green where it stands to this day, a rather forlorn Imperial relic which has been reduced to a pathetic eyesore by the action of wind, weather and vandals.

Kelvingrove House staged an exhibition entitled the Queen's Presents. Farther north, the focal point was the great Fairy Fountain, a sight to behold after dark when it was illuminated by that wonder of the decade, electric light, and played spectacularly before an enthralled audience. The North Band Stand and the Royal Bungalow Dining Rooms provided non-stop musical entertainment and round-the-clock sustenance. A nod at the medieval history of the area was provided by the very realistic re-creation of the Bishop's Palace on the slopes between the University and the Kelvin's north bank, and of course there was also the Bishop's Palace Cafe in which that rising young entrepreneur Joseph Lyons held the catering concession. Rather incongruously flanking Kelvingrove House were the Photographic Studio, Van Houten's Cocoa pavilion in the medieval Dutch style and the McDowall Steven Fountain. Within the Main Building the Main Avenue ran east and west, with exhibition stands on either side. Under the dome at the centre point, there were the press rooms and royal reception room and on the opposite side the bank and branch post office. Tucked in a corner adjoining Gray Street was the hall devoted to women's industries.

The Kelvin was a prominent feature of the Exhibition grounds. The Prince of Wales Bridge was refurbished and the Prince of Wales himself reprised his visit of twenty years earlier by making a grand entrance from the north side of the Park, where a triumphal arch had been erected approximately where Kelvin Way begins. Incidentally, near this spot still stands an ornately banded stone pillar surmounted by wrought-iron light fittings which I used to think was part of the arch from the 1888 Exhibition but which I later discovered had been one of four decorating the gateway to the old Woodlands mansion. Two other temporary bridges were erected, side by side, roughly where the Kelvin Way Bridge now stands, leading to twin kiosks selling Howell's tobacco and Assafrey's chocolate respectively. The bridges were quite unlike each other and appear to have been deliberately created in this manner to demonstrate the different methods of construction. The river played its noble part as the venue for regattas and swimming galas, and there was even a Venetian gondola and a steam pinnace offering short excursions.

The river also provided a discreet barrier between the serious and the frivolous. Yet another temporary structure, the Military Bridge, led from the main showground across the Kelvin near the western end, where the fairground aspects were to be found. As well as a shooting gallery and a rifle range there was the Switchback Railway, probably the first roller-coaster in Scotland and the attraction that, for many people, really stole the show. Reading the breathless and breathtaking accounts of the Exhibition, in which every superlative was done to death, one is left with the impression that this is where the rather dour Calvinist Glasgow of the period really began to loosen her stays and let her hair down.

When the Exhibition closed on 10 November, however, the buildings were dismantled and the site was rapidly cleared. By the spring of 1889 it seemed as if it had never happened. Its closure left an aching void in Glasgow, and an appetite for grand spectacle that would not be satisfied again for thirteen years. In the meantime, however, the Association for the Promotion of Art and Music busied itself with the plans for the creation of the Art Galleries and Museum, described in Chapter 10. The profits from the 1888 Exhibition were more than matched by public donations, while the Corporation provided the Kelvingrove site. In 1897, the year of Queen Victoria's Diamond Jubilee, her eldest grandson the Duke of York (later King George V) came north to lay the foundation stone and it was at that time that the notion of staging a second great International Exhibition was apparently first mooted. At the turn of the century the tempo of world fairs quickened and in the intervening years there had been the truly stupendous Paris Expositions of 1889 (for which the Eiffel Tower became a permanent reminder) and 1900, as well as vast shows in Chicago (1893) and Buffalo (1901), the latter made sombrely memorable by the assassination of President McKinley. Compared to the vast sprawling 350 acres of Buffalo's Pan-American Exposition, Glasgow's contribution that year was a puny 73 acres, but in terms of attendance, Glasgow saw eleven and a half million pass through the turnstiles, compared with the eight million at Buffalo. In terms of costs and revenue, Glasgow was dwarfed by the millions of dollars involved at Buffalo, but there was one salient difference: while Buffalo incurred a loss of almost a million dollars, Glasgow recorded a handsome profit. The Exhibition cost a modest £350,600 but yielded a revenue of £404,105 which more than justified the faith of those public-spirited individuals and companies which had stood as guarantors against any loss. The death of Queen Victoria that January and the fact that the war in South Africa seemed to be dragging on inconclusively may have put a damper on the Exhibition to some extent; on the other hand Glasgow's industries were booming, there was full employment and everyone seems to have been intent on having a really good time.

The opening ceremony on 2 May 1901 was performed by Queen Victoria's daughter Princess Louise and her husband the Duke of Fife. Although a part of the 1888 site was now occupied by the newly opened Kelvingrove Museum and Art Gallery the actual Exhibition grounds were now some 13 acres larger as a result of much more extensive use of the Park as far east as La Belle Place. Significantly, this area was given over in the main to the self-standing pavilions of the leading industrial nations, including Japan, whose pavilion (occupying the shell of the partly demolished Kelvingrove House) was on a prime site near the

The main pavilion at the Glasgow International Exhibition, 1901

Kelvin and just to the north of the main Industrial Hall. On this occasion the focal point was a huge fountain designed by Walter Macfarlane and constructed by the Saracen Foundry. Farther north was the Rockery Band Stand with its cascades and rock pools and an updated Van Houten's pavilion. A great novelty was the working replica of a lighthouse perched on the slope below the University. Beyond the Japanese pavilion were the Grand Concert Hall and the adjoining high-class (and expensive) Grosvenor Restaurant. In the bend of the Kelvin in front of the Art Gallery were Miss Cranston's Tea Rooms and the Band Stand. The Industrial Hall, designed by James Miller, was a startling building, with a huge central dome flanked by four ornate towers and a grand covered piazza at the front. The dome was surmounted by a tower on top of which stood a colossal gilded statue of Light, reminiscent of the Reichstag in Berlin about that time. It was designed to complement the Art Gallery, which was formally inaugurated at the same time, and certainly from the north end of the showground these buildings made a brave show. At the east end of the showground the largest contribution was provided by Russia which had several pavilions. To the south, fronting Royal Terrace and La Belle Place, were the horticultural and agricultural displays, including a Model Farm complete with cattle and poultry. Only a generation earlier, there were still several working farms within the City boundary and Balgray Farm in Kelvinside, operated by Semple's Dairy, continued till shortly before the Second World War.

As in 1888, the Kelvin itself played a major role in the Exhibition, although this time the Venetian gondola had to compete with several electrically operated launches, but a popular new attraction was the water chute. The Switchback Railway, which had made such a hit in 1888, was considerably enlarged but still charged only threepence a ride. There was the usual assortment of sideshows and shooting galleries but the public of 1901 was more sophisticated than that of 1888 and there was widespread criticism of the fact that the entertainment aspects of the Exhibition left much to be desired. A feature of the Exposition Universelle at Paris the previous year had been the staging of the second Olympic Games of the modern series. Undoubtedly sport was a major draw, so the organisers of the Glasgow Exhibition arranged with the University to create a splendid stadium, complete with grandstand and cycle track, on ground to the west of the University buildings, and extending from the bank of the Kelvin all the way north to University Avenue. The pitch in the centre of this recreation ground was used for football matches and, appropriately, the 'Old Firm' of Rangers and Celtic kicked off in rousing style on the opening day of the Exhibition. This ground was also used for Glasgow's first-ever car rally. The recreation ground continued to provide a valuable amenity for the University for many years, until the land was required for further buildings, and today the only legacy from the turn of the century is the gymnasium at the lower end of University Avenue.

A decade later Kelvingrove was the venue of the third and last great pre-war Exhibition staged in Glasgow. This was much smaller and, at 62 acres, nearer the size of the 1888 show, but in character it was vastly different from its predecessors. Whereas they had been international in scope, with the emphasis on commerce and industry, the 1911 Scottish Exhibition of National History, Art and Industry was specifically national, and its industrial aspects were relatively muted. Like its predecessors, however, the 1911 Exhibition had a purpose, and this was to raise the money to endow a Chair of Scottish History and Literature at the University. Inevitably, with such a serious purpose, the purely entertainment aspects were much less in evidence, and perhaps that explains why the attendance figure was well down, a total of 9,369,375. With the same admission charges as before, the Exhibition made a modest yet comfortable profit of about £20,000 which was quite sufficient for the purpose, Robert Sangster Rait being appointed the first Professor of Scottish History in due course.

Whereas the 1901 Exhibition had been overshadowed by the death of Queen Victoria, the opening of the 1911 Exhibition was much more upbeat as people looked forward to the Coronation of King George V a few weeks after the grand opening; but the new King was too preoccupied at the time to do the honours himself, so in the end it fell to minor royals, the Duke and Duchess of Connaught, to fill the bill. Prince Arthur, Duke of Connaught, was King

George's uncle. By 1911 international exhibitions were alarmingly frequent: in that year alone Berlin hosted the International Travel Exhibition (March-June), Dresden held the International Hygiene Exhibition (May-October), Posen had the International Exhibition of Industry and Agriculture (May-September) and Turin staged the International Exhibition of Industry and Labour (April-November), while closer to home London was the venue for the Festival of Empire at the Crystal Palace and the Coronation Exhibition at White City, both from May till October. By comparison, the Glasgow Exhibition was quite a parochial affair, but it enabled the Scots to indulge to the full their passion for tartan, bagpipes and all the pageantry from William Wallace to Bonnie Prince Charlie associated with their colourful if turbulent history.

The principal building (and the only one fronting Sauchiehall Street) was the Palace of Industry, occupying the square of ground on the west side of Gray Street (where the tennis courts now stand). The main entrance to the Exhibition was at the northwest side of this building, close to the Kelvin. Across the bridge the showgrounds were bounded by a roadway which more or less followed the line of Kelvin Way, although it meandered along the contour line and curved westward below Gilmorehill to encompass the Auld Toon, a re-creation of a Scottish burgh. The houses had quaint, crow-stepped gables and bottle-glass windows while the main landmarks included a crenellated and turreted keep, the main square and mercat cross whose effect was marred by such unfortunate lapses as Ye Olde Toffee Shoppe. Beyond the Auld Toon were the Irish dairy cottages farther north. On the east bank of the Kelvin, near the Eldon Street entrance, was laid out An Clachan, the Highland Village, remembered to this day by an inscription to that effect on a huge rounded boulder by the riverside footpath.

The Exhibition occupied the whole of the Park, but was dominated by the gleaming white Garden Club which, with pavilions at either end containing restaurants, occupied the slope immediately below Park Terrace. In front of this long curved building was the vast auditorium and bandstand of the Grand Amphitheatre where so many of the historical pageants and tableaux were staged that summer. In the triangle bounded by Park Gardens and La Belle Place there was an illuminated fountain surrounded by the Palace of Art, the Palace of Music (Concert Hall) and the Kelvin Hall. Immediately to the northeast of the Palace of Industry was the Palace of History, a turreted structure in best Baronial style combining elements from the palaces of Falkland and Holyrood, which contained the astonishing array of historical relics, real or imagined, brought together frae a' the airts by Professor John Glaister and his indefatigable committee. This palace was actually erected around what still remained of the old Kelvingrove House which had somehow survived its transformation as the Japanese pavilion of 1901.

There was no separate Women's Section (a salient feature of the previous Exhibitions); instead women's participation was more evenly spread throughout the entire show, notably in the Ecclesiastical and Decorative Arts which even had a woman convener.

The high-tech aspects of the Exhibition, however, excited the greatest interest. The Kelvin Hall (no relation of the building of that name opposite the Museum and Art Gallery at the present day) contained the electrical and engineering exhibits and was, in fact, named in honour of Scotland's most celebrated scientist, Lord Kelvin, whose biography appears in the next chapter. Lord Kelvin had died four years previously, but he was the presiding genius of this building, both in spirit and in his statue which was surrounded by a wide range of instruments and machines that directly or indirectly owed much to his research and development. Lord Kelvin was the first, though by no means the last, of the scientists at Glasgow University who managed very successfully to combine his academic career with entrepreneurial flair and hard-headed business acumen, and it is significant that the commercial section of this hall was dominated by Kelvin and White (founded in 1859) which mustered an impressive display of electrical, precision and navigational instruments, developed from Kelvin's many patents.

In the northeast area, flanked by the Canadian Pacific exhibit and the rifle range, was the Aviation Building which housed actual aeroplanes as well as scale models, and appropriately gave prominence to the late Percy Pilcher as a worthy pioneer. This pavilion occupied the highest point of the Exhibition grounds, roughly where the statue of Lord Roberts now stands. Below it was an area designated disconcertingly as Ehrlich's Baby Incubators, demonstrating the latest technology for the care of premature babies, but also thoughtfully incorporating a series of creches where mothers could park their infants while they toured the Exhibition. Beyond the rifle range there was the Joy House, the Joy Wheel, the Mysterious River Rides and the Mountain Scenic Railway, though the lastnamed was tame by comparison with the switchback of earlier Exhibitions. By way of compensation, however, there was the Aerial Railway devised by William L. Hamilton, a local engineer. Twin tracks spanned the valley between Gilmorehill and Woodlands Hill with cable cars heavily disguised as dirigible balloons sailing over the river at an altitude of 40 metres (130 ft). For those unable to pay for a brief hop in a real aeroplane at the Lanark Aviation Meeting the previous year, the Aerial Railway provided the sensation of flight at a fraction of the cost. Beyond the fairground aspects of the show, on the northern slopes of Woodlands Hill, were the compounds where visitors could gape at 'lesser breeds without the law' – an assortment of ethnic groups including Lapps (complete with reindeer) and tribesmen from French West Africa. It is difficult at this remove in time to assess whether the Wallofs and Mandingoes excited greater wonderment than the Gaelic-speaking Hebrideans and Highlanders in their primitive blackhouses in An Clachan, although to many first or second generation Glaswegians this sight must have struck a chord.

North of the duck pond, there was a very charming Japanese teahouse on the bank of the Kelvin. As on previous occasions, the Kelvin rose nobly to the occasion, although the excursion boats of previous exhibitions gave way to the daily pageant of historic vessels, an enormous collection of scale-model replicas of ships, old and new. The Exhibition more or less coincided with the centenary of steam navigation, if one stretched a point. At least this provided a good excuse to review the progress of shipbuilding on the Clyde (and the Kelvin itself), from Henry Bell's *Comet* onwards, while at the same time manufacturing a shipping industry of far greater antiquity which included 'the type of vessel probably built by King Robert the Bruce in his days of retirement at Cardross on Clyde' and a fanciful replica of the Spanish galleon lying at the bottom of Tobermory Bay. This pageant came right up to date with a working model of the *Lusitania* and the latest Super-Dreadnought battleship.

Later, people would look back on that long lazy, hazy summer of 1911 as one of the happiest times at the end of the halcyon Edwardian era and before the shadows of war began to gather. Indeed, the weather that summer was remarkably fine with a much lower rainfall than average; but on 4 November, the very day the Exhibition closed, the elements raged with sudden fury. Heavy rain all that day gave way to a terrible storm, nature lending a savage hand to the task of demolition. By the following morning the Exhibition grounds were a sorry sight, the damage to the temporary structures having been extensive. Most spectacular (and appropriate) of all was the roof of the Aviation Pavilion which took off in the direction of Park Terrace.

By the following summer, the Park was back to normal. Even the much battered Kelvingrove House was still standing as late as 1913, although it was now a mere shell, boarded up until such times as the Corporation could decide what to do with it. It continued to feature on the large-scale Ordnance Survey maps for several years, designated 'Kelvingrove Museum', although this function had ceased more than a decade earlier. It was finally demolished later that year in the course of laying out that part of the Park and the erection of the Children's Shelter farther east.

CHAPTER NINE

Glasgow University

Glasgow has the distinction of possessing the fourth oldest university in the British Isles (ranking after Oxford, Cambridge and St Andrews). It dates its foundation from the Bull of 7 January 1451, granted by Pope Nicholas V at the behest of King James II, which enabled Bishop William Turnbull to institute a course of higher learning along the lines of that pursued at the University of Bologna. It is interesting to note that the Bull expressly commended Glasgow which was, 'by the salubrity of the climate and the abundance of all the necessaries for life, peculiarly adapted for such an establishment'. In its earliest years the University was a very modest institution, occupying premises in the Rotten Row commonly known as the Auld Pedagogy. The academic administration was in the hands of the Chapter, which appropriately met in the Chapter House of the Friars Preachers (on the site of which the later College Kirk was erected). The great majority of the forty members were clerics, and David Cadzou, Precentor of the Cathedral, was appointed Rector, with Bishop Turnbull as Chancellor. Various endowments from the Crown and wealthy landowners eventually put the University on a sound footing, and by the end of the fifteenth century it consisted of a number of buildings on several acres of land near the Cathedral on the banks of the Molendinar. The College of the Faculty of Arts was still under construction in 1560 when the Reformation erupted and the University's Chancellor, Archbishop James Beaton, was forced to flee to France (where he acted for many years in the interests of Mary Queen of Scots, especially after her confinement in England). Beaton fled with all the valuables of the Cathedral as well as the University. Ironically, when the University fell on hard times as a result of the Reformation, it was the Queen, hard-pressed herself, who took a keen interest in saving it from extinction. As a practical demonstration of her concern, she immediately endowed five bursaries for poor scholars, and settled 13 acres of land on the University, together with various rents and annuities which had formerly belonged to the Friars.

Nevertheless, by 1570, the University really hit rock bottom. In that year the professors, students and lay members numbered only fifteen in all, and its annual income had fallen to £300 Scots (£25 sterling). In the nick of time, however, Andrew Melville joined the faculty in 1574 and by his energy and administrative abilities he turned the situation around, encouraging King James VI to grant a new constitution. More importantly, the King now settled on the University the income from the rectory and vicarage of Govan parish. Under the new charter, a Principal, three professors and thirteen other staff (bursars and servants) were appointed. Soon students flocked from all parts of Scotland, despite the very spartan regime. Students still abed by five in the morning, or not in bed by nine at night, were publicly flogged by the Principal in the Common Hall. While golf, archery and 'dramatic representations' were encouraged, 'Carding, Dicing, Billiards and the indecent exercise of Bathing' were strictly forbidden. The severest punishments, however, were reserved for the most heinous crimes which included scrumping the apples from the Principal's orchard, familiarity between Masters of Arts and the undergraduates, being caught conversing in Scots instead of Latin and raiding the kitchens. On the other hand, the students were beyond the reach of the civil power, only the University Court having any powers to try and punish them in all matters civil and criminal. In 1670 a student went on trial before the Rector for murder and was duly acquitted. As recently as the mid-nineteenth century, it was argued that messengers-at-arms and sheriff officers could not serve a warrant on a student within the walls of the University.

Despite the liberating influence of the Reformation which permitted its clergy to marry, the old University was a bastion of monasticism. As late as the seventeenth century it was decreed that:

> Inasmuch as *Women* are vain, frivolous, and gifted with an exceeding great Gift of Words, and by their Blandishments are apt at times to distract the minds even of grave Professors, therefore these latter are strictly counselled *not* to Marry; but, in the event of their being compelled by untoward Force of Circumstances to choose between two Evils, they are Prohibited, on pain of removal from their Chairs from bringing their *Better-Halves* within the College walls.

The University began to expand considerably from about 1680 onwards and its heyday on the original site was the second half of the eighteenth century when many fine buildings were erected. This process continued into the early nineteenth century, the Inner Quadrangle being completed in 1812. The front of the University, extending along the High Street, had a central doorway bearing the date 1658. Above and behind it was the bell-tower which rang for classes as well as tolling the hours. At either end of the main frontage were great archways leading to the quadrangles at the rear. Through these portals passed many of the great men of Scotland over a period of more than three centuries. Latterly the students included Archibald Campbell Tait, who succeeded Dr Arnold at Rugby and went on to become Archbishop of Canterbury (the first of three Scots to attain the primacy), the great Orientalist Cotton Mather, and Joseph Hooker, the foremost British botanist of his time. James Watt, father of the Industrial Revolution, began his brilliant career as instrument maker to the University.

While the older universities were still bogged down in the classical curriculum, Glasgow was already forging ahead in the sciences, under the redoubtable Dr James Thomson and his even more eminent son William, the future Lord

Kelvin. Students came from all over the world to study naval architecture and marine engineering, two of the early specialities which arose out of the development of shipbuilding and steam navigation. But the University seemed doomed by its very success, and by the middle of the nineteenth century was bursting at the seams with no room in the congested city centre for further expansion. Furthermore, the University was by that time located in the middle of a district that contained some of the worst slums, where dram shops, thieves' kitchens and brothels were all too likely to corrupt the morals of the students. From time to time proposals to uproot the University and relocate it in the western suburbs were mooted, but nothing positive was done until 1845 when the Glasgow, Airdrie and Monklands Railway offered a very tempting deal whereby, in exchange for the site on the High Street, they would erect a new university in the up-and-coming West End. The University obtained the necessary sanction of Parliament and as a result the railway company purchased the estate of Woodlands (including Woodlands Hill) in 1847, commissioning John Baird Senior to draw up suitable plans. On three occasions Baird submitted drawings and each time the Senate, on the advice of William Lyon Playfair and Augustus Welby Pugin, rejected them. In desperation, the Senate then consulted Edward Blore with a view to procuring a less expensive scheme, but by the time he came up with a suitable design, in 1849, the railway was in financial difficulties and no longer able to honour its commitments.

It seemed as if the University was doomed to remain in the High Street, and there were plenty of influential men at the time who argued cogently that instead of running off to the West End and selling their souls to the railways, the professors should do something about clearing the adjacent slums and restoring the existing buildings, which then constituted the foremost group of seventeenth-century edifices in Glasgow. This argument raged back and forth until 1863 when the City of Glasgow Union Railway approached the University authorities with an astounding suggestion. The Railway needed a site for its terminus and goods yards and made an offer of £100,000 which the University could not refuse. Another Act of Parliament was required, but by June 1864 the deal was concluded and on that basis the University began looking in earnest for a new site, the original Woodlands Hill location having, by that time, been developed by Charles Wilson. In July 1864, the University laid out £65,000 on the estate of Gilmorehill on the west bank of the Kelvin. By the end of the year, the adjoining estates of Clayslaps and Donaldshill were also acquired. Part of this land was subsequently sold to the City and formed the site of the Western Infirmary.

Professor Allan Thomson, Convener of the Senate's Removal Committee, had the honour of cutting the first sod at Gilmorehill on 6 June 1866. Allan Thomson ignored the plans of Baird and Blore and went behind everyone's back to secure designs from a London architect George Gilbert Scott. There was considerable ill feeling when the Senate awarded the commission to Scott, much to the chagrin of the Glasgow architects, especially Alexander Thomson who expressed himself very forcibly on the subject in the newspapers of the period. Scott had made his name as an ecclesiastical architect and his design for the University was strongly influenced by this. Perhaps that was what swayed the Senate in his favour, for the monastic quadrangles must have suggested the Auld Pedagogy to them. Whereas 'Greek' Thomson was a committed classicist, Scott was a disciple of the Gothic Revival which was all the rage in the 1860s.

The task of construction began in November 1866 when the site on the ridge of Gilmorehill overlooking the Kelvin was cleared and levelled. Gilmorehill House was retained for a time, and served as the offices of the master of works and the builders while the work was in progress, being demolished eventually to make way for the west quadrangle in 1872. By 1868, work had sufficiently progressed for the ceremony of laying the foundation stone to take place. Actually, there were two stones, laid by the Prince and Princess of Wales (the future King Edward VII and Queen Alexandra) on 8 October 1868. For some time there had been talk about Queen Victoria herself coming to Glasgow to perform the ceremony, but in the end she delegated this pleasant duty to her son and daughter-in-law. These long-running rumours explain the apparent excess of royal sentiment in Dowanhill, which was then in course of development, reflected in Albert Gate, Prince Albert Road, Victoria Cross, Crescent and Circus, Prince's Gardens and Terrace, Queen's Gardens and all those Crowns (Circus, Terrace, Gardens and Road North and South) as well as the temporary renaming of Byres or Byars Road as Victoria Street.

When the great day came Glasgow was fortunately enjoying an Indian summer, and the West End was *en fête* for the royal occasion. The Prince received the Freedom of the City and then rode in an open carriage with the Princess, accompanied by civil dignitaries along a route that was gay with flags and bunting. From the Old College, whose gateway was embellished with the Latin motto *Resurgat in Gloria* (may it resurge in glory), the royal cavalcade passed along Sauchiehall Street and entered the Park through a floral arch beside Kelvingrove House. They drove along the carriageway and crossed the river by the temporary Prince of Wales Bridge, previously noted, and thence entered the grounds of the University. At this point, they passed through a second floral arch, roughly where the north end of Kelvin Way now stands and proceeded up the driveway to Gilmorehill House where they were formally received by the Court and Senate. Honorary law degrees were conferred on the Prince and Princess of Wales as well as Prince John of Glucksburg, (Alexandra's uncle). Thus, the first graduation ceremony of the new University took place two years before it was inaugurated.

The last classes in the Old College concluded on 29 July 1870 and the new

The professors of Glasgow University leave the Old College for the last time in 1870

University opened its doors to students and staff on 7 November. The work of construction continued by fits and starts, depending on the availability of cash. Fortunately, the Senate was adept at getting some of Glasgow's wealthiest and most prominent citizens to stump up, especially if there was a prospect of getting their name perpetuated. In 1885, therefore, the remnants of the doorway from the Old College were incorporated in Pearce Lodge, marking the entrance to the University at the eastern end of University Avenue. Designed by Alexander G. Thomson, it was named Pearce Lodge in honour of the distinguished Admiralty architect, Sir William Pearce. The inscriptions, including the date 1658 and crossed swords surmounted by the royal cypher CR2, are picked out in gold. The Randolph and Bute Halls, used for examinations, graduation ceremonies and a wide variety of academic functions, commemorate the generosity of Charles Randolph and the third Marquess of Bute. George Gilbert Scott died before he could execute the plans for these noble chambers, but they were carried out by his son J. Oldrid Scott, assisted by Edwin Morgan between 1878 and 1884.

Adding insult to injury the Scotts, father and son, ignored the prior claims of local building contractors and employed John Thompson of Peterborough, with whom they had worked in connection with the erection of the Foreign Office in London and many churches in England. At least Thompson was quite content to work with local materials, some of the stone being quarried on Gilmorehill itself. Actually the composition of the fabric of the main buildings is an interesting geological mixter-maxter, with freestone from Kenmure, Old Red Sandstone from Bonhill, Dunbartonshire, and pink granite from the Ross of Mull for the pillars flanking the great medieval doorway on the south front. Extensive repairs to the stonework in the past decade have contributed to the patchwork-quilt effect, although the new masonry will eventually weather and blend with the old. John Tweed published an engraving entitled 'The College of Glasgow, Gilmorehill, opened 1870', which appears to have been based on Scott's impression of how the finished building would look, but which differs from it in a number of respects. The first thing that is immediately apparent, is the surprisingly level park in front of the University, unlike the steep slopes down to the Kelvin in reality. This gives a curious perspective to the balustrades running along the front of the building. Less apparent nowadays is the general impression of the building whose chief feature is its magnificent tower, but in fact this was not actually completed (by Oldrid Scott) until 1891. Photographs of the 1880s show the tower at various stages of construction, usually with an oddly truncated form (rather like Renfield St Stephen's Church in Bath Street which lost the upper part of its steeple in the severe storm on Boxing Day 1998). George Gilbert Scott had envisaged a lead-covered spire incorporating clock faces, but Oldrid's version is a great improvement.

Scott the father considered that he had evolved a distinctly Scottish brand of Gothic in creating the University, and certainly there are nice touches of Scots Baronial in the corbelled turrets at the corners of the main building as well as on the raised blocks at either end, with crow-stepped gables for good measure. At the eastern end of the main block there was, as late as my time as an undergraduate (1954-8) a strange little detached building. Intended as the chemistry laboratory, and set apart from the main building to keep noxious gases at bay, this structure was allegedly inspired by the Abbot's Kitchen at Glastonbury, but it always reminded me of the library of the Parliament Building in Ottawa. Sadly, it was demolished in 1958 to make way for the James Watt Engineering Building by Keppie, Henderson & Partners. I feel that the original John Keppie and Graham Henderson would be turning in their graves at the very idea. The majestic buildings of the 1870s are such an impressive sight that it seems a shame that the architects who have tacked on so many high-rise blocks in recent years have not kept faith with the original, but we have seen a blatant disregard for the glories of the past elsewhere in Glasgow, so it was probably expecting too much to hope for any attempt at uniformity. Some years ago there was correspondence in the *Glasgow Herald* (as it was then known) soliciting the views of readers regarding what they would regard as a building that was symbolic of the City as a whole. Strangely enough, the consensus seemed to be that the giant Clyde crane filled the bill; but a crane is a crane is a crane, and I have always strongly felt that the University Tower is the City's most obvious landmark. Wherever you are in Glasgow itself, it stands out, and it is the one building which is immediately recognisable from the air, or viewed from many miles away, on the Campsies or the Renfrewshire Hills. At one time it was possible to ascend the 30-metre (100 ft) tower by a cramped spiral stairway, the stunning views from the summit in all directions being well worth the climb. Nowadays the same panoramic views can be obtained by taking the elevator to the twelfth floor of the University Library which has a viewing gallery all round the reading room where the Special Collections may be studied.

Within the main building are the two great quadrangles, paved all round with grass in the centre. Connecting the quads is a large, vaulted passageway, which leads to the Bute and Randolph Halls. On the north side of the east quadrangle is the entrance to the staircase (in cast and wrought iron) which leads to the

West End Park and University, Glasgow. 4040/817

Glasgow University from the West End, or Kelvingrove, Park

Hunterian Museum on an upper floor. The museum, one of the great glories of the University, was founded in August 1804 and originally occupied a fine neo-classical building, part of the High Street campus, regrettably demolished in the late 1860s to make way for the High Street railway station. The museum owes its existence to the munificence of Dr William Hunter, born in May 1718 at East Kilbride, the seventh of the ten children of Hunter of Long Calderwood. William and his younger brother John became two of the most celebrated surgeons of the Georgian era. William became Surgeon to King George III and as one of the most fashionable medical men in London he became extremely wealthy, enabling him to indulge in his passion for collecting fine books, manuscripts, paintings, coins and medals, antiquities and natural curiosities. His collections, the accumulation of half a century, were valued at over £130,000 at the time of his death. The library alone contained upwards of twelve thousand volumes, including rare incunabula. The coin cabinet was ranked second only to the Royal Collection in Paris, while the paintings showed the discernment and taste of the true collector. In bequeathing his remarkable collections to his alma mater, Dr Hunter attached the sum of £8,000 to provide a suitable museum to house them. During the construction of the railway station in December 1870, workmen discovered the foundation stone of the original museum, beneath which was a sweetie jar from the Verreville Glassworks containing a set of coins and other contemporary relics, which were immediately handed over to the University authorities for inclusion in the new museum. Hunter's collection of stuffed animals included a giraffe and a rhinoceros, a lion and a tiger, whose flitting to Hillhead by railway goods wagons excited much jocular comment at the time, Gilmorehill being likened to Mount Ararat where Noah's Ark came to rest.

To the left of the Museum at the top of the stairs was the original University Library but following its relocation in the great tower block on the other side of University Avenue, this part of the main building became surplus to requirements. After a delay of several years it was refurbished and integrated into the Hunterian Museum, effectively doubling its size in the 1990s and providing scope for new display galleries. At the same time the lower part of the central core of the building was extensively renovated and restyled in the 1970s and 1980s to provide an excellent Visitors' Centre and cafeteria.

The west quadrangle remained incomplete on the west side until 1923-7 when the War Memorial Chapel was constructed to a design by Sir John James Burnet, fortunately in the same Scottish Gothic genre as Scott's main building. At the side of the Chapel was re-erected the Lion and Unicorn Stair from the Old College, dating from 1690 and intended to provide access to the quadrangle from the Professors' Square, the row of houses separated by a little park from the main building. This terrace of lofty houses occupying three sides of the square was intended as residences for the professors, and I recall frequently visiting my old friend Christian Fordyce and his wife Kitty at number 3 up to the time of his retirement. Perhaps his position as Clerk to the Senate enabled him to hang on to this residence long after most of the neighbouring houses had been taken over as offices by the University administration, and latterly only the Principal's residence at the south end continued to fulfil its original function.

The Fordyces had no children and the house would have seemed unduly large but for the fact that successive rooms were given over to his extensive collections. Unlike Dr Hunter and Sir William Burrell, however, Christian Fordyce's collections consisted mainly of articles whose common denominator was in the 'something for nothing' category. His chief passion was undoubtedly railway tickets, of which he must have had millions from every part of the world. It was always a mystery how he had acquired British tickets, which were normally surrendered at the end of a journey, but there was a tale (not entirely apocryphal) that he had acquired a ticket collector's uniform, wearing which he coolly parted many passengers from their tickets. Allied to the tickets was a prodigious collection of postcards and photographs of railway stations, large and small, ancient and modern, all of which, sadly, appear to have been dispersed soon after his sudden death in 1972. A true magpie, he had a schoolboy's fascination for stamps (mounted rather haphazardly in University examination jotters), but he was also a dedicated collector of postmarks long before this branch of the hobby became at all fashionable. There was also a huge collection of hotels' crested notepaper, a staggering accumulation of business reply envelopes whose telegraphic codes greatly intrigued him, and an equally vast collection of the blazer badges of every school, college and university in the British Isles, for heraldry was another of his interests and, indeed, he personally designed the armorial bearings for several of the new universities created in the 1960s. A brilliant classical scholar and an authority on the works of Catullus, he was a gifted amateur thespian. To students, staff and Senate colleagues he could be a holy terror, but I only ever knew the softer, gentler side and above all the surreal humour of the last of the great University eccentrics. It may be no accident that the Humanity Classroom, where Christian Fordyce taught for many years, has now been preserved as a typical example of a nineteenth-century lecture hall, with its serried ranks of benches.

On the north side of the main building, fronting on to University Avenue, stands the McIntyre Building and adjoining main gateway, erected between 1886 and 1908 to designs by Sir John James Burnet. This building, described in the Glasgow Buildings volume as 'an exercise in English collegiate Gothic', was designed as the original Students' Union, but when the male students moved out in 1931 to a much larger building on the corner of University Avenue and Bank Street, the McIntyre Building was extensively redesigned in order to convert it into Queen Margaret Union for lady students. The ladies moved to a monstrous tower block at the end of University Gardens in 1968 and the old QM was transformed yet again, to serve mainly as offices of the Students' Representative Council, a university shop and the campus branch of Smith's bookshop. Above the main doorway on University Avenue are the heraldic emblems of the four 'nations' into which the academic staff and students are divided according to their place of birth: Glottiana (Glasgow and Lanarkshire), Rothseiana (the former counties of the Clyde Coast, Ayr, Bute and Renfrew), Transforthana (the west of Scotland generally, as well as the country north of the Forth) and Loudoniana (southeast Scotland). A wall plaque also explains that the building was presented to his alma mater by Dr John McIntyre of Odiham, Hampshire, in memory of his wife Anne. For good measure, the gable at the east end has a sculpture of St Mungo, alias Kentigern. Alongside stand the Quincentenary Gates erected in 1954, the wrought-iron railings embellished with a gilded representation of the University mace and tablets bearing the names of twenty-eight famous persons and alumni over the past 500 years, from King James II and Bishop Turnbull in the fifteenth century, to Andrew Cecil Bradley (1851-1935), the professor of English Literature who earned international fame for his Shakespearean commentaries. The side gates are decorated with panels alluding to the four nations and the stonework bears the name of the institution in Latin (*Universitas Glasguensis*) and its motto *Via, Veritas, Vita* ('the way, the truth, the life'). Between the gates and the main building is located the grandiose Hunter Memorial designed by Burnet, with sculpture by George Henry Paulin to the memory of William and John Hunter. As well as the portrait medallions, the memorial is replete with heraldic imagery, the arms of the Royal College of Surgeons of England, and those of the Royal Faculty of Physicians and Surgeons of Glasgow flanking the insignia of the University.

The first of the 'outbuildings' constructed at the turn of the century and later in order to accommodate additional departments was the Anatomical Building of 1900-1, tacked on at the north side of the east quadrangle. Designed by Burnet, it was an honest attempt to produce a modern building that was in keeping with the main building, although the experts describe it as a Scottish Renaissance structure, but in the late 1950s it was dwarfed by the James Watt Engineering Building which bore no relation to anything else nearby. In the early twentieth century, however, most of the new development took place on the land to the west of the main building. James Miller designed the Materia Medica and Physiology Department buildings of 1903-7, as the result of an open competition which decisively favoured the architect who would come closest to the Scott ideal. Miller also designed the Natural Philosophy Building of 1906 (now the Kelvin Building after the University's most illustrious scientist), the first of the major structures to encroach on the Recreation Ground. Situated along a high bank opposite the west wing of the professors' terrace, it asserted its individuality with a Jacobean centrepiece topped by a cupola. Farther north, fronting on University Avenue and adjoining a gateway opposite the top end of Ashton Road, stands the headquarters of the Officers' Training Corps, built about 1900 to designs by H. & D. Barclay. On the east side is the Botany Building of the same period, by Oldrid Scott and Sir John James Burnet, representing the last throw of the nineteenth century in its lavish mixture of Renaissance and Baronial features. This has been renamed the Bower Building, in memory of Professor Frederick Bower.

The buildings erected after the First World War, however, marked a clear watershed in design and materials; being farther away from the main building, they were freed from any pre-war constraints and represent an interesting medley of styles that reflect the decades in which they were built. The first of these was the Zoology Building (now the Graham Kerr Building), designed by Burnet and erected in 1923. It contains the Zoology Museum formed around the collections of William Hunter, and is open to the public although this fact seems to be almost a state secret. The building is an interesting blend of his turn of the century style with elements of Bauhaus functionalism. This attained fruition in the Institute of Chemistry (now the Joseph Black Building), erected in 1936-9 to designs of Harold Hughes and D.S.R. Waugh but considerably augmented in the early 1950s and again in 1963-6. A plaque on the outer wall commemorates Joseph Black (1728-99), who discovered carbon dioxide in 1754 and deserves to be better known for his researches that led to the development of steam-power.

Hitherto all of the University buildings had consisted of stone, but this was the first structure to make free use of brick and concrete, although a concession to the past was the carved frieze on the south wall tracing the origin of species.

In the period since the Second World War, the University has expanded considerably to the north and west. Anticipating further development, the University authorities pursued a policy of buying up properties in adjacent roads and streets as they fell vacant and latterly this became a wholesale operation. In this manner much of Southpark Avenue, Oakfield Avenue, the north end of Gibson Street, Hillhead Street, University Gardens, Bute Gardens, Lilybank Gardens and Ashton Road was taken over, first as accommodation, then as offices and classrooms, and finally, in many cases, being demolished to make way for higher and higher concrete blocks from the 1960s onwards. As a result, the north side of University Avenue has been transformed beyond recognition but without the slightest evidence of any sense of overall purpose, far less planning. From the vantage point at the top of the University Library, itself the loftiest of the group, one forms the impression of a jumble of gigantic packing cases dumped down any old how and that when the powers that be finally get around to unpacking them everything will be all right. The compilers of the Glasgow Buildings volume prefer the analogy of a pincushion, with pins stuck in haphazardly, adding that 'the hilly nature of the area provides a necessary foil to this apparent lack of cohesion'.

There are the three interlinked blocks of the Mathematics Building (1969), the skyscraping glass and reinforced concrete Boyd Orr Building (1972), the rather untidy Adam Smith Building (1967) and the Geology or Gregory Building (1980). By contrast, the Hetherington Building (1983) is a refreshing return to buildings of a more conventional stature. The jewel in the crown, of course, is the complex at the southern end of Hillhead Street, comprising the University Library, with Hunterian Museum and Art Gallery extension and the almost surreal Mackintosh House, with its front door stuck inconsequentially half-way up the wall and serving no function whatever. The core of this complex was completed in 1968 with an ugly rectangular outline which rivals Oldrid Scott's Gothic tower in height, if not in grace and beauty. The interior was refurbished and substantially rejigged in the late 1990s, greatly improving the main entrance with state of the art electronic card-controlled turnstiles and better facilities for high-tech information retrieval. The chief feature of the Art Gallery is its massive cast-aluminium doors designed by Sir Eduardo Paolozzi in 1977. In the courtyard stands the cupola which Charles Rennie Mackintosh designed for the top of Pettigrew & Stephen in Sauchiehall Street, salvaged for posterity when that much-loved department store was demolished in the 1970s. By contrast, the long low building opposite the entrance to the Library is the Refectory with assorted shops and a bank, although it now seems to have a semi-derelict air. A flight of steps run past the side of this building to Southpark Avenue, with the University Reading Room on the right set in attractively landscaped grounds. This building is circular, with the reading room on the ground floor surrounded by a gallery off which are located various departmental libraries. It has a rather squat rotunda which was to have been surmounted by a clock tower, but the main structure was completed in 1940 and the tower had to be postponed for the duration of the war. Now, six decades later, there is no intention of getting back to the original plan.

One street, which has miraculously retained its original appearance to some extent, even if its houses are no longer in private occupation, is University Gardens, running in a northwesterly direction from University Avenue. It consists of a double row of terraced houses around a long narrow strip of garden. The houses on the north side were mainly designed by Sir John James Burnet and erected in 1882-4, although the corner house (number 1) by Robert Ewan dates from the turn of the century and is quite distinct. On the south side only numbers 11 and 13 now remain, the rest of the terrace having been demolished to make way for the Mathematics Building, while the houses at the end on the north side have long since given way to the Modern Languages Building. Number 7 is still intact and is now known as Hepburn House. For many years the private residence of Colonel Charles A. Hepburn (1890-1971), the whisky magnate, it was bequeathed by him to the University. His monogram is carved on the wall, alongside the mottoes *Be mindfu* and *Keep tryst*, although his greatest memorial is *A Hillhead Album*, which he funded and masterminded, though sadly he did not live to see this invaluable if idiosyncratic record of his native district in print.

Virtually the only building in this area which is not part of the University is Wellington Church, on the corner of University Avenue and Southpark Avenue. The last magnificent death-throes of classicism, it was built in 1882-4 to a design by Thomas Lennox Watson, then a young man barely out of his twenties but the last disciple of 'Greek' Thomson. Faithfully imitating a Grecian temple, it was actually modelled on the Madeleine in Paris and built for one of Glasgow's most prominent independent congregations, who could trace their history back to 1754, when the Seceders opened a church in Havannah Street. The original members were mostly handloom weavers in Anderston and in 1792 they broke away to form the Associate Congregation of Anderston. Their first minister, the Revd Dr John Mitchell, laboured on their behalf for almost half a century, during which time he was instrumental in the congregation moving to more commodious premises in Wellington Street in 1827. The congregation continued to expand and, in turn, the Wellington Street church ceased to be adequate. The building and land were sold to provide the location for the Alhambra Theatre, and the congregation moved westward again, this time fixing on the site in the up-and-coming West End. In 1881 the congregation purchased Oakfield House which, with the actual design and construction of the church, set the church members back the then colossal sum of £26,468. Remarkably, the ordinary collections at the morning, afternoon and evening services on Sunday 12 October 1884, the day the new church was inaugurated, brought in the tidy sum of £11,171 which more than wiped out the deficit between the costs and the sale of the former church. By that time the congregation had affiliated with the United Presbyterian Church which, in turn, rejoined the Church of Scotland at the beginning of the twentieth century. The first minister under the new regime was Dr George H. Morrison (1866-1928) who became Moderator of the General Assembly in 1926 and was the first Scottish clergyman to broadcast regularly on the religious services of the BBC (whose first Scottish Director, incidentally, was a man of the cloth, the Revd Melville Dinwiddie). Born and bred on the banks of the Kelvin, Morrison was educated at Glasgow Academy where his uncle, Dr Donald Morrison, was the first Rector. Wellington was singularly fortunate to have such a powerful personality as its minister. The story goes that in the 1920s the great Fleet Street journalist Hannen Swaffer paid a visit to Glasgow and was getting the guided tour from one of the local scribes. When they turned the corner from Kelvin Way into University Avenue and the great man beheld Wellington Church in all its Athenian splendour he cried out, 'What god do they worship in this temple?' This prompted the response, 'A god by the name of Morrison!'

The congregation of the 1880s had come a long way from its Secession forebears, for it installed an organ from the very outset and this instrument, by Forster & Andrews of Hull, is one of the church's glories, along with the communion table by Sir David Cameron and the interior war memorial created by Sir John James Burnet in 1920-1.

Wellington Church is an enclave, sandwiched between University buildings. Farther east along University Avenue is the Rankine Building (1969) and behind, facing Gibson Street, the Stevenson Physical Education Building (1960). On the eastern side, fronting on the junction with Kelvin Way and Bank Street, is the University Students' Union, originally erected in 1929-31 but now dwarfed by its enormous extension of 1965. On the opposite side of the street stands the Gilmorehall. It started life in 1876 as Anderston Free Church, designed by James Sellars in the Normandy Gothic style although the projected tower was never completed. Later it became Gilmore Parish Church under the auspices of the Church of Scotland, then Gilmorehill Halls and is now the place where undergraduates sweat over the end-of-term examinations.

Next door, on the corner of Gibson Street, is the former Hillhead Congregational Church, designed by H. & D. Barclay in the best French Gothic tradition and opened for worship in September 1890. Like Wellington, this non-conformist congregation had a long history, going back to 1799 when its first church opened near the Broomielaw. The growth of the congregation led to the inevitable move west, and in the course of the twentieth century it had a succession of very distinguished ministers as well as world-class visiting preachers such as the Revd Silvester Horne, the father of the much-loved comic genius Kenneth Horne. For many years the church organist was the late and sadly missed Sir Alexander Gibson, who went on to become conductor of the Scottish National Orchestra. The church also had the distinction of the Revd Vera Kenmure as minister in 1936-45, the first woman to be ordained in Scotland, and later she went on to become President of the Congregational Union, another first for her sex. Sadly, the congregation closed down some years ago, but the building continues to serve spiritual needs in a truly ecumenical manner as the Glasgow Christian Fellowship.

The southwesterly end of the University complex is approached from Dumbarton Road, just across the Kelvin in Partick, by means of an elaborate gateway with a porter's lodge in the same style. Alongside is the entrance to the Western Infirmary, established as a teaching hospital connected with the University. Actually, proposals to open a general hospital in the West End go back as far as 1846, about the time that the move of the University from the High Street was also being mooted, but plans for both institutions proved abortive, and it was not until 1867 that John Burnet Senior was asked to reconsider the project. The year after the University moved to Gilmorehill work on the Western Infirmary began on an adjoining site, between the lower end of University Avenue, Church Street and Dumbarton Road. This rectangular ground was formerly known as the Brewlands from the fact that the bishops of Glasgow had their brewery there, utilising water from the Brewster Burn. Now built over, this stream ran down the west side of Byres Road and along the line of Cooperswell Street in Partick to enter the Kelvin shortly before its confluence with the Clyde.

The original hospital in the prevailing Baronial style was completed in 1874 but over the ensuing years additions and extensions greatly altered the original concept. The east range was added in 1881, complete with a turreted centrepiece allegedly inspired by Glamis Castle. The three-storey surgical wing by Burnet was added in 1897 but demolished in 1989-90 to make way for one of several massive tower blocks of recent vintage which have utterly dwarfed the original structure. Within the Infirmary complex is the intriguing Alexander Elder Memorial Chapel by the Burnet partnership, erected in 1926 in a blend of various styles, although predominantly Norman, with stained-glass windows by Robert Anning Bell.

On the northwest side, fronting Church Street, are the Pathological Institute of 1894-6, the Dispensary and Outpatients Department of 1902-5, the Tennant

Memorial Building of 1933-6 and the Gardiner Medical Institute of 1937-8. All of these pre-war buildings had a certain symmetry and uniformity of materials, but the post-war buildings have broken ranks with a vengeance. Between 1965 and 1974 the eleven-storey Accident and Emergency Department was erected to a design by Keppie, Henderson. On the east side stands the former Staff Nurses' Home overlooking the river, erected just after the war and now used as offices by the Infirmary's burgeoning army of managers and administrators. Keppie, Henderson designed the new Nurses' Home of 1970, with the Nurses' Training School alongside.

Next door to the Dumbarton Road entrance of the Infirmary stands Anderson's College of Medicine, all that now remains of what was once Glasgow's original second university. It came into existence in 1799 as a result of a bequest from Professor John Anderson, a brilliant man of independent mind who did not suffer fools lightly. He was at one time professor of physics at the Old College but quarrelled with his colleagues when they strongly disapproved of him permitting workingmen to attend his classes and, what was worse, allowing them to turn up in their ordinary working clothes and not the red gowns demanded of undergraduates at the time. Anderson believed passionately in education for all, and not just a privileged few. Having brushed the dust of the University off his feet, he went to the Continent at the time of the French Revolution and served as a military adviser to the Convention during the opening campaign when the Austrians invaded France. When Britain declared war on France in 1793, however, he returned to Scotland and died three years later. In his will, he left all his possessions for the establishment of a second university where emphasis would be given on practical subjects, such as physics, chemistry, engineering and medicine. As it happens, Anderson's bequest did not amount to very much but it was a classic example of a leveraged project, his money priming the pump. His ideas were well received by the Town Council (which had sympathised with him in his dispute with fellow academics) and by 1799 the Andersonian University was opened. By organising part-time and evening classes, the Andersonian became the prototype for mechanics institutes all over the British Isles. Dr George Birkbeck, a former member of the Andersonian teaching staff, later went on to found a smaller institution in London which survives to this day as Birkbeck College of London University. Thanks to Anderson's brilliant concept, many poor but clever workingmen got their chance and repaid society by their achievements in many fields. Among the graduates of the Andersonian University, for example, were the millhand David Livingstone who studied medicine there before becoming a missionary explorer, and James 'Paraffin' Young, a cabinet-maker who became one of Britain's leading industrial chemists.

Out of the Andersonian University would develop the Glasgow and West of

Scotland Technical College of 1886, renamed the Royal College of Science and Technology in 1912, but the wheel came full circle when it was renamed the University of Strathclyde in 1964. When the Andersonian University changed direction in 1886 its medical faculty, which enjoyed a higher reputation than that of Glasgow University, was hived off to form a separate college, with its own building, designed by James Sellars but completed by John Keppie and erected in 1888-9. An outstanding blend of Scots Renaissance and Italianate features, this building is also of interest on account of the sculpture by Pittendrigh MacGillivray over the main doorway, showing a professor examining a patient while nine medical students hover in the background. Although adjacent to the Western Infirmary and Glasgow University, Anderson's College of Medicine maintained its independence until 1947 when it was absorbed by the University.

Associated with the University buildings are several freestanding sculptures. Among the more recent is Three Squares Giratory by George Rickey, erected in the west quadrangle in 1972. By contrast, in the open space in front of the main building at the east end, there stands the Terrestrial Globe, a huge stone sphere with a slate dial which tradition maintains was made by Lord Kelvin himself. Near the Geology Building stands a massive chunk of Ballachulish granite, retrieved from a demolished railway bridge and presumably symbolising the ancient rock of Scotland. Outside the Rankine Building is a colossal stainless-steel sculpture by Lucy Aird, erected in 1990 to celebrate the sesquicentennial of the Regius Chair of Civil Engineering and Mathematics. In front of the Refectory are two tall blocks of concrete, sculpture in the ultra-modernist idiom created by Zeyad Dajani and Robin Lee in 1996. The remaining statues or monuments associated with the University are to be found in that part of Kelvingrove Park immediately south of the main building on the west side of Kelvin Way. On the grassy bank on the right-hand side as you walk south on Kelvin Way there is the Suffrage Oak which was planted on 20 April 1918 by the Women's Suffrage organisations in Glasgow to celebrate the granting of votes to women. A small plaque, erected in 1995, gives the details. The women of Glasgow and the West of Scotland played a prominent part in the long-running struggle to win political equality with men, although it was only with the formation of the Women's Social and Political Union in October 1903 by Emmeline and Christabel Pankhurst that the campaign became really focused. At first the WSPU tried to achieve its aims by peaceful means but when that failed, it engaged in arson and bomb outrages. Several violent incidents took place in and around Glasgow in 1913-14, including an attempt to burn down one of the mansions on Woodlands Hill as well as bombs in the Kibble Palace and Belmont Church, Hillhead. Following the outbreak of the First World War, the suffragettes channelled their energies into war work, and it was this contribution, rather than militant action, that eventually won the day. It is heartening to note that the tender sapling of 1918 has now grown into a mighty tree. It has, of course, nothing whatsoever to do with the University, but it leads to the corner of the Park where several statues are grouped in a pretty dingle above the loop of the Kelvin.

The first statue is that of Lord Kelvin, by Archibald Macfarlane Shannon, erected in 1913. William Thomson was actually born in Belfast on 26 June 1824, the second son of James Thomson, a Glasgow man who was then Professor of mathematics at the Royal Academical Institution. In 1832 James was appointed professor of mathematics at his old university and the family then returned to Glasgow. At the tender age of ten William enrolled at the University and studied under his father before going to Peterhouse College, Cambridge where he was the first winner of the Smith Prize in 1845. He spent a year in Paris, carrying on his researches into thermodynamics under the great Regnault, but in 1846 he returned to Glasgow. Not long after his twenty-second birthday he became Professor of natural philosophy and occupied this chair for more than half a century, bringing distinction and renown to Glasgow University and making it the world centre for research into all branches of physics. Thomson, the greatest physicist of his generation, three times turned down an offer to leave Glasgow to head the Cavendish Laboratory. Instead, the world's great scientists beat a path to his door on the banks of the Kelvin. After the move to Gilmorehill in 1870 he occupied number 11 in the Professors' Square, still regarded as a shrine in which the great man's enormous clock can be seen, with its face on one floor and its pendulum going down to the basement below. Appropriately, this is believed to have been the first house in Glasgow lit by electricity. A plaque on the outer wall notes that William Thomson, Lord Kelvin, held the chair of natural philosophy from 1846 to 1899 before becoming Chancellor of the University and is buried beside Isaac Newton in Westminster Abbey.

As a young man, Thomson became embroiled in controversy with the religious fundamentalists. Just as Charles Darwin fell foul of the zealots over his theories on the origin of species, so also did Thomson incur their wrath with his calculation that the Earth was at least a hundred million years old. Later researches were less controversial but no less far-reaching, and by 1851 he had propounded the Second Law of Thermodynamics. If he had done nothing else, he would have left his mark on the history of science, but his illustrious career was just beginning. In the 1850s, he turned his attention to electricity and electromagnetism which he first applied to telegraphy. He was not just a brilliant theorist but also a man of an eminently practical turn of mind, solving the problem of sending signals by submarine cable which revolutionised global communications. For his services to transatlantic telegraphy he was knighted in 1866. From his researches into the properties of electricity developed a wide range of precision instruments adapted to every aspect of electricity, and from his numerous patents, developed commercially through his own company, he became a very wealthy man. He could easily have retired to live the life of the leisured classes, but to his credit he worked till the end of his long life. He played a leading role in the British Association for the Advancement of Science; although he attained the greatest eminence in the world scientific establishment, he remained a very simple man, a brilliant lecturer and communicator who, as early as 1873, was writing articles on popular science for *Good Words*. He redesigned the mariner's compass and invented numerous other navigational instruments as well as contributing over three hundred papers to the world's leading scientific journals. He was raised to the peerage in 1892 as Baron Kelvin of Largs (where he had his country residence at Netherhall). The golden jubilee of his professoriate triggered off a spate of honours, including the Grand Cross of the Royal Victorian Order and the Freedom of the City of Glasgow. He was one of the original members of the Order of Merit when it was created in 1902 and two years later became Chancellor of the University. After relinquishing his chair in 1899, he devoted his time to travelling the lecture circuit but still found time to commence research into electronics. He died at Netherhall on 17 December 1907. He left no heir so his title died with him, but it lives on in countless ways and, through him, the humble tributary of the mighty Clyde has attained international recognition out of all proportion to its actual importance. The earliest biographies of Lord Kelvin, by Andrew Gray (1908) and S.P.Thompson (1910) are unanimous in extolling the merits of his personal character: 'Extreme modesty, amounting almost to diffidence, was combined with the utmost kindliness in Lord Kelvin's

bearing to the most elementary student, and nothing seemed to give him so much pleasure as an opportunity to acknowledge the efforts of the humblest scientific worker.' These are admirable traits which, sadly, have all too often been lacking in the groves of academe.

In 1849 James White of Glasgow founded a company to manufacture mathematical, optical, industrial and scientific instruments, but ten years later he entered into a working relationship with William Thomson and over the ensuing half-century manufactured many instruments to Thomson's patent specifications. Eventually the company was reformed in the 1890s as Kelvin & White and later

William Thomson, Lord Kelvin

traded under the name of Kelvin, Bottomley & Baird, considerably diversifying its range of products and including electrical machinery and gadgets for the domestic market, notably the Kelvinator brand of refrigerators. In the 1920s the firm branched out into aircraft instruments but transferred this operation to a dedicated factory in the south of England, close to the major aircraft manufacturers. In 1947 the company merged with the London instrument makers, Henry Hughes & Son, to form Kelvin, Hughes, with a large factory on the Hillington Industrial Estate on the southwest side of Glasgow.

Lord Kelvin's example was in due course followed by two of his colleagues, Professor Barr and Professor Stroud who, responding to an announcement by the War Office in 1888, began working on a practical instrument for calculating the range for artillery. Their first range-finders were produced for them by Kelvin & White, but the demand for their instruments became so great that they decided to branch out and form their own company. In 1895 they began moonlighting with one man and a boy in a tiny workshop at the back of Byres Road. Business boomed with the outbreak of the Boer War and by 1900 Barr & Stroud had over a hundred men in their employment. Eventually they outgrew their workshops in Ashton Lane (now part of the re-aligned University Avenue) and moved out to a greenfield site at Anniesland where my father was employed as a precision toolmaker for many years. By the Second World War the company was employing over 1,550 people. Latterly the company diversified into all kinds of hydraulic, electrical, mechanical and electronic instruments in addition to the original range of optical equipment.

Beyond the figure of Lord Kelvin is the statue of Lord Lister, sculpted by G.H. Parkin and unveiled in 1924. Joseph Lister was born in Upton, Essex on 5 April 1827, the son of Joseph Jackson Lister, a pioneer of optics who invented the achromatic lens and perfected the compound microscope. His son trained at University College, London, and qualified as a physician. In 1853 he went to Edinburgh, became house surgeon to Professor Syme and married his daughter in 1856. The following year he became assistant surgeon at the Edinburgh Royal Infirmary and began lecturing on surgery as well as conducting research into the coagulation of blood and the infections that led to gangrene. He was appointed Professor of surgery at Glasgow University in 1860, but succeeded his father-in-law in the chair of clinical surgery at Edinburgh in 1869, so he was never actually one of the incumbents at Gilmorehill. During his Glasgow period, however, Lister made one of the greatest breakthroughs in surgery. At that period, the old Royal Infirmary at the top of the High Street near the Old College had a very bad track record for losing patients through post-operative infection. The public was convinced that some terrible pestilence lurked in the wards of the Infirmary, but it was Lister who suspected that these fatal infections were caused by airborne microbes. Consequently he developed a system of antiseptic surgery, using a carbolic spray of his own invention, as well as insisting on sterilised instruments and absolute cleanliness in the operating theatre. Lister published his seminal papers on the subject in 1867. Ten years later he returned to England as Professor of surgery at King's College, London. After a baronetcy (1883) and a peerage (1897), he joined his old colleague Kelvin as one of the first dozen members of the Order of Merit. He died at Walmer, Kent, in February 1912.

CHAPTER TEN

Kelvin Way to Pointhouse

Beyond the statues of Kelvin and Lister is the figure of the Psalmist, sculpted by Benno Schotz. He was born in Estonia in 1891 but left Tsarist Russia in 1911 to study engineering at the University of Darmstadt, Germany. In the aftermath of the 1905 Revolution, however, his elder brother had fled from Russia and settled in Glasgow. Many of these asylum seekers (as we would now call them) travelled from Hamburg or Rotterdam to Leith. In this case, Scotland appears to have been the intended destination, unlike many other Jews who thought they were landing in America, the land of opportunity, but were duped and dumped at Leith. Perhaps they could not afford the full transatlantic fare and came to Scotland as the next best thing. Benno only came to Scotland to visit his brother and obtain news of him, but soon enrolled at the Technical College and continued his engineering studies there. Incidentally, in Yiddish *Schotz* means a Scotsman, but this does not imply that Benno's family had Scottish blood. There were so many Scottish pedlars in eastern Europe by the seventeenth century that *Schotte* and *Szocz* had become synonymous with 'pedlar' in German and Polish, and there are numerous examples of local regulations aimed at controlling the movements of 'Scots, Jews and other vagabonds'. During the First World War Benno prudently anglicised his name to Shotts but later reverted to the German spelling of his name. In his adopted land, Benno qualified as an engineer in 1914 and went to work at John Brown's shipyard in Clydebank where he remained for nine years. At the same time he enrolled at the Glasgow School of Art under Fra Newbery studying art in evening classes before becoming established as one of Scotland's foremost portrait sculptors. His studio at Kirklee near the Botanic Gardens was a mecca for artists prior to his death in 1986. As the Psalms of David were at the core of worship in the Scots Kirk as in the Jewish faith, the choice of subject for this statue is singularly appropriate. Nearby is the little memorial to Dr Tom Honeyman (1891-1971); during his time as Director of the Museum and Art Gallery (1939-54) he did much to raise the artistic consciousness of his fellow citizens.

From the sculpture garden on the bank below the University, follow the riverbank footpath in a westerly direction. This affords the opportunity to view the Kelvin close to the water level, and it is even possible to scramble right down to the water's edge. It was here that I had that traumatic encounter with the bronze skull more than fifty years ago, and I chuckle at the memory every time I pass the spot. If I remember correctly, this is also the place where I first came across a strange and rather luxuriant plant which I afterwards learned was called Japanese Knotweed. Nobody knows how it got here, but in the period immediately after the Second World War it spread rapidly along the banks in the lower reaches of the Kelvin; so perhaps it began as a few seeds inadvertently brought ashore from a ship docked in the Clyde nearby. The high bank leading up to the University has been generously planted with rhododendrons and azaleas which are a riot of colour at the appropriate season.

Presently you come to the substantial remains of yet another weir which had a sluice on the opposite side and was still in use in connection with the aquatic activities at the Exhibitions of 1888-1911, although it would originally have been created to regulate the flow of water to one of the many mills hereabouts. A few metres farther on the path slopes down and runs along the water's edge. At this point there was at one time a footbridge, another legacy of the exhibition period, but it has long since disappeared, leaving only parts of the masonry rising from the river bed. Near this point, on the north bank, there was a chalybeate well, still marked on maps as late as 1861, but of which there now appears to be no trace. Past the western end of the Museum and Art Gallery on the opposite bank you come to the largest of the weirs across the Kelvin and still substantially intact. Farther down is a low-level freestone bridge of three arches, picturesquely festooned with ivy. It was the original Partick Bridge, erected about 1800 but closed to vehicular traffic since 1878 when the new bridge was constructed a few metres downstream. There are still gates in the railings, which apparently were opened in the depths of winter so that snow could be shovelled off the bridge straight into the river. Unlike Kelvinbridge, the old Dumbarton Road Bridge has been allowed to remain and it provides a convenient method of crossing to the bank on the south side. You should retrace your steps along this bank and examine this end of the weir, with the mill lade and sluice alongside, which effectively created a long narrow island. These weirs, sluices and lades are all that now remain as memorials to the milling carried on in this neighbourhood up to the 1870s.

At that period there was a road continuing in a straight line from Parkgrove Terrace, which eventually joined up with Old Dumbarton Road just before the bridge. This road has long since vanished, but it ran quite close to the driveway of Kelvingrove House and then straight past Clayslaps Flour Mills served by the first of the weirs and lades on this stretch of the river. The great weir dammed the water diverted into the long mill lade farther down which ran under the bridges to Bunhouse Flour Mills, and beyond that there was yet another weir with a lade which served the Slit Grain Mills at Thornbank. At least, that was the name by which this mill complex was known in the 1870s, but in fact it derived its name from an earlier use of the mills for slitting iron bars, the preliminary process involved in the manufacture of nails. In the 1790s, when iron-slitting was in progress, the Regent Mill (named in honour of the Prince of Wales at the time of the regency crisis of 1787) had no fewer than eight wheels, several operating the enormous hammers that pounded the iron pigs into strips and the others powering the machinery involved in the slitting. In an even earlier period this was the site of the Bishop's Grain Mills and the mill dam marked the highest point to which the ordinary spring tides flowed, unimpeded by any other obstructions downstream.

The creation of the Regent Mill dam in the late eighteenth century caused considerable anxiety to the fishermen on the Kelvin and their fears were articulated by the Revd Robert Rennie, in his account of Kilsyth parish for the *Old Statistical Account* (1790): 'Before the Regent Mill dam was erected over the Kelvin, salmon in spawning time came up as far as Kilsyth, and were to be found in every pool'. What the damming of the Kelvin to serve the mills higher up initiated, the discharge of industrial effluents by the bleachers, dyers and paper-makers completed, and within a few years the river was no longer inhabited by life of any kind, let alone salmon and trout. In *Notes and Reminiscences Relating to Partick* (1873), James Napier commented on the fact that the Slit Mill had recently converted to steam-power and, as a result, the mill lade was no longer used:

> 'For several months of the year,' he wrote, 'the bed of the River Kelvin, under the dam to the breast of the slit mills, lies as a receptacle for waste water, stagnating and creating a nuisance which has caused great expense to the burgh, it being obliged to carry a pipe sewer along the bed of the Kelvin, for the lower part of the town. The proprietor along the immediate banks of the Kelvin, not having taken action against the diversions of the waters of the river in time, have allowed the slit mill proprietors a prescriptive right.'

Regrettably, there were no ginger groups like FORK around in those bad old days to exercise constant vigilance in asserting people's rights.

The old bridge crosses the Kelvin at right angles, which explains why it appears to run almost due north and south, whereas the modern bridge runs almost east and west. During the westward expansion of Glasgow in the 1870s, the main road (Argyle Street) was re-aligned which explains why the modern bridge crosses the Kelvin at a wide angle. In the triangular space between the ends of the two bridges on the west bank was located the Lighting and Heating Pavilion at the 1901 Exhibition, demolished very soon after the event; but if you follow the driveway from the old bridge that leads up towards the University along the top of the ridge you pass the Old Men's Shelter (1935) and then come to a pair of mock-Tudor cottages which seem thoroughly out of place in this setting. They were, in fact, erected by Lever Brothers in connection with the 1901 Exhibition where they were billed as the Sunlight Cottages and were intended to show the enlightened attitude of the soap manufacturers in housing their workers at Port Sunlight. The cottages were designed for the Exhibition by James

Miller and, equipped with electric lighting and indoor plumbing, they were one of the sensations of the show. Afterwards they were presented by Lord Leverhulme to the City of Glasgow and stand on the original site overlooking the Kelvin to this day, certainly incongruous, ludicrous perhaps, but a mute testimonial to the benevolent despotism of *Bodach an-tSapuinn* (the old man of soap), as his tenants in Harris derisively named him a few years later, when he turned from soap to fish and made a misplaced but well-meaning attempt to revitalise his Hebridean estate. The little port of Leverburgh on the Sound of Harris (formerly Obbe) and the MacFisheries chain of fish shops were the only tangible legacy of this experiment in social engineering.

This is a convenient point at which to make the slight detour to the Glasgow Art Gallery and Museum, to give it its proper title of the present day. It has been known by variants such as Kelvingrove Museum and Art Gallery or Galleries, and no two maps ever seem to agree on the name. To most Glaswegians the building is known simply as the Art Galleries. This, the most exotic structure in Glasgow (although the former Templeton carpet factory replicating the Doge's Palace in Venice must come a pretty close second), consists of Locharbriggs sandstone from the Dumfries area. To appreciate the dazzling qualities of this bright red stone (which was cleaned to startling effect by Elder & Cannon in 1986-8) you have to view the Art Gallery on a cloudless day, when the deep rich colour contrasts vividly with the Mediterranean blue of the sky. If non-Glaswegian readers raise their eyebrows in scepticism, I hasten to add that it was this startling post-industrial sky colour which attracted me back to Glasgow after an absence of thirty years. Walk back from Partick Bridge and take the carriageway that runs off Argyle Street and approach the south entrance. Along the bank, there are several interesting monuments and memorials.

On the right is a tree whose plaque informs us that it was planted on behalf of a Greek lady, Panagioita B. Katsirea (1911-89) 'in her memory and out of her love to the people of Glasgow'. Opposite is the Hiroshima Tree planted on 6 August 1984 to commemorate the dropping of the first atomic bomb by Colonel Paul Tibbetts in his Flying Fortress *Enola Gay* (named after his Mom apparently). I believe that remorse for what he did drove Tibbetts insane, although the blame really lies with warmongers, politicians and the perversion of science. About eighty thousand people were killed at the time, though God alone knows what suffering was endured by countless others in the years since 6 August 1945. The sight of the Hiroshima plaque seems to add a touch of irony to the main memorial at this end of the park, the Cameronians War Memorial, sculpted by P. Lindsey Clark and erected in 1924 to commemorate the men of this historic infantry regiment who were killed in the First World War. Raised at Douglas, Lanarkshire in 1689 and named in memory of the extreme Covenanting sect led

The Glasgow Art Gallery and Museum at Kelvingrove, with the Kelvin in the foreground

by Richard Cameron, it later became the 26th Foot or the Scottish Rifles, but the original name was the most preferred. Having survived the onslaught of the Highlanders at Dunkeld in 1690, the regiment's baptism of fire, it went on to cover itself in glory in both world wars as well as many lesser conflicts, but eventually fell victim to War Office retrenchment and was disbanded in 1959. Most war memorials of the First World War are rather dreary and stereotypical, but this is one of the most imaginative and shows a Cameronian going 'over the top' with fixed bayonet, while a machine-gunner crouches behind his Lewis gun. Only one other war memorial ever moved me more, and that is the Vietnam Memorial in Washington DC. At the back of the Cameronian Memorial is a list of the battles in which this gallant regiment fought in the First World War. The original railings were removed as part of the Second World War drive for scrap metal, and in the immediate post-war period the memorial suffered at the hands of vandals, but it was subsequently restored and the railings replaced. Alongside is the Normandy Veterans' Association Monument which was unveiled on the fiftieth anniversary of D-Day and is inscribed 'to the eternal memory of our comrades who laid down their lives in the Battle of Normandy 6th June to 20th August 1944'.

Nearby is the Amnesty International Tree, planted in 1986 'to commemorate 25 years working for human rights' and beyond that is the plaque unveiled in 1988 to mark the fortieth anniversary of the massacre at Deir Yassin, Palestine, when the Jewish terrorist organisation Irgun Zvai Leumi destroyed an Arab village and thus triggered off a mass exodus of Arabs from northern Palestine. It was by far the worst atrocity perpetrated by the Jews in their War of Independence, and Deir Yassin has since become a festering sore in Arab-Israeli relations, although it pales into insignificance when compared with man's inhumanity to man in more recent times.

In the gardens in front of the south entrance there is a fascinating three-dimensional model of Glasgow's West End sculpted by Kathie Chambers, and well worth a close examination for the very realistic impression one gets of the actual terrain on which the City's most select suburbs were laid out. It also provides an excellent introduction to the Kelvin itself, and its windings around the district to the confluence with the Clyde can easily be traced. The only other monument in the surroundings of the Art Gallery is on the north side overlooking the Kelvin and consists of Michael Snowdon's fountain dedicated to the children of Glasgow. Very pretty when it was inaugurated in 1991, especially at night when the lights played on the cascades of water, it has, like virtually every other fountain in Glasgow, long since dried up, so that the vandals and graffiti artists can deface the column without getting their feet wet. The most recent of the public sculptures in Glasgow, it was created in the aftermath of the National Garden Festival of 1988, and 1990 when Glasgow was designated European cultural capital, and civic pride was at an all-time high.

As mentioned in a previous chapter, the Art Gallery and Museum was the outcome of the 1888 Exhibition whose handsome profit was doubled by public subscription and then topped up by the City Corporation. It was designed by Sir John William Simpson and E. J. Milner Allen, acting in conjunction with the Museum Committee established in 1886. The choice of an English firm of architects, however, provoked a storm of protest akin to that which had been unleashed when the commission to design the University went to George Gilbert Scott twenty years earlier. At least on this occasion Glasgow contractors and masons were employed to carry out the work. The original scheme envisaged a concert hall and an art college, but those parts of the project were dropped and then later realised in other parts of Glasgow. Work on the construction began in 1891 but was subject to interminable delays, and it was not until 1897 that the foundation stone could be laid. Thereafter the building proceeded smoothly and was completed just in time for the 1901 International Exhibition. During the Exhibition, the building was merely designated the Fine Arts Section and was not formally christened as the Kelvingrove Art Gallery and Museum until the following year.

The authors of the Glasgow volume in *The Buildings of Scotland* neatly describe the structure as 'Hispanic Baroque', the central block on the north front (which was intended to be the main entrance) being closely modelled on Santiago della Compostella at Obradoiro; but grafted on to this was an assortment of wings, towers, pavilions, flying buttresses and cupolas incorporating elements of every style and period imaginable. Not surprisingly, the design was severely criticised by Glasgow's architectural establishment at the time, but the people of Glasgow took it to their hearts, and it is arguably the City's most popular building for local as well as out-of-town visitors, and regarded by Glaswegians with great affection. In keeping with the profusion of diverse architectural features, the exterior of the building has been lavishly adorned with sculpture. Sir George Frampton sculpted the seated bronze statue of St Mungo surrounded by allegorical figures, which was erected outside the north entrance. Elsewhere symbolic sculpture has the British Colonies saluting the arms of Glasgow, Love teaching Harmony to the Arts, and the rather comical Industries of Glasgow at the Court of Mercury. Derwent Wood sculpted the allegories of Music, Architecture, Painting, and Sculpture that decorate the end pavilions, while Science was sculpted by William Birnie Rhind, Religion by Johann Keller, Literature by E.G. Bramwell and Commerce by S. Fabrucci. At one time there was also a figure of Victory above the north entrance, with Immortality and Fame atop the flanking towers, but they have mysteriously disappeared. There is also a vast amount of sculptural ornament elsewhere including the arms of all the Scottish counties and gilded names of outstanding painters, sculptors and architects. For many years the north entrance was kept locked, and only the south entrance fronting Argyle Street was used, especially after the gardens were landscaped and red sandstone terraces erected in 1913-14, with a re-alignment of the carriageways to create a more graceful sweep than in the original arrangement. In more recent years, however, the north entrance was restored to proper use, at about the time that the main hall (formerly used for the vast collection of ship models) was refurbished to create the present open space, flanked by cloakroom, cafeteria and souvenir shop.

The interior lives up to the expectations created by the exterior, but is constructed mainly of white Giffnock stone, much embellished with gilding, florid ornament and architectural sculpture. The huge main hall is surrounded by open galleries on three levels. The names of forty-six composers in rococo cartouches continue the theme of the exterior and is appropriate to a hall which is often used for organ recitals, but there are also sculptures honouring the first members of their professions: Pheidias the sculptor, Ictinus the architect and Apelles the painter. The insignia of Glasgow's fourteen trades also embellish the main hall, although in recent years some of these features are often obscured by gigantic wall-hangings. Off the main hall are various exhibition galleries. Firm favourites are the displays of arms and armour and the stuffed animals and birds which include a Great Auk and the figure of an elephant which formed part of a visiting circus in the late nineteenth century and which died during the Glasgow stint. It was skinned by a local taxidermist, but the huge carcase itself was buried on the banks of the Kelvin near Kelvinbridge; perhaps some day an archaeological dig will bring the bones to light and cause endless speculation as to how they got there.

In the upper galleries is Glasgow's incomparable collection of paintings and sculpture, the nucleus of which was presented to the City by Archibald McLellan and originally housed in the McLellan Galleries in Sauchiehall Street, but a judicious combination of donations, bequests and purchases over the intervening years has resulted in probably the finest and most comprehensive assemblage of European art, to be found anywhere outside the great national galleries such as the Tate and the Louvre. All periods, from the Middle Ages to the present day, are represented, although the strength lies in the nineteenth and early twentieth centuries, with the French Impressionists rivalling the works of the Glasgow Boys. This priceless collection reflects the immense wealth of the City in its industrial heyday.

The most controversial purchase was 'Christ of St John of the Cross' by Salvador Dali which the Corporation purchased shortly after the Second World War for a four-figure sum. This extravagance in a period of great austerity excited considerable adverse comment at the time, but with commendable sagacity the Corporation put the painting on display at Kelvingrove and charged the public a shilling a time to view it. Intrigued by the controversy in the local press, Glaswegians flocked to Kelvingrove in their thousands and within a few weeks the money outlaid on the painting had been recouped. When the Museum of Religion opened near the Cathedral, this painting was transferred thither, much to the annoyance of aficionados of Kelvingrove where it was for many years one of the chief attractions. The galleries on the ground floor include areas where temporary and travelling exhibitions are staged, notable examples in very recent years being devoted to the Dead Sea Scrolls and the island of St Kilda (evacuated in 1930).

West of the Kelvin Way Bridge, the Kelvin (which has so far been flowing in a roughly southerly direction), suddenly swings round in the broad curve at the base of Gilmorehill and for some distance pursues a westerly course before turning south again to join the Clyde. The area to the south and east of the Kelvin, bounded by Finnieston Street and Argyle Street, is schizophrenic or chameleon-like, for it has changed its name and its character many times. In the past it was known variously and rather vaguely as Sandyford or Kelvinhaugh, both names eminently descriptive of salient features such as the sandy ford in the lower reaches of the Kelvin on the track from Glasgow to Partick and all points west, or the low-lying land between the Kelvin and the Clyde which was prone to flooding. Other names associated with this area when it was very sparsely populated were Overnewton, from an estate of that name and later bestowed on

Overnewton Road and Overnewton Street. But the name which has survived the longest, and by which this district is now generally known, is Yorkhill. This was the name given to a mansion house erected about 1800 on a hill at the western end of the Overnewton estate. In 1813 Andrew Gilbert purchased the mansion and its grounds, together with adjoining land extending down to the Clyde, and gave the name Yorkhill to the whole area. During the landscaping of the grounds about the middle of the nineteenth century, workmen stumbled across a small hoard of Roman coins including a 'large brass' of Trajan (98-117) commemorating his conquest of Dacia in Hungary. Other artefacts unearthed about the same time gave rise to the assertion that Yorkhill had been a Roman signal station in the second century.

While the eastern parts of Overnewton lost their rural character in the last quarter of the nineteenth century, as the area was given over to closely packed streets of workers' tenements to serve the rapidly developing shipyards and engineering works along the Clyde, Yorkhill remained an oasis of country life. Alexander Stephen & Sons had their shipyard at Kelvinhaugh between 1859 and 1869 and built some of the greatest (and latest) of the clipper ships before they gave way to steam. Stephen moved downstream to Linthouse in 1870 and the Queen's Dock and Yorkhill Quay were constructed on the site. Even after the construction of Yorkhill Quay on the Clyde in 1868-70, and the inevitable spread of shipyards and machine shops, ropewalks and steam-powered cotton mills in succeeding years, Yorkhill remained as a large country house, with its wooded policies, parklands and formal gardens high above the surrounding district. By the early years of the twentieth century, Kelvinhaugh was one of the most congested districts in Glasgow and it consequently suffered when post-industrial decay set in. Most of these crowded tenements and run-down alleys were swept away in the 1960s when this part of the city was cleared to make way for the Clydeside Expressway.

In 1914 Yorkhill House and its grounds were acquired for the Royal Hospital for Sick Children, an impressive red sandstone structure with a crenellated tower reminiscent of Inverness Castle and just as bogus. In the 1960s it was demolished to make way for the present Sick Children's Hospital, with the Queen Mother maternity hospital alongside. Regrettably, although these hospitals were designed by different firms of architects, (Baxter, Clark & Paul and J.J. Gleave & Partners respectively), neither edifice is particularly distinguished. Architecturally the most interesting part of this area lies to the south, in the wharfs and warehouses of the Yorkhill Basin which was created in 1907 for the Clyde Navigation Trust. Actually there are two basins, known as the East and West, and they are chiefly memorable these days as the anchorage of the very few ships that venture this far upriver, notably sail training ships and such whimsies as the replica of Sir Francis Drake's *Golden Hind* which was tied up here for some time in 1996.

On the south side of the hospitals, the slopes have been laid out as a public park stretching between Ferry Road and Gilbert Street. At the eastern end stands the Territorial Drill Hall, formerly the Volunteer Headquarters erected by William Leiper in 1900-1. A large part of the costs was covered by Sir Thomas Lipton who was Honorary Colonel of the Lanarkshire Rifle Volunteers. In March 1901 he returned to Glasgow briefly to lay the foundation stone and was subsequently dined right royally by Colonel Drummond Young and the regimental officers, in recognition of his generous contribution. To the east, the former tenements have been cleared and are now occupied by office accommodation. On the north side of Kelvinhaugh Road is the Glasgow University Hall of Residence, built in 1988-9 to designs by Cooper Cronmar Architects, a pleasing confection in striped brick and painted timber, within easy walking distance of the University by way of Haugh Road which leads on to Kelvin Way.

Of the churches in this district, the only one which has survived in its original function is the Sandyford Church (now the Sandyford-Henderson Memorial Church) at the corner of Argyle Street and Kelvinhaugh Street. Work began in 1854 but the superintending architect, J.T. Emmett, died before it was finished and so the work was supervised by John Honeyman, who added some touches of his own, and it opened for worship in 1857. It was a Church of Scotland building from the outset, which explains the relatively enlightened attitude regarding the inclusion of stained-glass windows during the incumbency of the first minister, the Revd J.R. MacDuff, notably the splendid 'Raising of Lazarus with Saints Peter and Paul' executed by William Wailes in 1859. Henderson Memorial Church, erected in 1878 to a design by John Burnet, was a Free Church edifice. It became a Church of Scotland building in the 1920s and continued as a separate congregation until 1938 when it was accidentally burned down. Thereafter the two congregations joined forces. The church halls and manse survived the blaze and are still located in Lumsden Street. Nearby is the former Overnewton School, built in 1876-7 to a design by John Burnet, with crow-stepped gables and castellated towers suggesting Gothic influence. The school closed some years ago and was taken over as offices by the Social Work Department.

Just around the corner from Sandyford-Henderson Memorial Church is Corunna Street, running south from Argyle Street to St Vincent Crescent, a surprisingly elegant terrace commenced in 1849 by Alexander Kirkland and completed in 1855. Early maps of the area, soon after the terrace was laid out, indicate that there was a large park extending all the way down to the north bank of the Clyde, but first the shipyards and later the engineering works gradually encroached on this land, and finally a slice was taken by the Caledonian Railway for its line west to Partick. All that now remains is the relatively small bowling green. The Crescent continues eastwards along the northern section of Minerva Street which joins Argyle Street near the top of Finnieston Street.

North of the hospitals is Old Dumbarton Road which runs in a gentle westerly curve to join Ferry Road, so called because it terminated on the bank of the Clyde where there was at one time a vehicular ferry to Govan. On the north side of Old Dumbarton Road is the rear of the Kelvin Hall, one of Glasgow's great institutions. During the 1901 Exhibition this site, south of Dumbarton Road, was occupied by the great Machinery Hall with, at its south side, a convenient access to the Caledonian Railway station bringing excursionists from the City. It was a matter for regret that this structure was not preserved after the Exhibition and by the time that Glasgow had wakened up to the fact that a permanent exhibition hall for heavy engineering was desirable, the First World War had erupted. In 1920-1 a large exhibition hall was erected on this site and enjoyed a moderate success as a venue for the Heavy Industries Section of the British Industries Fair, but it burned down early in 1926. Plans were immediately drawn up to replace it with something bigger, better and more fireproof. The new Kelvin Hall, designed by the City Engineer, Thomas Somers, had a frontage on Dumbarton Road in the same Locharbriggs red sandstone as the Museum and Art Gallery across the road, the long, low main block being flanked by towers surmounted by bronze globes. The ferro-concrete roof by Considere Constructions, supported by twenty-two massive columns, covers an area of 15,885 square metres (171,000 sq. ft) – about the same area as Olympia in London and all on one level. In its heyday, the Kelvin Hall was the venue for the annual motor show and other industrial exhibitions, but in the depths of winter it changed character and was given over to the Circus, with a vast array of side-shows and funfair attractions. During the Second World War, the enormous interior was ideally suited to the manufacture of barrage balloons and it was rapidly transformed into the country's chief balloon factory. In the post-war period it returned to the usual fare of trade exhibitions and winter carnival, although it was also memorable as the venue for the Tell Scotland Crusade of the Revd Dr Billy Graham in the 1950s.

When it was superseded by the Scottish Exhibition and Conference Centre in 1984, the Kelvin Hall was converted over the ensuing four years to become a vast sports complex known as the Kelvin Hall International Sports Arena and accommodating the widest programme of sporting events including indoor athletics. As well as hosting contests at national and international level, it offers a comprehensive range of training facilities on a permanent basis. It was a happy decision to utilise a portion of the building at the side for the new Museum of Transport, with its entrance on Bunhouse Road. This museum had its genesis in the extraordinary collection of locomotives, tramcars, all forms of road transport, ship models and associated memorabilia which had at one time been housed across the way in Kelvingrove. In the 1960s the Corporation handed over the former tram depot on Albert Drive to provide a more adequate location, but in 1986 the ever-expanding collections crossed the Clyde again and are now

The Bishop's Mill, on the right, with the Kelvin Hall in the background

housed in the Kelvin Hall. The exhibits are rotated regularly, so the Museum is always worth a visit. Inside the entrance is George Wylie's whimsical bronze of the Tramcar in the Sky, and nearby stands the oldest pillar-box in Glasgow; mail posted therein gets a special rubber stamp to signify the fact. On the left side is Kelvin Street, a re-creation of a typical Glasgow street from the early twentieth century, complete with Lipton's Dairy and other shops, the Regal Cinema (in full working order), a sub-post office and even a Subway station (very realistic, although the pong of Archangel tar which greased the cables is lacking). To judge from the posters and cinema advertisements, this street has been frozen in time on 9 December 1938.

Naturally, the Museum has examples of the original subway carriages. Each train consisted of two cars, one for smokers and the other for non-smokers. Both my parents were heavy smokers but my sister and I detested the habit, and took great delight in pointing out to Mum and Dad the startling difference in the paintwork of the Subway carriages: one gleaming virginal white and the other heavily patinated with several shades of brown from beige to darkest sepia. If tobacco smoke did that to Corporation paintwork, we asked rhetorically, what must it be doing to your lungs? Smelly it may have been, but the much-loved old Subway was a great deal more reliable than its reincarnation of the 1980s, known to Glaswegians as the Clockwork Orange on account of the colour of its rolling stock. A recent three-stop trip from West Street to Buchanan Street took forty minutes. In the bad old days you could go for a 'hurl' round the entire circuit in under half an hour. When the service re-opened in 1980, the names of most of the previous stations had been retained, even if the stations themselves were altered out of all recognition; but, in the West End, Partick Cross had become Kelvinhall, while Merkland Street had metamorphosed into Partick – all rather confusing especially as Kelvinhall station is nowhere near the Kelvin Hall.

Partick Bridge was designed by the civil engineers R. Bell and D. Miller on behalf of the trustees of the Glasgow and Yoker Turnpike Roads and constructed by Hugh Kennedy between 1876 and 1878. It has a single cast-iron arch, with a side channel to cope with flash floods and topped by cast-iron parapets painted bright green with heraldic shields in the spandrels bearing the arms of Glasgow and Partick. Alongside, but downstream, is a gigantic steel tube supported by its own lattice-roof bridge of steel girders with red sandstone housing at either end. This was the pipe erected about 1873 to carry the main sewer to the pumping station on the Partick side, although the present lattice-girder bridge dates from 1904. Running down the east side from Partick Bridge is Bunhouse Road, fronting the Museum of Transport. It owes its unusual name to the fact that, in bygone times, there was a hostelry on the turnpike road known as the Bun and Yill (ale) House. The Bunhouse Grounds, extending to six and a half acres, were acquired by the City at the end of the nineteenth century and provided the site on which the Kelvin Hall now stands. The Bunhouse Flour Mills stood on the east bank of the Kelvin, roughly where the car park for the Museum of Transport is located. A line of the Caledonian Railway at one time ran westwards under Argyle Street and emerged into daylight at the west end of Yorkhill where it crossed the river by an iron plate-girder bridge erected in 1896, and soon afterwards joined up with the Clyde line at Partick station. After 1922 this line was operated by the London, Midland and Scottish Railway, hence the name LMS Bridge by which this disused railway bridge is now known. It is still passable on foot but much more could be done to make it a viable amenity for river ramblers. This stretch of the Kelvin could hardly be more urban, and yet kingfishers have been seen skimming the waters and not so long ago it was the haunt of an otter, until the wretched animal was knocked down while trying to cross the road.

At the south end of Bunhouse Road, where it joins Old Dumbarton Road, there was for centuries the original Partick Bridge. A ford of large stepping stones was superseded by a stone bridge in 1577, by far the oldest bridge in this part of Glasgow, for the convenience of the Bishop commuting between the Cathedral and his Palace on the west bank. By all accounts it was a very solid construction, with narrow arches of massive masonry. It was demolished as recently as 1896, but its passing was not mourned at the time, because it was simultaneously replaced by the Benalder Street Bridge built along the same line. This bridge, together with the Slit Mill dam and the railway bridge, forms a gigantic

N shape criss-crossing the Kelvin, and from the east side of the Benalder Street Bridge you get the best view of the former dam, now generally known as the Bishop's Weir, and the railway bridge beyond. Continuing southwards along Ferry Road, past the bluff of Yorkhill with the Queen Mother Hospital above, there is an impressive new development of luxury housing on the right, overlooking the river. Not so long ago, it was possible to walk along the top of the river bank, although it was heavily overgrown with brambles, but now the site has been cleared, fenced in and bulldozed to make way for the Riverbank Estate. As some consolation, however, the grounds around the new houses have been nicely landscaped with a railed viewing platform at the end.

The Kelvin joins the Clyde: Govan shipyards on the left, with Meadowside on the right

South of the Expressway is that part of the riverbank known as Pointhouse, from the ferryman's cottage which formerly stood at the Point where the Kelvin meets the Clyde. Judging by early descriptions, as well as old paintings and engravings, the Clyde was quite wide at this point, but very shallow. In some parts there was only fifteen inches of water at low spring tides so that it was possible to cross the Clyde on foot. The channel was occupied by several islands, such as the Sand Inch, King's Inch, Buck Inch and White Inch and innumerable sandbars, all of which vanished when the Clyde was deepened from the late eighteenth century onwards. As late as the 1860s the ferry from the Point across the Clyde to Govan was operated by open rowing boats, but when one of these boats capsized in 1861 with the loss of seven lives, and another sank near

Anderston three years later with the loss of nineteen lives, the Clyde Navigation Trust installed a chain-driven steam ferry capable of transporting carriages and wagons as well as pedestrians. This was succeeded by a tall variable-level vehicular ferry in 1912 which made a modest charge for conveying cars and lorries across the river. A free service for pedestrians was operated by a small steamboat that ran alongside. For Southsiders a trip on the little Govan ferry to Pointhouse was the start of many a Sunday afternoon excursion to the Art Gallery and Kelvingrove Park. This service ceased on 22 January 1966, but vestiges of the timber uprights, steps and winding gear can still be seen.

Thomas B. Seath founded the Pointhouse Shipyard about 1845, specialising in relatively small vessels which were launched from the east bank of the Kelvin. In 1862 Seath moved his operations upstream to Dalmarnock and sold the Pointhouse yard to Anthony and John Inglis who had previously operated an engine works in Anderston. They expanded the shipyard, and in 1865 cut a slip dock on the east bank of the Kelvin; part of the retaining timbers are still evident although this part of the bank is now heavily overgrown. This firm's speciality was ship's engines and boilers and this aspect of their operations survived till the 1960s, long after shipbuilding had been discontinued. The Pointhouse yard constructed many of the Clyde steamers, including the *Waverley* of 1899 which served as a minesweeper in the First World War and was sunk in May 1940 while evacuating the British Expeditionary Force from Dunkirk. Her replacement, launched in 1946, is now the world's last surviving sea-going paddle-steamer, still a splendid sight on the river as she heads from her berth at Lancefield Quay for a trip 'doon the watter'.

Ferry Road passes under the Clydeside Expressway, from which a slip road at a roundabout gives access from the motorway to the Yorkhill Basin whose warehouses now accommodate Glasgow's largest collection of antique and second-hand furniture showrooms, a real browser's paradise. There is a low-level road bridge with sidewalks giving pedestrian access to the west bank. This is the last of the Kelvin's bridges, if we discount the structure high above our heads that carries the Clydeside Expressway, and the railway bridge alongside carrying the line from Glasgow Central, via Anderston and the Exhibition Centre, to Partick and all points west.

On the corner of this low-level bridge and Ferry Road is a modest monument which signifies that this is the start of the Kelvin Walkway which follows the track through the parks and sticks to the river whenever it can, all the way to the canal basin at Maryhill. It seems somehow symbolic that the Walkway starts here, and not farther south at the confluence of the Kelvin and the Clyde, for it reflects the rather half-baked nature of the Walkway. I long for the day when it will be possible to walk the full extent of the urban Kelvin along one if not both banks, and a good start with realising this ambition would be to clear some of

the jungle that now makes the path to the Point so hazardous. The true aficionado of the Kelvin and protector of its wildlife, however, would argue that
this stretch of the riverbank should be left as it is. A determined rambler can still
traverse it, whereas to clean it up and lay a proper footpath with trim lawns and
neat shrubbery would destroy the habitat. Perhaps some middle ground can be
found between the opposing arguments. The area in the immediate vicinity of
the main road has been attractively landscaped and to continue this along the east
bank of the river would surely not disturb the wildlife.

As it is, once you pass the end of the cobblestones which marked the site of
the former Inglis slip dock the path can be very tricky as a result of the decay of
the timbers forming the retaining wall, resulting in subsidence and severe erosion
of the riverbank, but with care once you negotiate this treacherous stretch, the
rest is plain sailing. What was once a bustling shipyard is now a wilderness backing on to the warehouses lining the West Basin. Not too many decades ago Ferry
Road turned sharp right at the bank of the Clyde and continued about a hundred
metres downstream to the Point where the ferry ran across the river to Water
Row in Govan. Indeed, from this vantage point, where the Kelvin joins its big
brother, you get the best view of Govan. Gone are the cranes and scaffolding of
countless shipyards and factories. Instead, Govan has been redeveloped, with
low-rise mixed housing and lots of trees, above which the spire of Govan's old
parish church rises serenely, as it has done for hundreds of years.

Richardson's map of 1795 shows a double line of trees running along the
east bank of the Kelvin to the Pointhouse where the ferryman resided, and there
are several paintings and engravings of the early nineteenth century which show
how rural this district once was. In post-industrial decay, Nature has reclaimed
this once-important hub of the river traffic. Self-sown trees vie with the beautiful but deadly Giant Hogweed whose trunks are as thick as a man's thigh and
standing ten metres tall. There is a controversy about whether intruders such as
Giant Hogweed, Japanese Knotweed and Himalayan Balsam should be ruthlessly
extirpated or left to assimilate with native plants. For years the former argument
held sway, but now ecologists are coming round to the view that Nature knows
best and will find the right level of peaceful co-existence. They point out that
such invasive monsters create ideal conditions in which many other plants can
shelter and thrive, and, in turn, support a very varied fauna of birds, insects and
small mammals. Personally, I believe in leaving Nature to its own devices, and am
much more concerned about controlling the intrusion of Man. Beholding the
monstrous soup of decaying, putrescent rubbish intermingled with all manner of
plastic containers and old supermarket trolleys that clutter the little coves at the
mouth of the Kelvin where the scour of the tide and current does not reach, I
rail against those thoughtless individuals who use the river as a rubbish dump. Of
course, the Kelvin and the Clyde are infinitely cleaner than they were when I was

a boy, as the presence of thirty-seven varieties of fish, from minnows to salmon, proves; but we need to be constantly vigilant for any misuse, as recent disturbing reports of the discharge of heavy-metal effluent affecting the sexual balance of fish indicate. At least the east bank of the Kelvin is passable right down to the Point – which is, unfortunately, more than can be said for the opposite bank, with its monstrous heap of wrecked cars and rusting scrap metal, now the worst eyesore on the entire course of the river.

CHAPTER ELEVEN

Partick

The area west of the lowest reach of the Kelvin is Partick. At the 1931 census it had a population of almost seventy thousand, which, had it been a separate town, would have placed it quite far up the Scottish list, but it lost its separate identity in 1912 when, along with Govan, it was absorbed by the City of Glasgow. The old saying that Glasgow made the Clyde and the Clyde made Glasgow always had a hollow ring to the good citizens of these burghs because, they argued, the biggest vessel ever made in Glasgow was a rowing-boat. It was the bustling yards of Govan and Partick which made the Clyde the world's leading shipbuilding centre.

Partick's rise to industrial fame was, however, relatively short-lived. The map of 1795 shows 'Partik' as a mere cluster of houses on the west bank of the Kelvin at the end of the bridge carrying the medieval packway west from Glasgow to Dumbarton. According to monastic tradition, Pertnech was the seat of Rydderch, King of Strathclyde and his consort Queen Languoreth. She it was who indirectly left her mark on Glasgow's coat of arms, alluding to one of the miracles of St. Mungo, or Kentigern as he was originally known. The King had given her a fine ring, but the Queen was foolish enough to bestow it on a young courtier with whom she was infatuated. In one version of the story the King, having learned of the affair, confronted the courtier, whom he slew, ripped the ring from the corpse's finger and in a fit of rage tossed it into the river. When he calmed down he went to Languoreth and demanded to see the ring, which he had given her. The Queen managed to fob him off with some tale, but immediately went to Mungo, her priest, and confessed her sins. Mungo granted her absolution and when she asked in desperation what she should do, he sent one of his acolytes to catch a salmon and bring it to him. On cutting open the fish Mungo found the ring in its stomach. He handed it to the Queen who slipped it back on to her finger and thus confounded her jealous husband. In this manner the salmon, with the ring in its mouth, came to appear on the civic arms.

Of course, this tale first appeared in the late twelfth-century biography of St Kentigern by the monk Jocelyn of Furness, so we cannot be a hundred per cent certain that the facts are as stated, but why let the bare facts get in the way of a good story? Apart from monastic fables, Partick first appears in written records in 1136 when that Sair Sanct for the Crown, David I, granted the lands of Perdeyc to the church of Glasgow at the time when it was being solemnly dedicated to St. Mungo or Kentigern. In return, the Archdeacon of Glasgow had to pay an annual rent of one silver mark, though later on this was waived and the lands of Partick were held of the King 'in pure alms'. Eventually the lands in Partick, as well as

Govan across the Clyde and other grants to the Church in the time of King William the Lyon, were combined to form the district known as the Barony and Regality and transferred from the Archdeacon to the Bishop, successive prelates administering their territory with all the power of a feudal lord. It was from his stronghold at Partick Castle that Archbishop James Beaton left for France in 1567, taking with him all the valuables of the Archdiocese as well as the University.

Following the Reformation in 1560, the lands enjoyed by the Church reverted to the Crown and thereafter the boundaries of civil administration were redrawn. Because of the close connection between Govan and Partick which had been simultaneously granted by David I to the Church, however, Partick was regarded as part of Govan parish, and thus Renfrewshire (to which Govan belonged) was extended north of the Clyde. Interestingly enough, Govan parish also included a few acres at Pointhouse on the east bank of the Kelvin and this, though in Govan parish, was regarded as part of Lanarkshire. Despite this anomaly, the Kelvin was regarded as the traditional boundary between the parishes of Glasgow and Govan and explains why Partick developed quite separately from Glasgow until its absorption in 1912.

The northern boundary of Partick, however, was an artificial one, and therefore it varied from time to time. According to Richardson's map of 1795, the parish of Govan ran all the way along the west bank of the Kelvin as far as the aqueduct and then followed the Forth and Clyde Canal westwards as far as the Bearsden Road, then south along Crow Road but veering west to encompass Whiteinch. In 1852, when Partick was created a burgh, its limits were much more narrowly defined. The burgh boundary ran from Partick Bridge up the east side of Church Street, then along University Avenue and down Ashton Road to Byres Road, then west along Ruthven Lane. It turned left to run along Victoria Terrace (now Victoria Crescent Road) and Prince Albert Road, then along the line of present-day Clarence Drive (still undeveloped farm land at the time) as far as the Stobcross Railway line which it followed in a northerly direction, skirting the Royal Lunatic Asylum (Gartnavel) then down the east side of Crow Road and Balshagray Avenue to Ferryden on the north bank of the Clyde. The old burgh boundaries, in fact, virtually coincide with the G11 postcode area of the present time, although it also included a generous slice of Dowanhill. When Partick became a parliamentary constituency, the northern boundary was much simpler and ran along Highburgh Road, then down Clarence Drive. Broadly speaking, if Hillhead and Dowanhill were middle-class, mainly inhabited by professional men and their families, Partick was essentially working-class, its crowded tenements thrown up in the late nineteenth century to accommodate the vast numbers of shipyard workers, dockers and others whose livelihood depended on the Clyde and the Kelvin. Partickhill and Broomhill in the north of the burgh, however, developed as 'select' suburbs at the turn of the century.

For seven centuries after the grant by King David, Partick remained a small village, surrounded by rolling country. To the south lay the lands of Meadowside, as good a description as any for the fairly level ground that sloped gently down to the confluence of the Kelvin and Clyde. Partick owed its existence to its ecclesiastical connections. It next appears as 'Perthec' in a disposition of 1227 drawn up there in connection with a promise by the Lord of Luss on Loch Lomondside to supply timber for the repair of the church of Glasgow. Probably not long after the original grant by King David the clergy of Glasgow erected a corn-mill on the west bank of the river on the east side of Partick Bridge Street, the cul-de-sac which became truncated when Old Partick Bridge was demolished in 1896. This is, at the present time, the site of Bishop Mill, a luxury apartment block created in 1987 by converting flour-mills which in fact go back no earlier than 1839 when they were erected for William Wilson. The elaborate wheatsheaf ornaments on the gable ends presumably date from that period. To reinforce the historic importance of the building, however, one of the large grindstones has been incorporated into the surrounding gardens. Wheatsheaf finials apart, however, this is a rather grim building which cannot disguise its industrial origins. Old maps indicate a mill on the riverbank near the weir, which experts aver contains masonry of considerable antiquity and probably predates the old bridge.

Even if nothing has survived of the medieval mill, its importance is well-attested in documents. The bishopric of Glasgow had exclusive rights to the milling of grain in Partick right up to the Reformation of 1560 and this was an extremely valuable perquisite. After the Reformation, however, the Bishop's Mill passed to the Crown and in 1573 King James VI gave it to Thomas Crawford of Jordanhill in recognition of the fact that he had captured Dumbarton Castle from rebels two years earlier. Crawford subsequently figures in the records of the University to whom he made a gift of 'sixteen bolls of good and sufficient oatmeal' to sustain a poor student for a whole year. Interestingly the Crawford Bursary still exists, although it was commuted to a cash payment in 1890.

In 1608 the Town Council of Glasgow, teetering on the verge of bankruptcy, persuaded the then Archbishop to let them have control of the Partick Mill. He then leased it to them for nine or ten years in exchange for a nominal rent amounting to fifty bolls of malt yearly. The Council used this in order to reassert the law of thirlage whereby the citizens were obliged to bring their grain thither to be ground. As the brewers were likewise forced to obtain their malt there, the town's finances quickly recovered as a result, despite the fact that the Baxters Incorporation was exempted from this regulation and continued to grind 'quheit and rye in thair awin mylnis'. The Council later leased the mill for 4,400 merks (£244 sterling) per annum to James King who got into bother for misusing the mill, unhygenically stabling his horse there. He was also censured for exceeding the privilege of sustaining 'his knave upon his bonok' whereby a miller was allowed one knave or assistant, who was entitled to a ripp of corn from each sack brought for milling. King not only employed two 'knaves', contrary to rule, but also gave them 'the run of their teeth' without proper supervision. Thereafter Partick Mill, according to a report of 1660, was of little profit on ordinary occasions, 'but verie stedable to the toune in tyme of ane drouth and frost'. The system known as thirlage, by which the tenants of an estate had to bring their grain to the laird's mill for grinding, was open to abuse. It was abolished by Act of Parliament in 1799 and this opened the grinding of corn to healthy competition.

According to Robert Renwick in his *Glasgow Memorials* (1907), the sale of Partick Mill to the Slit Mill across the river in 1809 was precipitated by the vast improvement in the flow of the Molendinar whose mills, being much more convenient to the town, were quite sufficient to Glasgow's purposes and therefore the Kelvin mills were surplus to requirements. This building burned down in 1836 and was replaced by the present structure three years later. This reverted to the original function as a flour-mill, switching to a steam turbine in the 1870s and latterly being electrically operated.

In nearby Scotstounmill Road stand the Scotstoun Flour Mills, the last flour-mill operating in the district and now part of the Rank Hovis organisation. The oldest part of this complex is the building on Thurso Street, erected in 1909 to a design by J.W. & J. Laird and distinguished by its red-brick tower with crenellated battlements in the best Baronial tradition. This structure is now dwarfed by the vast factory buildings of more recent years. This mill derives its name from John White of Scotstoun (a district farther down the Clyde) who acquired it about 1847 and considerably extended his premises over the ensuing half-century. The White family played a very prominent part in the development of Partick, John being Provost in 1857-60 and his son John holding office in 1905-8. Thus the Whites, father and son, were the second and the second last of the chief magistrates of the burgh during the sixty years of its existence (1852-1912) and between them also served for fifty-one years on the burgh council. The memory of this public-spirited pair is perpetuated in White Street. Just downstream from Scotstoun Mills there was a modest plant known as the Wee Mill which apparently continued to function by water-power. This appears to be the mill which was granted to the Baxters Incorporation of Glasgow in 1569 as a reward for their services against Mary Queen of Scots at the battle of Langside in 1567. Close by was the Partick Waulk Mill which dated back at least as far as 1517 when it was leased to Donald Lyon and referred to in the document as 'the new walk-myll of Partik'. This mill, which served to finish cloth, passed in 1554 to Donald's son Archibald who then converted it into a corn-mill, 'on condition that the thirlage of Partick Mill should not be prejudiced, and that the lessee should grind such wheat as was required for the bishop's house free of multure'. Lyon's Mill was sold off to the Incorporation of Bakers in 1771 and they continued to operate it until 1874 when the City purchased it for incorporation in Kelvingrove Park.

Although Partick was later to attain importance as a shipbuilding centre it was previously a seaport – a very modest one, to be sure, especially when compared with its neighbours Port Glasgow and Greenock. The records of the Customs House reveal that, in 1800, 98 ships passed through Port Glasgow, compared with 556 ships at Greenock; but Partick, the only other Clyde port listed, mustered six ships with a total tonnage of only 262. This sounds quite laughable, until it is remembered that the upper Clyde was shallow and navigable only to small vessels with little draught. Not until John Golborne began his great work of dredging the Clyde and virtually canalising it could ships of any size get up as far as Glasgow. The port of Partick was, in fact, the mouth of the Kelvin which had low wooden jetties on both Meadowside and Pointhouse banks.

In 1795 the only other settlement in the parish dignified by the name of village was Byres, a cluster of cottages around what is now Partick Cross at the foot of Byres Road. The name alludes to the stables where the bishops of Glasgow and their associates kept their horses. In olden times the clerics rode north along this track, then turned right where it joined Dobbie's Loan (now University Avenue) and continued eastwards along this ancient road into Glasgow. Dobbie's Loan still exists, and frequently figures in the traffic reports on national radio on account of the congestion on that arterial thoroughfare, but the present-day Dobbie's Loan is no more than a short stretch of road north of the city centre.

No trace of the Bishop's Castle now remains. After the flight of Archbishop Beaton, it seems to have been uninhabited and fell into disrepair. At the beginning of the seventeenth century the site was acquired by George Hutcheson, who built an impressive structure in the standard tower-house style, complete with crow-stepped gables, and this came to be known as Partick Castle. It was designed and erected by William Millar of Kilwinning, a town which, since the Middle Ages, had been renowned for its mason-architects (and also as the birthplace of the Masonic movement). The builder's contract has been preserved and stipulated a house 11 metres (33 ft) high, with the kitchen, cellars, pantry and girnal (grain store) on the basement and ground floor levels, a grand hall on the first floor and bedrooms on the upper floor, connected by a turnpike stair 3 metres wide. James Napier's *Notes and Reminiscences Relating to Partick* (1873) are rather vague concerning the later history of Partick Castle, although by 1770 it was inhabited by 'common tradespeople' who let out the first floor as a dance hall, probably not unlike Morton's Ballroom in Mauchline where Robert Burns, in the best Scottish tradition, met his future wife, Jean Armour. By the early nineteenth century, however, the Castle was no longer in use and Andrew MacGeorge's charming sketch of 1828 shows it as a roofless ruin. It provided a handy source

Engraving of Partick Castle, by Andrew MacGeorge

of masonry when Merklands farmhouse was built some way to the southwest, but it too has long since vanished from the scene. After flour-milling, this part of Partick was the first to become industrialised, Meadowside becoming a bleachfield in the 1770s, then a calico printworks at the beginning of the nineteenth century and later a chemical bleach and dyeworks whose factories were erected in 1824. The Castlebank Laundry took its name from the castle site and, in turn, gave its name to Castlebank Street. This old-established business has also vanished, although its buildings, with their tall chimney, still exist and now form part of the Castlebank Vehicle Storage and Recovery Company whose graveyard of wrecked cars lines the lower reach of the Kelvin. On the opposite side of Castlebank Street the Lancefield Spinning Company established a steam-powered textile mill which, for a brief period, was the main employer of labour in the village. Napier records how the company employed a drummer to rouse the workers at five o'clock each workday morning, and then sent round a bugler half an hour later to catch the sluggards.

With the development of textiles and related industries, the village of Partick began to expand in the early years of the nineteenth century. By 1829, James Napier estimated that the village consisted of 247 families, totalling 1,235 men, women and children. Starting from the west side of the Old Partick Bridge, the original roadway ran north along what is now Benalder Street to Partick Cross and thence up Byres Road. Just across the bridge, on the left, was the Knowe Brae which ran northwest to join the Meadow Road (later Castlebank Street). Parallel to it were two other tracks known as the Horse Brae and the Kiln

Brae. East from the top of Knowe Brae ran Well Street to Partick Cross. At the top of the Kiln Brae, north of Meadow Road, was the Goat. This thoroughfare had nothing to do with goats, but was a phonetic spelling of gott, an old Scots word for a drainage ditch and which, in this case, was the open sewer which ran down the east side of the street towards the Kelvin. By the time that proper streets were being laid out this insalubrious thoroughfare became Kelvin Street and later Keith Street. At the north end of this street was the Cross Loan, where it crossed over the main road from Glasgow to Dumbarton, and this is now the foot of Hyndland Street. Until the middle of the nineteenth century, the town of Partick was contained within the triangle formed by what is now Dumbarton Road, the Kelvin and the Clyde. The villagers drew water from Cooper's Well or the nearby Brewster Burn which ran down the side of Well Street (now Cooperswell Street).

Partick has had a long connection with the Quakers and now boasts the only Quaker burial ground in Scotland, although there were at one time Quaker cemeteries in Chapelton and Lesmahagow, both long gone. The Society of Friends is thought to have had a meeting-house in Glasgow during the Commonwealth period, but, like other non-conformists, they were increasingly persecuted following the Restoration in 1660 and by the 1680s were suffering for their beliefs almost as grievously as the Covenanters. After the Revolution of 1689 they were given liberty to worship in their own way, and in the ensuing decades the congregation in Glasgow rose rapidly. Even so, there was still a great deal of prejudice against the Quakers and they were not permitted to bury their dead in the parish kirkyards. At the beginning of the eighteenth century land at the Brigend of Partick belonged to John Purdon whose wife Margaret was a Quaker. When she died in 1711 Purdon got around the burial problem by giving a piece of his land to the Quakers for a cemetery, 'Quaker Meg' being the first person interred there. The small burial ground in Keith Street has been preserved, although it was last used for burials in December 1857. Even when they were no longer discriminated against, the Quakers continued to be regarded by the local people with awe, and there arose the belief that Quaker Meg's ghost haunted the burial ground. The decision to terminate burials there was precipitated by the fact that a Quaker funeral was regarded as a public spectacle. It is deplorable to recall that this invariably brought out a large throng of villagers, mostly women and children, who clambered on to the wall of the cemetery to watch the proceedings. Their loud comments and jokes, accompanied with much swearing, caused great distress to the peaceable Quakers who felt that they had no alternative but to close the cemetery. Thereafter, their dead were buried in the City's Necropolis. Considering the enormous development that took place in Partick in the second half of the nineteenth century (and the fact that the other Quaker cemetery, dating from 1733, in North Albion Street, has completely vanished) it is miraculous that the Quaker Burial Ground in Partick should have survived, and today it is an attraction, if not to tourists in general, certainly to local historians and genealogists. Although it is in the care of the Parks Department, it is heartening to note that its flowerbeds are tended by some of the residents of Keith Court, perhaps subconsciously making amends for the profanity of 150 years ago. Purdon Street (which actually features in one of Emma Blair's romances) was named in honour of the Quakers' benefactor.

The only building of note in the village was Burnbank House which stood in its own grounds atop the hillock between Well Street and Bridge Street and is believed to have been the residence of the mill manager. Inevitably, Partick had a number of taverns from the earliest times. James Napier records that an inn with a stone above the lintel dated 1619 was still standing in Castlebank Street. The tavern known as the Ark was a substantial stone building with crow-stepped gables, picturesquely perched on the riverbank just to the left of the old bridge. It was a sufficiently kenspeckle landmark for William Simpson to include a sketch of it in his *Glasgow in the Forties*, the picture being doubly interesting for the recently erected Bishop Mill in the background. Napier also recalls the Old Bridge Inn run by a Mrs Craig and the Bun and Yill House whose landlord was a Mr McTyre. These establishments specialised in roast duck (from the birds that flocked to Partick to feed off spilled grain from the mills) and attracted a large and appreciative clientele from Glasgow, especially at the weekends. At the western end of the village was the hostelry known as Granny Gibb's Cottage from the fact that it was managed by a widow named Granny Gibb and her two daughters, known facetiously to the cattle-drovers who frequented it as Mother Gibb and Auntie Gibb. It was one of the last thatched structures in Partick at the time it was demolished in 1894.

Crow Road (and its continuation south along what is now Balshagray Avenue) was one of the ancient drove roads down which came the Highland cattlemen taking their beasts on Saturdays to the Glasgow meat market, Meadowside being a popular grazing ground *en route*. Overnight, while the sheep and cattle grazed in the fields at the back of the cottage, the Highlanders, up to a dozen at a time, slept in Granny Gibb's windowless loft, arguably the roughest accommodation in the entire Glasgow area. The Glasgow butchers would drive out early on Sunday mornings to inspect the animals. The cattle-dealers and drovers salved their Sabbatarian consciences by peppering their business deals with a set formula. 'If it were not the Sabbath, how much would you be asking for that beast, Donald?' a butcher would ask, and Donald, in reply, would say, 'If it were not the Sabbath, I would be wanting...' Why this extraordinary performance was not delayed till Monday is explained by the fact that there were no tolls on the roads and bridges on Sundays, and so the dealers could take the beasts into town free of charge.

Granny Gibb died in 1851 and, as luck would have it, the day of her funeral was the very day that the Duke of Atholl was scheduled to lay the foundation stone of the Victoria Bridge at Stockwell Street. The minister of Govan parish was in a quandary, as he had an invitation to the ceremony as well as the civic banquet that followed. In the end he deputed his assistant to handle the obsequies for Granny Gibb and, salving his conscience that he would be at the graveside in spirit if not body, he went off to the civic function. Granny Gibb was a very popular figure in Partick and there was a huge turnout for her funeral. Among the mourners was a band of Freemasons in full regalia who, having paid their last respects, promptly headed off to Glasgow and gatecrashed the banquet, the stewards mistaking them for some of the official party just arrived from the foundation-stone ceremony.

Meadowside was, for a time, the estate of the McLehose family whose ne'er-do-well son James married pretty little Agnes Craig but later ran off to Jamaica abandoning poor Nancy and her sons. She might have been consigned to oblivion had it not been for her encounter with Robert Burns and the passionate Clarinda-Sylvander correspondence that ensued. In the eighteenth century the Craigs were near neighbours, Nancy's father, an eminent Glasgow surgeon, having his country house at Overnewton on the eastern side of the Kelvin. It is not recorded when or where James McLehose and Nancy Craig first met, but Andrew Craig did not like the cut of his jib and eventually forbade James the house. Nothing if not resourceful, James discovered that Nancy was about to take a trip to Edinburgh and not only managed to board the same stagecoach but bought up all the other tickets, so that they had the carriage to themselves. Teenage Nancy was compromised as a result and, despite the misgivings of her father and uncle (later a Court of Session judge with the title of Lord Craig), Nancy was wed at the age of seventeen.

After the erection of the Dumbarton Road bridge in 1800 the village began to expand along the south side of this road, although there were nursery gardens between the west end of the bridge and the riverbank until the late nineteenth century. On the north side, however, the ground was feued off to some of Glasgow's new rich, who erected their mansions there. Dowanvale, Dowanside and Dowanhill House would later be remembered in Dowanvale Terrace (White Street), Dowanside Road and Dowanhill Street, while Hillside House gave its name to Hillside Gardens off Turnberry Road and North Gardner Street. Rosevale, Stewartville and Muirpark have also given their names to streets, the last named having been for many years the residence of the paper-maker Edward Collins before he moved to Kelvindale House.

The first *Statistical Account of Scotland*, published in the 1790s, contains conflicting opinions about the effects of the recently concluded American War of

Independence. While the minister of Port Glasgow considered that the war had caused the stagnation in trade and economic depression, his counterpart in Greenock took a much more positive view, shrewdly pointing out that since Scotland was cut off from the shipyards of Maine and Massachusetts it had been forced to develop an indigenous shipbuilding industry. Very few vessels were built on the Clyde before 1780 but after that date the demand for shipping resulted in shipyards in the Clyde ports. This development more or less coincided with the advent of steam navigation, beginning with the experiments of Patrick Miller and William Symington in 1788 on Dalswinton Loch, Dumfriesshire, and continued by Symington the following year when he put the first steamboat on the Forth and Clyde Canal. Although the latter experiment was unsuccessful, Symington persevered and in 1802 launched the stern-wheel steamboat *Charlotte Dundas* which towed two heavily laden barges nineteen miles in six hours. As the wash from the vessel seemed likely to erode the canal banks, this interesting venture was soon abandoned. Henry Bell, who had witnessed the 1802 trials, had himself taken a keen interest in the possibilities of steamships as far back as 1786, and by 1812 he saw his dream come true, with the launching of the Comet at Port Glasgow. Bell must have been a remarkable man, virtually bankrupting himself in pursuit of his magnificent obsession and having to put up with the jeers and ridicule of his peers. But when his steamboat took to the water no one realised how this ridiculous little paddle-boat would revolutionise the world.

To be sure, there were others engaged in the same pursuit, and the American-Scot Robert Fulton got his *Clermont* on the Hudson River five years earlier, having worked with Symington and obtained a steam engine from Matthew Boulton and James Watt, but the *Comet* was the first practical steamer in service anywhere in Europe. The wooden vessel was constructed by Woods of Port Glasgow and engined by John Robertson of Glasgow, but the boiler and engine blocks were cast at the Camlachie foundry of David Napier, who subsequently went into partnership with his cousin Robert whose maternal grandmother was a Denny of Dumbarton, a name which would also achieve world fame in the development of great ships. In 1818 David Napier designed the steamboat *Rob Roy*, built by William Denny for the Greenock-Belfast route though it later plied between Dover and Calais. In the early 1820s he designed and engined larger and larger wooden vessels, but went on to build the first iron ship in Scotland, the tiny *Aglaia* of 30 tons of 1827, which plied on Loch Eck and thus opened up communications in the West Highlands. In 1831 John Neilson constructed the *Fairy Queen*, the first iron vessel to ply on the Clyde. It was built in Neilson's foundry in Garscube Road and must have been the very first 'abnormal load' to take to the City's streets, its painfully slow progress being observed by huge crowds *en route* to the Broomielaw where it was hoisted into the river by a steam crane.

Various schemes for dredging the Clyde and creating quays were promoted from the seventeenth century onwards, but it was not until 1773 that John Golborne was empowered to carry out the first practical project of constructing jetties that would narrow the course of the river and therefore make the tides much more effective in keeping the channel clear. On the recommendations of Rennie and Thomas Telford between 1799 and 1806, the work of canalisation was taken a step further, but it was not until the 1830s that the Clyde became truly navigable, at all states of the tide, as far upstream as the Broomielaw. Robert Napier, who had by now taken over from his cousin, was well poised to take full advantage of this development. In 1834, however, two of his under-managers, David Tod and John McGregor, left to form their own engineering business and very soon diversified into ship repairing and construction. Their first yard was at Mavisbank in Govan, from which they launched the *Royal Sovereign* in 1839, the Clyde's first iron ocean-going steamer. When the lease of Mavisbank expired in 1844, and the site was required for new quays, Tod & McGregor crossed the river and established a yard at Meadowside, a very shrewd move, as the mouth of the Kelvin gave them the necessary room to launch much bigger and longer ships than before. In 1858 they cut a slip for a graving dock and although this has long since been filled in, the slight inlet on the west bank of the Kelvin betrays its location. Slightly downstream, however, was the main shipyard and engineering workshops of the enterprise, which reached its peak at the time of the American Civil War when the firm specialised in fast screw steamships which were sold to the Confederacy to beat the Union blockade of Southern ports. John McGregor built himself a fine mansion on what had been Meadowside farm, and land-scaped the grounds, with a long driveway running northward to the junction of Clyde Street and Hosier Street. David Tod, on the other hand, preferred to live in Partickhill, where he occupied a villa named Ironbank, believed to have been designed by Charles Wilson about 1845. The steep hill below this villa was locally known as Tod's Brae for many years. As the largest employer of labour in Partick, David Tod was always conscious of his civic obligations. By 1851 Partick's population had passed the five thousand mark and it was largely as a result of his efforts that Partick was raised to the status of a police burgh the following year – twelve years before Govan itself attained that position. Fittingly, Tod who was the chairman of the board of commissioners, then became the first Provost (1852-5).

In 1872, both shipyard and graving dock were sold to Handyside & Henderson which had founded the Anchor Line in 1859. The shipyard began operations under the name of D. & W. Henderson, producing many fine steamers for the Anchor Line's North American and Indian services, which continued to run from Yorkhill Quay until the early 1960s. The firm also built several of the best-known coastal steamers, including both vessels named the *Lord of the Isles*

(1877 and 1891) and the *Ivanhoe* of the Firth of Clyde Steam Packet Company, the preferred medium of the douce middle classes for going 'doon the watter' because of its strict ban on alcohol. The seal on the company's success was set in the 1890s when the yard built the royal yacht *Britannia* for the Prince of Wales, later King Edward VII. Shortly after the First World War the Henderson yard was acquired by Harland & Wolff of Govan, but shrinking order books in the late 1920s led to severe retrenchment and the yard was mothballed. It got a new, but all too brief, lease of life during the Second World War when it built tank and infantry landing craft for the D-Day invasion of Normandy. By 1945, however, shipbuilding at the mouth of the Kelvin was a thing of the past, although ship repairing continued fitfully until the early 1960s. The graving dock was then filled in, ironically using rubble from the demolition of another Glasgow landmark, the Grand Hotel at Charing Cross. Scotway Haulage now occupy the site, and have preserved the building, erected in the French style by Bruce & Hay in 1895, originally used as the shipyard office block. To the west lie the great Meadowside Granaries, built in 1911-13 for the Clyde Navigation Trust and greatly expanded in 1936-7. Two other granaries were added in 1960 and 1967, but this complex closed down in 1988 and stands today as yet another forlorn reminder of Partick's past commercial and industrial importance.

Between 1851 and 1911 the population of Partick rose fourteen-fold and probably attained its peak around 75,000 during the First World War when many of its workforce daily crossed the Clyde to work in the Govan shipyards, as well as in the yards of Partick, Pointhouse and Whiteinch downriver. From the twenties it began to decline, in line with the national trend during the Depression, then picked up again during the Second World War. The present population is much lower, mainly as a result of the Clydeside Expressway, which has cut a broad swathe through the former industrial heartland of Partick, but also due to the redevelopment of former industrial sites which have now given way to attractive housing estates such as Keith Court and Burgh Hall Street.

The heyday of Partick was undoubtedly the sixty-year period when it was an independent burgh. Within the first decade, the village became a town, as tenements were erected along both sides of Dumbarton Road. Most of the development in the 1850s and 1860s took place on the south side of Dumbarton Road, and Partick was laid out on a grid plan with Douglas Street (now Purdon Street), Anderson Street, Orchard Street and Merkland Street running south from the main road at a slight angle towards the southeast. Parallel to Dumbarton road were Wilson and Castlebank Streets, but there were also many narrow side streets and alleys criss-crossing this area as the density of population rose sharply. In the 1870s the burgh spread westward and northward. Beyond Merkland Street, Hayburn, Rosevale, Crawford and Clyde Streets were laid out at right angles to Dumbarton Road, with Hosier Street parallel to the main road and joining up with Wilson Street. For many years Dumbarton Road was effectively the division between the working class and middle-class sections of Partick, although gradually the tenements began encroaching farther and farther up the hill.

Twenty years after its foundation, the burgh acquired a handsome suite of Burgh Halls on Maxwell Street (now Burgh Hall Street), designed by William Leiper in the style of a French chateau of the time of Francis I in the early sixteenth century, with a steep mansard roof crowned by an elaborate cupola more in keeping with the banks of the Loire. Significantly, Leiper's model for this building was displayed at the Paris Exposition of 1867 to illustrate the progress of British architecture. Architectural sculpture was provided by William Mossman who carved the three allegorical roundels of Mercy, Truth and Justice on the facade. Although its primary function ceased in 1912, the Burgh Halls were retained and extended at various times between 1936 and 1971, accommodating a wide variety of local services as well as providing function suites and assembly halls. By contrast, the Partick Police Building, erected in 1853 and for the first two decades the headquarters of the burgh administration as well as the police station, courthouse and cells, was for many years the headquarters of the Marine Division of Glasgow Police. It was designed by Charles Wilson in the style of an Italian palazzo and, as a listed building, survived the devastation of this area during the creation of the Expressway. For some years, it sat forlornly surrounded by dereliction but in recent years an attractive complex of light industrial premises has been created on the eastern side of the street. Beith Street became the location for several of the burgh's public services, the Fire Brigade, the power station and the Cleansing Department, all created about 1905-6 to designs by John Bryce or James Miller. Partick's public baths and washhouse – 'the Steamie' – were designed by Bryce and erected in Purdon Street in 1912, and are remarkably still functional, despite the enormous growth of indoor plumbing in the intervening years.

The kirk session records of 1652 reveal that the 'bairns in Particke' were running wild on the Sabbath, which suggests that their spiritual, if not also their educational, needs had been sorely neglected. There is no record of a school in Partick until 1715 when the kirk session voted £16 Scots for the purpose. This was probably the schoolhouse with adjoining playground, which was situated between the Goat and Dumbarton Road by 1750. Forty years later the inhabitants raised a fund for rebuilding and enlarging the school. In 1850 Partick Academy, a fee-paying school for the children of the rising middle classes, opened in Church Street. As this neighbourhood went down, the trustees disposed of the building to Govan Parish School Board and moved the Academy to more salubrious surroundings adjoining the West of Scotland Cricket Ground. The Academy ran into financial difficulties and closed down seven years later. Later a public school run by the School Board was erected at the top of Hamilton Crescent. In 1903 the school in Church Street was demolished and replaced by a red sandstone Italianate building designed by Bruce & Hay and incorporating swimming baths which were installed the following year. The original Church Street school was the 'drab school' described by Robert Service in *Ploughman of the Moon* (1946), where he started his primary education before moving to the 'dream school' (Hillhead) when it opened in 1885. Drab it may have been, but it had some very able pupils and a very high scholastic record. Service was there at the same time as the Bone brothers, sons of the radical journalist Drummond Bone. James Bone became the editor of the *Manchester Guardian* and was appointed a Companion of Honour in 1947. David, two years younger, went to sea and became the Commodore of the Anchor Line and was knighted in 1946. Baby of the family was Muirhead, born in 1876, who rose to fame and fortune as an artist and was knighted in 1937. The present school buildings are now used as premises by the Social Work Department. A Board school was erected in Rosevale Street in 1874 and an infants' department added thirty years later. The Board school was demolished some years ago and the infants' school closed in 1989. Elsewhere in Partick St Peter's Public School in Stewartville Street, erected at the end of the nineteenth century, was converted into flats in 1982-6. The decline of public schools in this district reflects the demographic pattern: with the fall in the number of pupils schools have merged or closed down.

The educational needs of Partick are also served by the public library at the corner of Purdon Street and Dumbarton Road. It was designed by Glasgow's Office of Public Works in 1925 but because of the hard times that followed in the wake of the General Strike it was not actually completed till ten years later. The single-storey building in the Renaissance style is set at an angle to the street corner with a rather attractive facade. It was revamped in the 1960s, which effectively means that it has far fewer books on its shelves than previously. Unlike neighbouring Hillhead, Partick has lost both of its cinemas. The Rosevale in Merkland Street was a fine modern cinema, in contrast with the fleapit (whose name mercifully escapes me) opposite the foot of Dowanhill Street. Even the best seats, by the late 1940s, were no more than sixpence (2 1/2p). For more energetic entertainment there was the F & F Palais de Danse, also on the south side of Dumbarton Road, which has now become some sort of emporium for cheap and cheerful knick-knacks.

Partick is home to the West of Scotland Cricket Club whose grounds are bounded by Peel Street and Fortrose Street (formerly Hamilton Crescent). One of the handsome villas of the 1860s has been transformed into the Wickets Hotel whose lobby and function suites are decorated with pictures of the cricket grounds in their heyday. Mention has already been made of the Caledonian

Cricket Club which functioned where Glasgow Academy now stands. The Clutha and Royal Cricket Clubs, both founded in the 1840s, shared the cricket grounds, and it was members of the former who founded the West of Scotland Cricket Club in 1862. Up to 1893 the ground was shared with the West of Scotland Rugby Club, which was very handy for the keen sportsmen who played rugger in winter and cricket in summer. It was even the venue for the first three international soccer matches between Scotland and England (1872-6).

At one time, the ferryboats ran on the Sabbath mainly for the purpose of taking worshippers across the Clyde to the parish church in Govan. As the ferry service consisted of open, undecked rowing boats, by the time the last parishioners had managed to take passage the service was almost over. As a result, there was very stiff competition to board these little vessels and the unseemly pushing and shoving often resulted in some people, including women and children, being toppled into the river 'to their great hurt and the spoiling of their clothes' as a petition of 1769 put it feelingly. This petition for a separate church in Partick was turned down and it was not until 1834 that a chapel of ease was erected on a site donated by Archibald Bogle of Gilmorehill. This was, in effect, a branch of the parish church and services were conducted according to the rites of the Church of Scotland. Partick was not separated from Govan parish until 1869. Ten years later a new church in the French Gothic style was erected at the foot of Church Street by Steele & Balfour who added the chancel and organ loft in 1896. Over the years the interior was beautified by a magnificent marble and onyx font and an attractively carved pulpit, but its crowning glory is undoubtedly the stained glass, including a fine rose window and side windows by the leading artists of the late nineteenth and early twentieth centuries in this medium. Later known as Partick Old Parish Church, it lost its primary role in the early 1990s and is now a furniture showroom.

A decade before the establishment of the chapel of ease, however, Partick had acquired two other places of worship, both used by non-conformist sects. The Secession Church opened in May 1824 and the Relief Church the following July. Previously, their adherents had had to cross the Kelvin and worship in the Dissenting chapels of Anderston. The Revd James Ewing of the Relief Church succumbed to cholera in 1837 at the early age of thirty-three. The only mark which he left on the parish was when he was censured for fooling about on the ice at the Slit Mill dam one Saturday, to the annoyance of the local curlers holding a bonspiel. The Relief Church was replaced in 1864 by St Mary's Church, designed by James Hamilton, with two neo-Gothic mission halls added in 1885. With the various amalgamations, which led eventually to the consolidation of the Church of Scotland in 1929, the congregation of this church was successively known as Partick West, Newton Place and latterly Partick South. A new church, the third on the site, was erected in 1988 by Fleming Buildings in the contemporary timber-framed idiom and inaugurated on 19 April that year.

The Secession Church lagged behind its rival in securing a minister and then the Revd John Skinner only stayed for two years before emigrating to the United States. His place was taken by the Revd Thomas Lawrie who made up for this by staying in Partick for almost half a century. During his long incumbency the congregation moved from its original church in Byres Road to a splendid new edifice at the junction of Hyndland Street and Partickhill Road, built in 1865-6 for what had now become a United Presbyterian church. The congregation put the design out to tender and the commission was awarded to William Leiper, his first important project. Externally its most outstanding feature is the tall spire, the tallest in the district, but remarkably the church was adorned with a magnificent rose window portraying the Old Testament prophets, with side windows to match bearing full-length figures of David and Miriam, all by Daniel Cottier. The original church then became a mission church under the name of Partick East, but moved to a new site at Lawrence Street in 1899, the original church being then demolished to make way for tenements. By 1986 the congregation of Dowanhill Church had dwindled to such an extent that it was no longer viable, and its members then merged with Partick East. Dowanhill Church was then sold and converted in 1989-90 by the Four Acres Charitable Trust, to re-emerge as the Cottier Theatre.

Partick probably has a higher percentage of Gaelic speakers than any other part of Glasgow, the cattle drovers being followed by hundreds of Highlanders who came to work in the new shipyards or join the police force, while Highland girls were enrolled as domestic servants. On Sundays they would congregate at the gates of the Botanic Gardens at the top of Byres Road, or if the weather was wet, under the railway bridge in Argyle Street, jocularly known as the Highlandman's Umbrella. Today the Park Bar in Argyle Street is the pub where Gaelic is commoner than English, although the pubs of Partick have their fair complement of Highland customers. At the turn of the century, when the Gaelic-speaking population of Partick was over 1,200, there were two Gaelic churches. Partick Gaelic Church in Gardner Street was built in 1904 to a design by H. & D. Barclay and catered for the adherents of the established church, whereas the Highland Free Church in Dowanhill Street was erected about 1880. For all I know, it may be the last church in Glasgow where the Devil's kist o' whistles has not been admitted and the singing of Psalms is conducted by a precentor. Partick seems to have been extremely well catered for by churches of different denominations. The Methodist Church on Dumbarton Road was erected in 1880-2 to a design by William McGibbon, Congregational Church in Stewartville Street was built in 1910 and the Baptist Church at the foot of Crow Road was completed in 1927. St Bride's Church in Rosevale Street, a Gothic structure of 1897, is now disused, as is St Silas, the Episcopal church in Hayburn Street, erected in 1874 to a design by John Honeyman.

The Polish Memorials, St Simons Church, Partick

Fortunately one of the oldest (and most interesting) of Partick's churches has survived. Just across the Benalder Street Bridge, on the right-hand side of Partick Bridge Street, stands St Simon's. Originally known as St Peter's, the first Catholic church in Partick was erected in 1858, flanked by a presbytery and a school, the latter added in 1864. The first parish priest was the Revd Daniel Gallagher, a native of Ireland, who worked as a millhand at Blantyre as a teenager where, despite religious differences, he became a close friend of fellow worker David Livingstone. Father Gallagher was a remarkable man and Partick was fortunate to have him. He ministered to the rapidly growing Irish population of the burgh, mainly employed in the shipyards. By the end of the century their numbers had been augmented by the many Italian families who had settled in the area and were engaged in the ice-cream, fish and chips and cafe industry as well as running barber shops. By the beginning of the twentieth century, the congregation had grown to such a size that a much larger church was required. A site was acquired on the east side of Hyndland Street and Peter Paul Pugin produced a design in his best Gothic style, interpreted in red sandstone. In 1903 the Catholic congregation took possession of the new St Peter's. Adjoining it is St Peter's School, on the corner of Chancellor Street and Dowanhill Street, which was erected in 1898. The original church on Bridge Street was retained and given a new lease of life during the Second World War when it was adopted by the Polish forces in exile as their church. After the war many Poles did not wish to return to a Communist homeland and settled in Glasgow, continuing the wartime connection with the church now known as St Simon's. It was extensively refurbished in 1956-7 by Gillespie, Kidd & Coia, and given new marble fittings. Above the Lady altar is a replica of the famous Black Madonna of Cestochowa, a gift from the Polish Army. In 1979 this precious memento was taken to Warsaw to receive the blessing of Cardinal Wyszynski. In May 1991 the Polish community erected two monuments outside the church. The larger one bears a shield showing the Polish eagle superimposed on crossed flags with Our Lady, Queen of Poland, above. The smaller monument is an engraved tablet which recalls the wartime period when Poles on leave came to worship here and listen to the word of God in their own tongue. 'I was a stranger and ye took me in' (St Matthew 25: 15) is inscribed near the foot.

In 1895 the Caledonian Railway's Lanarkshire and Dunbartonshire line from Glasgow was under construction. The following year, when it constructed the railway bridge and the new Benalder Street Bridge alongside, it also erected Partick Central Station at the west end of the road bridge, with its waiting room and booking hall at pavement level, and a long flight of steps down to the single platform which had up and down tracks laid on either side. In the early twentieth century this station was renamed the Kelvinhall Station but when the line was closed in the 1960s the tiny booking office survived, even though the surrounding area has been virtually derelict ever since. The former railway line has now been landscaped and forms part of the Glasgow to Loch Lomond cycleway.

To the south ran the line of the North British Railway (later part of the London and North Eastern Railway), opened in the 1870s, which crossed the Kelvin just below the Slit Mill by means of a high viaduct that crossed the Pointhouse Shipyard and Ferry Road. Until about thirty years ago there was an iron footbridge on the south side, supposedly maintaining an ancient right of way, although there does not seem to have been protest made when this bridge was quietly shut down. This line ran along a high embankment revetted with masonry, across the southwestern side of Partick, past St Silas Church to Dumbarton Road which it crossed by a high bridge. This was the original location of Partick Station, with flights of steps at the sides of the bridge giving access to the station buildings at trackside level. The station was relocated on Merkland Street during the extensive redevelopment of the area in the 1960s and subsequently, when the Underground was renovated, the new Partick Subway station was sited conveniently alongside. When the Subway was inaugurated in 1896 there was a station near here, and known as Merkland Street. One stop up the line was Partick Cross on Dumbarton Road at the foot of Dowanhill Street with a back entrance that led to Dalcross Street. In the re-organisation of the 1980s this station was rebuilt and on completion emerged under the new name of Kelvinhall Station. Thus this name has, in effect, gone all round the district in the past half-century. From Merkland Street the Subway line ran under the Clyde to emerge at Govan Cross and then head in a southeasterly direction to Cessnock (now Ibrox).

Street transport in this district began in 1844 when Wylie & Lochhead inaugurated a frequent service between the City centre and the west end of Partick at the junction of Dumbarton Road and Jordanhill Street (now the foot of Crow Road), where the company stabled its horses. When a tenement block was erected on this corner it was named Downie Place in honour of the wives of Wylie and Lochhead, sisters whose maiden name was Downie. James Walker (after whom Walker Street was named) began a rival service in 1847 and then the Glasgow and Partick Omnibus Company began a horse-bus service in 1860, operating from premises at the foot of Peel Street. Long before the burgh was absorbed by Glasgow the Corporation's tramcars began running along Argyle Street and across the bridge to Dumbarton Road and all the way to Dalmuir. The trams also ran up Byres Road from Partick Cross to Great Western Road. From Byres Road a tramline also ran along Highburgh Road into Hyndland Road, then down Clarence Drive to Broomhill and thence northwards on Crow Road to the terminus at Anniesland. The trams were hauled by a pair of horses, but from 1902 onwards the lines were gradually electrified. Motor buses followed soon afterwards. The tramcars ceased in 1962 and the bus services were deregulated in the 1990s, with the result that public transport is a shadow of its former self.

Partick was also well served by ferries across and along the Clyde, the Clyde Navigation Trust operating a dozen small, twin-screw steamers known as Cluthas (the ancient name for the river). In 1884 the Trust inaugurated a service up and down the Clyde, between Stockwell Street in the City centre and Whiteinch downriver from Partick, a distance of three and a half miles, with eleven landing stages (including Govan and Partick) *en route*. The entire journey took forty-five minutes and cost a penny. This service ended when the electric tramcars began running, but the cross-river services, by small, open-decked ferryboats, continued until the opening of the Clyde Tunnel in 1964 rendered them superfluous. The vehicular ferry ceased in 1965 and the passenger service the following January. It should be noted that ferryboat number 8 which served the Govan-Kelvinhaugh route was subsequently given a new lease of life as the *Ferry Queen* at Glasgow Bridge on the Forth and Clyde Canal (a pun on the old *Fairy Queen*), while ferryboat number 10, from the Finnieston-Kingston crossing, is now the *Caledonian* floating restaurant at the same place.

With the development of public transport, Dumbarton Road became the main shopping street of the burgh, and several local tradesmen eventually had large stores, mainly along the north side. In the 1930s the large multiple stores began to make their presence felt, and this trend has continued ever since, with the result that Dumbarton Road now resembles every other high street in the land although a sign of these more affluent times has been the appearance of a number of antique shops around Partick Cross. Here and there, however, Dumbarton Road has preserved little oases of individuality, such as Kelvin House, a haberdashery business that seems to be in a time warp. Its tiny walk-round arcade boasts a fine display of good old-fashioned bloomers, corsets and even liberty-bodices. A real institution, I doubt whether there is another shop like it anywhere in Glasgow, or the whole of Scotland for that matter.

Heading back eastwards on Dumbarton Road you pass a strange-looking building on the south side of the road, overlooking Partick Bridge. This is the Partick Sewage Pumping Station which was constructed in 1904 by Alexander B. McDonald. Built of the same Locharbriggs red sandstone as the bridge and the Art Gallery beyond, its exuberant Baroque style reflects the civic pride of the Edwardian era, when even something so mundane as a sewage works could be made to look architecturally interesting. At the rear or the building and teetering on the riverbank was a boiler house which once supplied steam for the central heating system of the Kelvin Hall (via the lattice-girder bridge), but this no longer exists. According to the Glasgow Buildings book the pumping station was derelict by 1989 but it appears to have been given a new lease of life, as you will be acutely aware when the wind is blowing in the wrong direction.

Works Consulted

General

Simon Berry and Hamish Whyte (eds) *Glasgow Observed, a Documentary Anthology* (1987)

A.D. Boney, *The Lost Gardens of Glasgow* (1988)

David W. Boyce, *The Bridges of the Kelvin* (1996)

Andrew Brown, *History of Glasgow* (1795)

R.G. Cant and I.G. Lindsay, *Old Glasgow* (1947)

John Chalmers, *One Hundred Walks Around Glasgow* (1988)

James Cleland,   *Annals of Glasgow* (1816)
                   The Rise and Progress of the City of Glasgow (1820)
                   The Former and Present State of Glasgow (1840)

James Cowan, *From Glasgow's Treasure Chest* (1951)

J. Cunnison and J.B.S. Gilfillan, *The Third Statistical Account of Scotland*, volume 5, *The City of Glasgow* (1958)

David Daiches, *Glasgow* (1977)

George Eyre-Todd and Robert Renwick, *History of Glasgow*, 3 volumes (1921-34)

Andrew Gibb, *Glasgow, the Making of a City* (1983)

R. Gillespie, *Glasgow and the Clyde* (1876)

Andor Gomme and David Walker, *Architecture of Glasgow* (1968)

J.F.S. Gordon (ed), *Glasghu Facies*, 3 volumes (1872)

F. Groome (ed), *The Ordnance Gazetteer of Scotland*, 6 volumes (1885)

John Gunn (ed), *The City of Glasgow: its Origin, Growth and Development* (1921)

Thomas Howarth, *Charles Rennie Mackintosh and the Modern Movement* (1953)

J. Stephen Jeans, *Western Worthies* (1872)

J. Knight, *Glasgow and Strathclyde* (1931)

Maurice Lindsay, *Portrait of Glasgow* (1972)

Hugh Macdonald, *Rambles Round Glasgow* (1854)

J.K. McDowall, *The People's History of Glasgow* (1899, reprinted 1970)

Andrew MacGeorge, *Old Glasgow* (1880)

George MacGregor, *The History of Glasgow* (1881)

Peter Mackenzie, *Reminiscences of Glasgow*, 3 volumes (1865-66)

K. Macleod, *Charles Rennie Mackintosh* (1968)

James MacLehose (ed.), *Memoirs and Portraits of a Hundred Glasgow Men* (1885)

D.M. Malloch, *The Book of Glasgow Anecdote* (1912)

J.D. Marwick, *Early Glasgow* (1911)
J.O. Mitchell, *Old Glasgow Essays* (1905)
Michael Moss and John Hume, *Glasgow as it Was* (1975)
C.A. Oakley, *The Second City* (1946, new edition 1975)
        Our Illustrious Forbears (1980)
Robert Renwick, *Glasgow Memorials* (1908)
J.M. Reid, *Glasgow* (1956)
Senex (Robert Reid), *Glasgow, Past and Present* (1851)
        Old Glasgow and its Environs (1864)
Sir John Sinclair,   *The Statistical Account of Scotland* (1791-99)
        The New Statistical Account of Scotland (1834-45)
John Guthrie Smith, *The Old Country Houses of the Old Glasgow Gentry* (1870)
Gavin Stamp, *Alexander Thomson, the Unknown Genius* (1999)
Thomas Stothers, *Glasgow, Lanarkshire and Renfrewshire Annual* (1911)
Joseph Swan, *Select Views of Glasgow and its Environs* (1828)
Andrew Wallace, *Popular Traditions of Glasgow* (1889)
David Williams, *The Glasgow Guide* (1998)
Elizabeth Williamson, Anne Riches and Malcolm Higgs, *The Buildings of Scotland: Glasgow* (1990)

1. From the Source of the Kelvin to Kilsyth

Robert Anderson, *A History of Kilsyth* (1901)
Peter Anton, *Kilsyth, a Parish History* (1893)
I.M. Smith, *The Story of Twechar* (1994)
Sydney Smith, *West of Scotland Rambles* (1979)

2. Kirkintilloch and the Luggie

A.I. Bowman, *Kirkintilloch Shipbuilding* (1983)
        Swifts and Queens: Passenger Transport on the Forth & Clyde Canal (1984)
        The Gipsy o' Kirky (1988)
Robert Buchan, *David Gray and Other Essays* (1868)
Olive Checkland, *Japanese Whisky, Scotch Blood* (1998)
David Gray, *The Luggie and Other Poems* (1868)
John Horne (ed), *Kirkintilloch by Select Contributors* (reprinted 1993)
D.E. McGuire, *Agricultural Improvements in Strathkelvin*, 1700-1850 (1987)
Don Martin, *The Garnkirk & Glasgow Railway* (1981)
        The Monkland & Kirkintilloch Railway (1992)
        The Forth & Clyde Canal: a Kirkintilloch View (1985)
        The Story of Kirkintilloch (1987)

The Story of Lenzie (1989)
Sue Selwyn and Don Martin, *Kirkintilloch Life & Times* (1994)
A.V. Stuart, *David Gray: Poet of the Luggie* (1961)
Thomas Watson, *Kirkintilloch, Town and Parish* (1894)
D. Weir, *Kirkintilloch as it Existed Fifty Years Ago* (1887)

3. The Campsies and the Glazert

John Cameron, *The Parish of Campsie* (1892, reprinted 1985)
Iain C. Lees, *The Campsies and the Land of Lennox* (1933)
James Lindsay, *Milton of Campsie: People & Places* (1992)
Leslie Gardiner, *Lunardi* (1984)
A.D. Morrison, *The Story of Free St. David's* (1926)
Loretta Mulholland, *Campsie Glen Picture Album* (1988)
B. Skillen, *Mines and Minerals of Campsie* (1985)
Sydney Smith, *West of Scotland Rambles* (1979)

4. Hayston to Summerston

Christina Bewley, *Muir of Huntershill* (1981)
T.C.F. Brotchie, *Some Sylvan Scenes Near Glasgow* (1910)
Michael Donnelly, *Thomas Muir of Huntershill* (1975)
E. Robertson and A.A. Maclean, *The Story of Baldernock* (1991)
J.A. Russell, *The Story of Bishopbriggs* (1979)
W. Ure, *Bishopbriggs, the Years of Growth* (1989)
Maureen Whitelaw, *A Garden Suburb for Glasgow* (1992)

5. Killermont to Kelvindale

Colin Harvey, *Milngavie in Pictures* (1975)
James Hastie, *Maryhill High Church Centenary,* 1848-1948 (1948)
Thomas Healy, *The Church of the Immaculate Conception, a Centenary Record* (1951)
John Robertson and Rachel Pateman, *Maryhill Road, from a Needle to an Anchor* (1986)
John A. Shearer, *In and Around Milngavie* (1908, new edition 1988)
Aileen Smart, *Villages of Glasgow,* volume 1 (Maryhill) (1988)
Sydney Smith, *West of Scotland Rambles* (1979)
Bill Taylor, *Glasgow North West* (1976)
Alexander Thomson, *Random Notes and Rambling Recollections of Maryhill* (1895)
Roderick Wilkinson, *Memories of Maryhill* (1993)

6. Kelvinside

Alison F. Blood, *Kelvinside Days* (1929)
Glasgow Academy, *The First Hundred Years* (1946)
Colin Menabney and Janet Darling, *Working Lives in Woodside and North Kelvinside* (1987)
H.B. Morton, *A Hillhead Album* (1973)
James Hamilton Muir, *Glasgow in 1901* (1901)
Benno Schotz, *Bronze in my Blood* (1981)

7. Hillhead and Woodside

J.J. Bell, *I Remember* (1933)
H.B. Morton, *A Hillhead Album* (1973)
John Robertson and Rachel Pateman, *Life in the Woodside Tenements* (1987)
Robert Service, *Ploughman of the Moon* (1946)

8. Woodlands and Kelvingrove

William Bentley, *Kelvin Grove and Other Poems* (1843)
Mark McManus and Glenn Chandler, *Taggart's Glasgow* (1989)
James Hamilton Muir, *Glasgow in 1901* (1901)
Perilla and Juliet Kinchin, *Glasgow's Great Exhibitions* (1988)
D. McLellan, *Glasgow Public Parks* (1894)
G.W. Muir, *River Purification* (1881)

9. Glasgow University

James Coutts, *A History of the University of Glasgow* (1909)
J.D. Mackie, *The University of Glasgow, 1451-1951* (1954)
David Murray, *Memories of the Old College of Glasgow* (1927)

10. Kelvin Way to Pointhouse

George Blake, *The Shipbuilders* (1935)
Derek Dow and Michael Moss, *Glasgow's Gain, the Anderston Story* (1986)
C.L.D. Duckworth and G.E. Langmuir, *West Highland Steamers* (1967)
       Clyde River and Other Steamers (1971)
A. McQueen, *Clyde River Steamers of the Last Fifty Years* (1923)
       Echoes of Old Clyde Paddle Wheels (1924)
Brian D. Osborne, *The Ingenious Mr Bell* (1995)

Jack Webster, *The Flying Scots* (1994)

J. Williamson, *The Clyde Passenger Steamer* (1904)

11. Partick

William Dickie, *History of Dowanhill Church, 1823-1923* (1926)

W. Greenhorne, *History of Partick, 550-1912* (1928)

C.D. Horne and J. Harris, *History of the West of Scotland Cricket Club* (1962)

J.D. Marwick, *The River Clyde and the Clyde Burghs*, 1909

James Napier, *Notes and Reminiscences Relating to Partick* (1873)

Partick History Group, *Mind These Days? Partick Between the Wars* (1985)

Aileen Smart, *Villages of Glasgow,* volume 1 (1988)

Bill Spaulding, *Bygone Partick* (1992)

                 Partick in Old Photographs (1993)

                 Partick Remembered (1996)

INDEX